SOLID GOLD 2

ENGELSKA 6

Eva Hedencrona
Karin Smed-Gerdin
Peter Watcyn-Jones

Studentlitteratur

Produktionsstöd har erhållits av
Specialpedagogiska skolmyndigheten.

Studentlitteratur har både digital och traditionell bokutgivning. Studentlitteraturs trycksaker är miljöanpassade, både när det gäller papper och tryckprocess.

Art.nr 37756
ISBN 978-91-44-10780-6
Upplaga 1:3

studentlitteratur.se
Studentlitteratur AB, Lund

Formgivning: Werner Schmidt
Omslagslayout: Jens Martin, Signalera
Omslagsbild: Masterfile

Printed by Interak, Poland 2017

Congratulations on choosing *Solid Gold!*

Solid Gold 2 will improve your English in a variety of ways – first and foremost it will help you meet the course requirements for English 6. You can access *Solid Gold 2* from your computer, iPad or mobile phone, whichever suits you best. The *Quick Guide to Solid Gold 2* on pages 4–5 will show you what there is and how everything works.

Solid Gold 2 covers the core content of English 6. The focus in the nine units is mainly on living conditions, social issues and cultural features in different parts of the English-speaking world. *Solid Gold 2* also aims to make you aware of how culture influences communication. There are a variety of texts in different genres such as fiction, non-fiction, biographies, magazine features, songs, etc. The section *Authors of the English-Speaking World* gives an introduction to further studies of literature.

In the *Resource Section* you will be introduced to different strategies to use when learning English. There is also advice on how to become a better speaker or writer. For example, you will learn how to adapt your language according to the purpose, recipient and situation. Your ability to summarise, explain, discuss and argue will all be practised in *Solid Gold 2*. The sections *On Speaking, On Writing* and *On Language* all contain useful information on how to progress.

The *Exercises* deal with the language and subject matter of the texts. Many of the exercises can be done either in the printed book or digitally and there are additional digital exercises, including intensive vocabulary practice.

Expand Your Vocabulary will help you increase your vocabulary while *Use of English* will improve your grasp of the language. If you need to revise some grammar, the *Grammar* section from *Solid Gold 1* is included in the digital material, backed up by interactive grammar exercises. *Want Some More?* offers texts for additional reading in the digital material.

We hope that *Solid Gold 2* will help you move ahead in your English studies, improving your communication skills and broadening your knowledge and understanding of the world in which English is used.

The *Solid Gold* team

Quick Guide to Solid Gold

'ALL-IN-ONE' BOOK – TEXTS, EXERCISES, RESOURCES AND MORE

Solid Gold 2 provides a complete base for your English course, offering a wide range of printed and digital materials. You may not have time to use everything in *Solid Gold 2* but we believe you will find all you need.

Reading

Nine chapters, each with a theme, containing a variety of texts from different countries. The authors of the texts are also presented and the illustrations are intended to provide extra food for thought and discussion.

Authors of the English-speaking world

Twenty or more important figures from throughout the world of English literature, from Shakespeare and Jane Austen to Margaret Atwood and Roddy Doyle. Thumbnail biographies plus an outline of literary history from the Renaissance to the early twentieth century. An exercise sections offers methods for reviewing, analyzing and discussing literature both orally and in writing, as well as suggestions for projects.

Resource Section

An invaluable handbook on how to improve your language skills. You can look up critical reading and reviewing of sources, letter writing, how to work with different genres and much more.

Exercises

In the exercise section of *Solid Gold 2* there is an extensive body of exercises on each of the texts, as well as listening and grammar exercises.

WSM (Want Some More?)

Under this heading there is a selection of extra texts for further reading, some of them printed in the book and others appear as extra texts in the digital material.

Expand your vocabulary

An opportunity to learn/revise important words which do not necessarily occur in the nine chapters. The exercises are divided into ten categories, e.g. British and American English, synonyms, easily confused words, phrasal verbs.

Use of English

This section will help you develop and sharpen your own use of English, with particular focus on the correct use of words and correct sentence construction.

Grammar

Interactive grammar exercises are included in the digital material to help you practise and consolidate the right level of grammar.

Word lists

Word lists for all the texts and listening exercises.

DIGITAL MATERIAL

Recorded texts and word lists

All the texts in *Solid Gold 2* are recorded with native voices from different English-speaking countries. The word lists are also recorded, both English and Swedish.

Listening comprehension

The listening comprehension passages are recorded with native voices from different English-speaking countries.

Digital exercises

Throughout the exercise section there are a number of links that give access to digital exercises as well as the listening exercises. Here you will find different kinds of exercises on vocabulary, comprehension, grammar and a great deal more.

Contents

TOSHIBA
TIMES SQUARE 2014
TOSHIBA
TDK
THIS AIN'T NO TEA PARTY
shameless
JAN 12 SUNDAYS 9PM
SHOWTIME
CHILL IN THE AIR
BARCLAYS
Budweiser
Superdry.
toxic
BAR
PALACE
W 50 ST
ONE WAY

GO-AHEAD 1

Cracking the Code
Letter to a Funeral Parlor
We Beat the Street
LISTENING We Beat the Street cont.

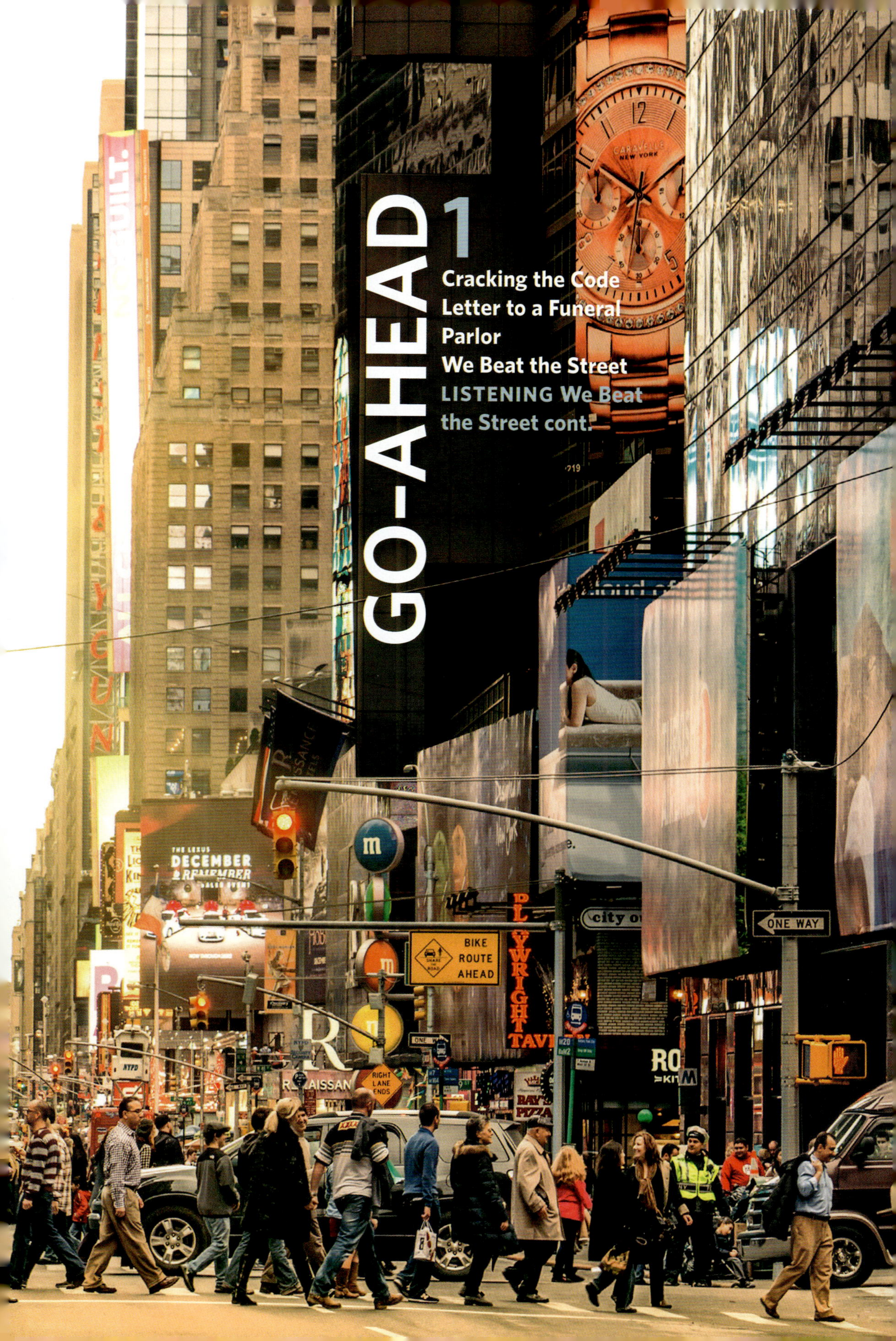

CRACKING THE CODE

BY ALLIE EDWARDSSON

Wouldn't it be wonderful if all you needed to succeed with effective communication was a perfect command of the language? If you could only master pronunciation, get your prepositions in the right place, and choose exactly the right word, then successful communication would be assured.

But think about the people you communicate with in your native language every day, your colleagues, boss, clients, suppliers, husband, wife, children, neighbours, parents, brothers, sisters and friends. Is your communication always effective? Do you always get the result you want? Do the people around you always understand you perfectly in your native tongue? Or do you experience misunderstandings? Do you sometimes feel that you just can't get your message across, even though it's perfectly clear – to you?

Deborah Tannen, an American and Professor of Linguistics at Georgetown University, has written several bestsellers on this subject, intended primarily for Americans communicating with other Americans in their native language. Titles include: *That's not what I meant!* and *You just don't understand!* So you see, even being a native speaker of English is no guarantee that you will succeed in your communication in English. All of us can recognise this frustration from meetings, discussions and conversations we've experienced.

COMMUNICATION IS SO MUCH MORE THAN LANGUAGE

Over the past decades there have been many studies showing how much of our communication is in fact *not* contained in the words we speak. You make your very first impression on someone within a fraction of a second, before you've had a chance to say anything. When you *do* speak, it is the tone, volume, pitch and so on of your voice that makes the next impression. *Then* there's the content of your actual words. One popular set of percentages, known as the 7–38–55 per cent rule, from the research of Albert Mehrabian, says that the impact of our communication is: 55 per cent body language, 38 per cent voice and 7 per cent words alone.

An important concept here is *congruence.* Do your words and body language 'match'? Do you look and sound enthusiastic when you want to show your enthusiasm, about a new project, for example? Do people find it easy to concentrate on your voice, or does it send them to sleep, even if the content of what you're saying is interesting and important?

THE CODE: FIVE PARTS

So how *do* we crack the code of international communication? People travel more than ever. The Internet has dramatically increased our means of communication with Facebook, Twitter, YouTube, etc. We are living in the information age. If you will be visiting Japan to do business you can just Google and find enormous amounts of information on both the country and culture. We can have webinars and teleconferences across all the continents of the world. You might think that we know enough about each other already.

Questions and exercises on the text are on page 186.

And yet succeeding with international communication can mean the difference between motivated employees, satisfied shareholders, and confident investors on the one hand or stranded negotiations, conflicts, and time lost on misunderstandings on the other hand. What we can find out on Google is just the tip of the iceberg.

Through my work with people I have identified five areas that need to be sufficiently developed for you to succeed with international communication. One or two of them are not enough. You need all five – in the right combination for *you* and your communication challenges and intentions:

- *Language skills.* Of course an adequate knowledge of the language is important. We have all experienced communicating primarily with our body language. It works for a while, especially in the beginning. The better you can express yourself, the more you increase your chances of communicating what you actually intend to communicate. An important part of rhetoric is choosing language that is persuasive and helps get your message across. But command of the language alone is no guarantee of success.
- *Intercultural skills.* We also need to understand what kind of communication will work with the culture we are communicating with. What does silence mean in that culture? How much emotion is it appropriate to show? How is a manager expected to behave with staff?
- *Communication skills.* This means understanding yourself as sender of the message, understanding your 'audience' which might be employees, customers or partners, and increasing your ability to adapt your message to maximise success.
- *Personal skills.* Personal skills include your self-awareness, for example of your cultural 'baggage'. It also includes your ability to create time in your schedule to prepare. Or to keep to an exercise schedule so that you look after yourself physically as well as mentally, especially when you have a demanding presentation to deliver. It includes your ability to keep your attention and focus on the task at hand and not be distracted by negative thoughts about how you're coming across in English.
- *Small talk skills.* Small talk is a kind of super-tool that helps with the other four skill areas. The main function of small talk is warming up relationships. However, it's also a great way to warm up your English, warm up to the other person's language and communication style, find out more about the culture you're dealing with and get useful background information.

LETTER TO A FUNERAL PARLOR

BY LYDIA DAVIS

LYDIA DAVIS (1947–) is an American author known for several short story collections and one novel, *The End of the Story*. She has also translated modern French literature and been named Chevalier of the Order of the Arts and Letters by the French government for her fiction and translations. In 2013 Davis was awarded the Man Booker International Prize.

Dear Sir,

I am writing to you to object to the word *cremains,* which was used by your representative when he met with my mother and me two days after my father's death.

We had no objection to your representative, personally, who was respectful and friendly and dealt with us in a sensitive way. He did not try to sell us an expensive urn, for instance.

What startled and disturbed us was the word *cremains.* You in the business must have invented this word and you are used to it. We the public do not hear it very often. We don't lose a close friend or a family member very many times in our life, and years pass in between, if we are lucky. Even less often do we have to discuss what is to be done with a family member or close friend after their death.

We noticed that before the death of my father you and your representative used the words *loved one* to refer to him. That was comfortable for us, even if the ways in which we loved him were complicated.

Then we were sitting there in our chairs in the living room trying not to weep in front of your representative, who was opposite us on the sofa, and we were very tired first from sitting up with my father, and then from worrying about whether he was comfortable as he was dying, and then from worrying about where he might be now that he was dead, and your representative referred to him as "the cremains."

At first we did not even know what he meant. Then, when we realized, we were frankly upset. *Cremains* sounds like something invented as a milk substitute in coffee, like Cremora, or Coffee-mate. Or it sounds like some kind of a chipped beef dish.

As one who works with words for a living, I must say that any invented word, like *Porta Potti or pooper-scooper,* has a cheerful or even jovial ring to it that I don't think you really intended when you invented the word *cremains.* In fact, my father himself, who was a professor of English and is now being called *the cremains,* would have pointed out to you the alliteration in *Porta Potti* and the rhyme in *pooper-scooper.* Then he would have told you that *cremains* falls into the same category as *brunch* and is known as a portmanteau word.

There is nothing wrong with inventing words, especially in a business. But a grieving family is not prepared for this one. We are not even used to our loved one being gone. You could very well continue to employ the term *ashes.* We are used to it from the Bible, and are even comforted by it. We would not misunderstand. We would know that these ashes are not like the ashes in a fireplace.

Yours sincerely.

Questions and exercises on the text are on page 189.

WE BEAT THE STREET

BY THE THREE DOCTORS

THIS IS A TRUE STORY. We are real people. We started out as kids in the toughest neighborhoods of Newark, New Jersey, and today we are doctors. We had to fight drugs and crime and hopelessness. We had to overcome obstacles like poverty and apathy and violence in our community. Individually we probably would not have succeeded, but together, we were able to make it through high school, college, and medical school.

We are Dr. Rameck Hunt, Dr. Sampson Davis, and Dr. George Jenkins. We call ourselves The Three Doctors. We now work in the same community where we grew up, trying to help the people in our neighborhoods.

We never thought our story was anything special. It wasn't until after we finished medical school that the public showed us what a remarkable journey we had made. In retrospect, it's probably best that it happened that way. If we had thought about how daunting the task was that we were undertaking, we probably never would have even tried.

In these pages we want to show the power of friendship and of positive peer pressure. We also want to show the necessity for strong role models in the lives of young people. The three of us suffered because we didn't have many, and we hope to offer young people today three strong, positive role models they can depend on.

Don't get us wrong – we made lots of mistakes. We often made foolish decisions, sometimes got involved in dangerous situations, and frequently suffered the consequences of impulsive behavior. But we weren't bad kids – just kids in need of focus and direction.

We want to show that obstacles can be overcome and how struggles can lead to success. We hope that by reading our story, young people can avoid some of the mistakes we made and perhaps can be inspired to reach for dreams of their own.

Many of the names of the real people who lived and died in our neighborhoods have been changed in this book to protect their privacy. But their stories are important and need to be shared.

We hope that our story will add a beacon of hope to young people

in particular and to society in general. Anyone with a dream can succeed and with that success return to where it all started and make the world just a little better.

THE WALKOUT

RAMECK, ELEVENTH GRADE "Yo, man, what's up with this? How come there's no black history classes taught at this school?" Rameck asked the history teacher as he flipped through the pages of their American history book. "All I see in here is white folks!"

"We teach the history of all Americans, Rameck," the teacher replied carefully. "We try very hard to be culturally diverse in our approach."

"Where?" Rameck asked bluntly. "I see a picture of some slaves, and three hundred pages later I see Martin Luther King. Didn't anybody black or Hispanic do anything important in all that time?"

The teacher changed the subject, saying it was time for class to begin, but Rameck seethed inside. He had recently helped organize a group at school called the United Students Organization, with Ahi and Amiri Baraka, sons of the famous poet Amiri Baraka, and another student named Hassan. The USO met regularly, not to cause trouble, but to try to work within the school and the community to make changes.

George and Sampson went to meetings occasionally, but Rameck, always questioning, was one of the leaders.

"Our history books should reflect our history," Ahi said.

"And we need more money in this school," Hassan added with passion. "Why do they always cut the budgets of schools in the city? Suburban kids have swimming pools and tennis courts and carpet in the halls. We get the leftover desks and old books and equipment. We deserve better!"

"We ought to walk out!" Rameck suggested at one meeting.

"And what would that do," George asked, "except get us in trouble?"

But Ahi seized upon the idea. "If just a few of us walk out, you're

right, we would get in trouble. But suppose we ALL walk out – the entire school?" he asked excitedly.

Rameck grabbed his excitement. "Suppose we get other schools in Newark to walk with us? They would *have* to pay attention to us!"

"It would have to be well organized," Ahi said. "We need flyers and coordinators and troubleshooters. We can do this!"

The USO worked for weeks organizing the walkout. It was to be peaceful, yet powerful. Rameck, George, and Sampson all participated in the planning.

On a cool morning in April, at exactly the same time, hundreds of students from University High School quietly walked out of the

building. They spilled onto the sidewalks and into the street. Some walked; some drove; some took busses to the Board of Education headquarters in downtown Newark. The buses and streets grew more crowded as, amazingly, students from Shabazz, Central, and other high schools joined the protest.

They locked arms and chanted. "We shall overcome!" they sang.

Police showed up and tried to stop them, but there were too many students to arrest. Besides, the students were peaceful, well behaved, and focused on their goal. Traffic was snarled as hundreds and hundreds of students marched toward the building.

"We want to speak to the superintendent!" Hassan and Ahi demanded of the timid-looking secretary who came out to greet them in the front of the building. "We have legitimate concerns, and we respectfully request a meeting to discuss them." The secretary scurried back inside with the message.

Of course, the superintendent refused to come out of his office. Students grew impatient and began pushing. A surge of students moved forward, and they entered the lobby of the building. They sat down and refused to move until someone came to speak to them. Hassan, the loudest and most outspoken, was arrested for disturbing the peace.

Eventually, the superintendent, an assemblyman, and a state senator showed up and spoke to the crowd, but the students' requests weren't addressed specifically or seriously. Hours passed. Gradually, students began to leave. They had jobs to get to, or family responsibilities.

"I gotta go, Rameck," George said. "I can't miss work tonight."

"Do what you gotta do, man. I'm staying," Rameck said with a smile. "It just feels right, you know?"

"I'm outta here, too, man," Sampson said. "Good luck."

Rameck and about fifty others refused to leave the lobby of the building that night. The police set up a guard, more to protect them than to detain them. Someone ordered them pizza. A parent brought blankets. But the students stayed the night, emphasizing the importance of their demands.

The next morning they went home, feeling victorious. Over the next few weeks, a committee was formed to develop the first curriculum at University High School that included African-American and Hispanic history.

Rameck was a hero at school and was even on the news briefly. He felt good about himself and what he had accomplished.

But that didn't stop him from getting in trouble.

Questions and exercises on the text are on page 191.

CHALLENGES 2

I Am Malala
LISTENING Indira Gandhi on Education
Friday 4th April
For a Laugh
No Plans at All

I AM MALALA

BY MALALA YOUSAFZAI WITH CHRISTINA LAMB

MALALA YOUSAFZAI (1997–) was born in Mingora, Pakistan. She came to public attention at the age of eleven by writing for BBC Urdu about life under the Taliban. Using the pen name Gul Makai, she often spoke about her family's fight for girls' education in her community. In October 2012, Malala was targeted by the Taliban and shot in the head as she was returning from school on a bus. She miraculously survived after surgery in Britain and continues her campaign for education. In recognition of her courage and advocacy, Malala was the winner of Pakistan's National Youth Peace Prize in 2011 and was awarded the International Children's Peace Prize in 2013. In 2014 she was awarded the Nobel Peace Prize, the youngest ever winner. Malala continues to champion universal access to education around the world.

The bus did two trips every day, and that day we took the second one. We liked staying on at school and Moniba said, "As we're tired after the exam, let's stay and chat before going home." I was relieved that the Pakistan Studies exam had gone well, so I agreed. I had no worries that day. I was hungry, but because we were fifteen we could no longer go outside to the street, so I got one of the small girls to buy me a corn cob. I ate a little bit of it then gave it to another girl to finish.

At 12 o'clock *Baba* called us over the loudspeaker. We all ran down the steps. The other girls all covered their faces before emerging from the door and climbed into the back of the bus. I wore my scarf over my head but never over my face.

I asked Usman Bhai Jan to tell us a joke while we were waiting for two teachers to arrive. He has a collection of extremely funny stories. That day instead of a story he did a magic trick to make a pebble disappear. "Show us how you did it!" we all clamored, but he wouldn't.

When everyone was ready he took Miss Rubi and a couple of small children in the front cab with him. Another little girl cried, saying she wanted to ride there too. Usman Bhai Jan said no, there was no room; she would have to stay in the back with us. But I felt sorry for her and persuaded him to let her in the cab.

Atal had been told by my mother to ride on the bus with me, so he walked over from the primary school. He liked to hang off the tailboard at the back, which made Usman Bhai Jan cross, as it was dangerous. That day Usman Bhai Jan had had enough and refused to let him. "Sit inside, Atal Khan, or I won't take you!" he said. Atal had a tantrum and refused, so he walked home in a huff with some of his friends.

Usman Bhai Jan started the *dyna* and we were off. I was talking to Moniba, my wise, nice friend. Some girls were singing, I was drumming rhythms with my fingers on the seat.

Moniba and I liked to sit near the open back so we could see out. At that time of day Haji Baba Road was always a jumble of colored rickshaws, people on foot and men on scooters, all zigzagging and honking. An ice-cream boy on a red tricycle painted with red and white nuclear missiles rode up behind waving at us, until a teacher shooed him away. A man was chopping off chickens' heads, the blood

dripping onto the street. I drummed my fingers. Chop, chop, chop. Drip, drip, drip. Funny, when I was little we always said Swatis were so peace-loving it was hard to find a man to slaughter a chicken.

The air smelled of diesel, bread and kebab mixed with the stink from the stream where people still dumped their rubbish and were never going to stop despite all my father's campaigning. But we were used to it. Besides, soon the winter would be here, bringing the snow, which would cleanse and quieten everything.

The bus turned right off the main road at the army checkpoint. On a kiosk was a poster of crazy-eyed men with beards and caps or turbans under big letters saying WANTED TERRORISTS. The picture at the top of a man with a black turban and beard was Fazlullah. More than three years had passed since the military operation to drive the Taliban out of Swat had begun. We were grateful to the army but couldn't understand why they were still everywhere, in machine-gun nests on roofs and manning checkpoints. To even enter our valley people needed official permission.

The road up the small hill is usually busy, as it is a shortcut, but that day it was strangely quiet. "Where are all the people?" I asked Moniba. All the girls were singing and chatting and our voices bounced around inside the bus.

Around that time my mother was probably just going through the doorway into our school for her first lesson since she had left school at age six.

I didn't see the two young men step out into the road and bring the van to a sudden halt. I didn't get a chance to answer their question "Who is Malala?" or I would have explained to them why they should let us girls go to school as well as their own sisters and daughters.

The last thing I remember is that I was thinking about the revision I needed to do for the next day. The sounds in my head were not the *crack, crack, crack* of three bullets, but the *chop, chop, chop, drip, drip, drip* of the man severing the heads of chickens, and them dropping into the dirty street, one by one.

Questions and exercises on the text are on page 198.

FRIDAY 4TH APRIL

BY SIOBHAN PARKINSON

SIOBHAN PARKINSON (1954–) is an Irish writer of books for both children and adults. She studied English and German Literature at Trinity College, Dublin. She writes both in Irish and English and has published more than twenty books since 1992 as well as translating books from German. Her books have won numerous awards.

Alva and I are going to paint her bedroom this weekend. I said I would buy the paint, instead of an Easter egg this year. I thought it would cheer her up.

I got Mum to leave us at the DIY shop yesterday, while she went off with her trolley in that distracted way of hers – she goes into a complete trance once she enters a supermarket, I don't know why – and we chose the paint. It's a very, very pale pink, so pale you could almost call it white.

The best part is that it was on special offer, so it didn't cost a fortune. I love getting things cheap. Money is a bit of a problem in our house. Mum's job is only part-time. In some jobs, part-time is fine, because you can get by on half a salary if you really put your mind to it and anyway you pay less tax, but Mum is a teacher, which means that there are three months in the summer, plus other holidays, when she doesn't get paid at all, so cash is always tight with us.

Dad pays our school fees. That's his contribution to the family economy, that and half the mortgage. He says he doesn't agree with single-sex education. The only mixed school in our area is a fee-paying one, but he insisted we go there anyway. I don't really believe it has anything to do with co-education. I think it's just snobbery, but I love our school, so I don't argue. That's the only extravagant thing about our lives. We are always having to plan our finances and budget for things.

I help Mum with all that side of things. She's not very good with figures, but we do it together and it's very satisfying, seeing the columns all adding up and balancing out. I've got her into the habit of using her credit card for most things, and we only keep enough cash for bread and milk and the paper, so we don't buy things we haven't planned for, like expensive magazines or sudden-impulse takeaways. We have an emergency fiver, in the bottom of a spaghetti

jar – one of those long ones, so it's hard to get it out unless you really need it.

TUESDAY 8TH APRIL

Alva is delighted with her bedroom. She gave me a big painty hug and half-smothered me in kisses on Sunday when we finished it and said I was the best big sister anybody ever had and that nobody ever had such a brillo bedroom ever ever before. It is nice, I must say, not too pink, just a nice soft rosy glow. She tore up all the old posters and pin-ups and postcards she'd had festooned over her walls, saying that they were all too raggy and dog-eared for such a beautiful room, and she went out and bought an enormous, shiny technicolour poster of Boyzone and put it up reverently with blu-tack. Mum and I had to act as consultants while she put it up, and she kept begging us to tell her whether it was properly centred and whether it would be in a glare when the curtains were open. At one point she even wished she had Dad's spirit level so she could be completely sure it was straight. Dad took all his DIY tools with him, which was a bit mean of him. We never have a hammer or a pliers or anything.

When the poster was exactly where Alva wanted it, Mum and I had to stand there and admire it, nudging each other secretly, and agreeing that the lads were just the pinnacle of male desirability. So there they are, like Matthew, Mark, Luke and John and a stray friend blessing the bed that she lies on, and grinning down with their toothpasty smiles at her all night long. I suppose they are quite good-looking, really, if you're going on fourteen.

(Extract from *Sisters ... No Way!* by Siobhan Parkinson, The O'Brien Press Ltd.)

Questions and exercises on the text are on page 204.

FOR A LAUGH

BY EUGENE SALOMON

In the summer of 1990 I was hailed on 6th Avenue in Greenwich Village by an attractive young lady who was pregnant. Perhaps that's an understatement. Actually, she was *too* pregnant: her belly was so huge it looked like she would soon be giving birth to an elephant. I noticed, however, that she slid into the back seat with the grace of a gazelle. It raised an eyebrow.

'I want to go to Tompkins Square Park in the East Village,' she blurted out immediately, 'but, you know, I'm nine months pregnant and I don't have any money.'

This was so up front and fresh that I found it rather disarming. I pulled out from the curb and made a right on West 4th Street, not knowing how long I'd be willing to keep driving for no exchange, but at least for the moment showing her that I was willing to keep listening to her justifications for why it was okay not to pay.

'So what you're saying is that if you're pregnant you get everything for free?' I inquired.

She displayed a wry smile.

'Well, no,' she said, 'but I *can't* pay you and as you can see I'm nine months pregnant.'

Actually what I could see was that she was nine months *pillow*! She was trying to use her gigantic bulge to push people's sympathy buttons and get stuff for free. Nevertheless, it was one of those times when you know someone is full of it, and the person knows that you know that she is full of it, but you don't care because of the entertainment value of the pretense. I continued driving.

'Well, you know, I have a strict policy when it comes to

giving rides,' I said in a friendly way, 'and that is that everyone has to pay something. No free rides. Strict company policy.'

'Yeah, but I don't have any money, man.'

'Well, maybe you can think of something else to offer me in exchange for the ride,' I said. 'It doesn't *have* to be money.'

She thought about this for a few moments. Then, as we came to a red light at LaGuardia Place, she had an idea.

'How about a joke?' she asked.

A joke! I thought right away that it would be a fair enough exchange. For one thing, there was the novelty of it: perhaps in the history of taxi driving, no one had ever before paid for a ride with a joke. And for another thing, it was a short ride. If someone was going to Kennedy Airport from Manhattan and wanted to pay with a joke, the only joke would be the one on me. But this was just a shortie to the East Village. I decided to accept her offer.

'Well, okay,' I said, 'but it has to be a joke I haven't heard before. Wooden nickels and used jokes are not accepted in this taxi!'

She was up for the challenge.

'Okay,' she said. 'Here goes.' And with that, she told me her joke:

'Why was Six afraid of Seven?'

'Why?'

'Because Seven ate Nine.'

I had not heard that one before and it brought a smile. I told her I liked it and I thought that my daughter, who was seven at the time, would like it too. And I told her that her fare had been paid.

In an interesting way this back and forth created a little bond between us. She saw that she had been able to give me something of value in order to receive something of value, and this at least for the moment had raised her self-esteem. She was no longer a cheat. She could contribute. And I was now a person who could be communicated with and could be trusted.

We began to talk and I learned enough of her story to understand how she came to be walking around Greenwich Village with a pillow under her dress. She was a middle-class kid who'd dropped out of some college that was somewhere else and had taken off with her artist boyfriend for New York City. They were both heavily into drugs and wound up establishing residence in Tompkins Square Park, which was something you could do in those days. I was able to get it across to her in a gentle way that she needed to make a decision to quit the shit, that the time for change had come for her, and that the only real change can come from within.

'I know,' she said, and she said it in a way that made me feel that she did indeed know it and that maybe she just needed the right person to tell her. Within a minute we arrived at the park and said our goodbyes.

'Thanks for the ride,' she said.

'Hey, thanks for the joke,' I replied.

She closed the back door, started to walk off, took a few steps, and then, before I could drive away, she turned around and said something else to me.

'I love you!' she called out with a big smile. I returned her smile, waved farewell, and headed off down Avenue A.

Looking back at it, she'd given me a joke which my daughter did indeed enjoy, a story which has been retold in my cab countless times, and a wonderful acknowledgment that I've never forgotten. Looks like *I* was the one who was short on the exchange factor here – she'd given me much more than I could ever have expected for a six-minute ride across town.

Questions and exercises on the text are on page 206.

NO PLANS AT ALL

BY SUE TOWNSEND

SUE TOWNSEND (1946–2014) lived in Leicester, England. She wrote *The Secret Diary of Adrian Mole 13 ¾* (1982) which has sold over 20 million copies worldwide. A number of books about the life of Adrian Mole followed. Other books include *Rebuildning Coventry, Ghost Children, The Queen and I. The Woman Who Went to Bed for a Year* was published in 2012 and became a great success. Townsend received several literary awards during her life.

On the second day Eva woke and threw the duvet back and sat on the side of the bed.

Then she remembered that she didn't have to get up and make breakfast for anyone, yell at anyone else to get up, empty the dishwasher or fill the washing machine, iron a pile of laundry, drag a vacuum cleaner up the stairs or sort cupboards and drawers, clean the oven or wipe various surfaces, including the necks of the brown and the red sauce bottles, polish the wooden furniture, clean the windows or mop the floors, straighten rugs and cushions, shove a brush down various shitty toilets or pick up soiled clothing and place it in a laundry basket, replace light bulbs and toilet rolls, pick up things from downstairs that were upstairs and bring them down or pick up things from upstairs that were downstairs, fetch dry-cleaning, weed the borders, visit garden centres to buy bulbs and annuals, polish shoes or take them to the key cutter, return library books, sort recycling, pay paper bills, visit one mother and worry about not visiting one mother-in-law, feed the fish and clean out the filter, answer the phone for two teenagers and pass on messages, shave legs or pluck eyebrows, give self manicure, change the sheets and pillow cases on three beds (if it was Saturday), hand wash-woollen jumpers and dry flat on a bath towel, pay bills, shop for food she wouldn't eat herself, wheel it to the car, unload it into the boot, drive home, put the food away in the fridge and the cupboards and, on tiptoe, place tins and dried goods on a shelf that exceeded her reach but was perfectly comfortable for Brian.

She would not be chopping vegetables and browning meat for a casserole. She would not be baking bread and cakes because Brian preferred the home-made to the shop bought. She would not be

cutting grass, weeding, planting and sweeping paths or collecting leaves in the garden. She would not be painting the new fence with creosote. She would not be chopping wood to light the real log fire that Brian sat next to after he came home from work in the winter months. She would not be brushing her hair, showering or hurriedly applying make-up.

Today she would not be doing any of those things.

She would not be worrying that her clothes were uncoordinated, because she could not see the time when she would be wearing clothes again. She would only be wearing pyjamas and a dressing gown for the foreseeable future.

She would rely on other people to feed her, wash her and buy her food. She didn't know who these people were but she believed that most people were longing to demonstrate their innate goodness.

She knew she wouldn't be bored – she had a great deal to think about.

She hurried to the lavatory, washed her face and under her arms, but it felt wrong to be out of bed. She thought that with her feet on the floor she would easily be lured downstairs by her own sense of duty. Perhaps in future she would ask her mother for a bucket. She remembered the porcelain potty under her grandmother's sagging bed – as a child, it had been Ruby's job to empty the contents early every morning.

Eva lay back on the pillows and quickly fell asleep, only to be woken by Brian asking, 'What have you done with my clean shirts?'

Eva said, 'I gave them to a passing washerwoman. She's going to take them to a babbling brook she knows and pummel them on the stones. She'll have them back by Friday.'

Brian, who had not been listening, shouted, 'Friday! That's no good to me! I need one now!'

Eva turned over to face the window. A few golden leaves were spiralling down from the sycamore outside. She said, 'You don't have to wear a shirt. It's not a condition of your employment. Professor Brady dresses as if he was in The Rolling Stones.'

'It's bloody embarrassing,' said Brian. We had a delegation from NASA last week. Every last one of them was in a blazer, collar and tie, and they were shown round by Brady in his creaking leather trousers, Yoda T-shirt and down-at-heel cowboy boots! On *his* salary! All the bloody cosmologists are the same. And when they're together in the one room, it looks like a meeting in a drug rehabilitation unit! I'm telling you, Eva, if it wasn't for we astronomers they'd be dead in the water!'

Eva turned back to him and said, 'Wear your navy polo shirt, your chinos and your brown brogues.' She wanted him out of her room.

She would ask her uneducated mother to show Dr Brian Beaver BSc, MSc, D Phil (Oxon) how to manipulate the simple dials on the washing machine.

Before Brian left the room she asked him, 'Do you think there *is* a God, Brian?'

He was sitting on the bed, tying his shoelaces. 'Don't tell me you've got religion, Eva. It always ends in tears. According to Steve Hawking's *latest* book, God's not fit for purpose. He's a character in a fairy tale.'

'Then why do so many millions of people believe in him?'

'Look, Eva, the stats are against it. Something *can* actually come from nothing. Heisenbergian uncertainty allows a bubble of space-time to inflate out of nowhere...' He paused. 'But I admit the particle side is ... difficult. The string theory supersymmetry boys *really* need to find the Higgs boson. And the wave function collapse is always a problem.'

Eva nodded, and said, 'I see. Thank you.'

He groomed his beard with Eva's comb and said, 'So, how long do you intend to stay in bed?'

'Where does the universe end?' asked Eva.

Brian fiddled with his beard, twirling the scraggy end between his fingers. 'Can you tell me why you want to retreat from the world, Eva?'

'I don't know how to live in it,' she said. 'I can't even work the remote. I preferred it when there were three channels and all you had to do was go duh, duh, duh.' She stabbed at the imaginary knobs on the imaginary television.

'So, you're going to loll about in bed because you can't work the remote?'

Eva muttered, 'I can't work the new oven stroke grill stroke microwave either. And I can't work out how much we're paying E.ON per quarter on our electricity bill. Do we owe them money, Brian, or do they owe us?'

'I don't know,' he admitted. He took her hand and said, 'I'll see you tonight. By the way, is sex off the menu?'

Questions and exercises on the text are on page 207.

3

IN TRANSITION

FASTER THAN LIGHTNING

BY USAIN BOLT

The scariest thing for me after Moscow 2013 has been planning my next move. What can I do next? Will I better myself? Can I continue winning? I know I've got another solid season in me, maybe two, but can I go all the way to the next Olympics in Rio? That's the only thing that makes me sit and wonder because it's a big challenge – the biggest yet, possibly. Two or three years feels like a long time in track and field because a lot can happen. It's scary and exciting at the same time. I love competition, I thrive off it. Just the thought of trying to get to Brazil gives me a spark.

If there's a possibility that I might make it, then I'm going to give it everything I've got. I've talked to Coach about our chances, and we've discussed the situation sensibly by looking at some of the other athletes around us. I'll be turning 30 when Brazil comes around. Some guys in track and field have run times of 9.80, 9.90 seconds at that age. If I take care of my body and if I can push myself to the limits, then I don't doubt my ability to make 9.60 seconds in 2016. The important thing for me is to land there and compete at a high level. At least then I'll be able to say, 'I attempted it, I got a silver, a bronze, whatever. I was in with a chance and I tried.' Imagine if I managed to win gold, though. The parties in Rio would be off the scale.

I've realised that getting there might be hard work. When I see the young cats coming up around me, I know it could be tough in the trials, even harder than 2012. There are some quick kids in Jamaica right now, but I genuinely want those guys to be the strongest they can be. I want to compete against the best, like I always do. That way, if someone beats me, then at least I can say that I was defeated by The Real Deal. If someone takes my title I want it to be an athlete with serious game.

For now, I want to run as fast as I can and be the best in the world. When I finish with track and field I'll change sports and move on. If I can't race at the top level by 2016, then I want to turn my hand to another game – football, most probably, because I can play, and with enough effort I can get better. I might even get good enough to earn a pro contract. I know that sounds crazy, but the way I look at it is that a manager should take a chance on a player every now and then. I reckon I could add something special to a team in England.

I've watched some wingers in the Premier League and they've not been that great. I've cussed them because they haven't been able to cross the ball with any accuracy. I can pick up a pass, take on a few players at speed and create a goal-scoring opportunity. I'm not saying I'm the next Cristiano Ronaldo, but I'm a speed guy with skill. Imagine what I could do with a lot of practice.

The thought of being a track and field coach doesn't seem like too much fun, though. I couldn't train another athlete, especially if they were someone like me. That would be some serious hell. Sure, if I could work with a kid like Blake, someone with dedication, someone who behaved themselves, then that would be fine. But I'd much rather inspire the younger generation from afar. To do that, I want to run faster for the next couple of years. I want to push the boundaries. Supposing I don't make any quicker times in the 100, I would love to be able to run 18-something seconds in the 200, even if it was an 18.99 race. Forget making the next Olympics and the medals, breaking that time would be an ever bigger success. I'd love to crack it, knowing that people were sitting in their homes and losing their minds at my achievement.

To reach that landmark pace, I would need to have the perfect season, like the one I had in '08. I think next year could be my shot at it, though the window of opportunity is getting smaller with every campaign. The older I get, the narrower that window becomes; the harder it is for me to reach peak fitness in time for a major race. But given what I've done in the past, I don't think it's totally out of reach in the next season or so. Seriously, who would be surprised if I did it? Who's going to stop me from going faster? The only man who can bring an end to my status as a star of track and field in the next couple of years is me, and I'm a phenomenon, a serious competitor – a legend for my generation.

Believe me, my time isn't up just yet.

Questions and exercises on page 212.

NEXT STOP ALABAMA

BY JOHN GREEN

JOHN GREEN (1977–) is an American author of fiction for young adults. He published his first novel *Looking for Alaska* in 2005. Among his books are *Paper Towns* and *The Fault in Our Stars,* both of which have received awards. John Green is also an active video blogger and promoter of charity projects.

ONE HUNDRED AND THIRTY-SIX DAYS BEFORE

The week before I left my family and Florida and the rest of my minor life to go to boarding school in Alabama, my mother insisted on throwing me a going-away party. To say that I had low expectations would be to underestimate the matter dramatically. Although I was more or less forced to invite all my "school friends", i.e. the ragtag bunch of drama people and English geeks I sat with by social necessity in the cavernous cafeteria of my public school, I knew they wouldn't come. Still, my mother persevered, awash in the delusion that I had kept my popularity secret from her all these years. She cooked a small mountain of artichoke dip. She festooned our living room in green and yellow streamers, the colours of my new school. She bought two dozen champagne poppers and placed them around the edge of our coffee table.

And when that final Friday came, when my packing was mostly done, she sat with my dad and me on the living-room couch at 4.56 p.m. and patiently awaited the arrival of the Goodbye to Miles cavalry. Said cavalry consisted of exactly two people: Marie Lawson, a tiny blonde with rectangular glasses, and her chunky (to put it charitably) boyfriend Will.

"Hey, Miles," Marie said as she sat down.

"Hey," I said.

"How was your summer?" Will asked.

"OK. Yours?"

"Good. We did *Jesus Christ Superstar.* I helped with the sets. Marie did lights," said Will.

"That's cool." I nodded knowingly, and that about exhausted our conversational topics. I might have asked a question about *Jesus Christ Superstar,* except (1) I didn't know what it was and (2) I didn't care to learn, and (3) I never really excelled at small talk. My mom, however, can talk small for hours, and so she extended the awkwardness by asking them about their rehearsal schedule, and how the show had gone, and whether it was a success.

"I guess it was," Marie said. "A lot of people came, I guess." Marie was the sort of person to guess a lot.

Finally, Will said, "Well, we just dropped by to say goodbye. I've got to get Marie home by six. Have fun at boarding school, Miles."

"Thanks," I answered, relieved. The only thing worse than having a party that no one attends is having a party attended only by two vastly, deeply uninteresting people.

They left, and so I sat with my parents and stared at the blank TV and wanted to turn it on, but knew I shouldn't. I could feel them both looking at me, waiting for me to burst into tears or something, as if I hadn't known all along that it would go precisely like this. But I *had* known. I could feel their pity as they scooped artichoke dip with chips intended for my imaginary friends, but they needed pity more than I did: I wasn't disappointed. My expectations had been met.

"Is this why you want to leave, Miles?" Mom asked.

I mulled it over for a moment, careful not to look at her. "Uh, no," I said.

"Well, why then?" she asked. This was not the first time she had posed the question. Mom was not particularly keen on letting me go to boarding school and had made no secret of it.

"Because of me?" my dad asked. He had attended Culver Creek, the same boarding school to which I was headed, as had both of his brothers and all of their kids. I think he liked the idea of me following in his footsteps. My uncles had told me stories about how famous my dad had been on campus for having simultaneously raised hell and aced all his classes. That sounded like a better life than the one I had in Florida. But no, it wasn't because of Dad. Not exactly.

"Hold on," I said. I went into Dad's study and found his biography of François Rabelais. I liked reading biographies of writers, even if (as was the case with Monsieur Rabelais) I'd never read any of their actual writing. I flipped to the back and found the highlighted quote ("NEVER USE A HIGHLIGHTER IN MY BOOKS," my dad had told me a thousand times. But how else are you supposed to find what you're looking for?).

"So this guy," I said, standing in the doorway of the living room, "François Rabelais. He was this poet. And his last words were, 'I go to seek a Great Perhaps.' That's why I'm going. So I don't have to wait until I die to start seeking a Great Perhaps."

And that quieted them. I was after a Great Perhaps, and they knew as well as I did that I wasn't going to find it with the likes of Will and Marie. I sat back down on the couch, between my mom and my dad, and my dad put his arm around me and we stayed there like that, quiet on the couch together, for a long time, until it seemed OK to turn on the TV, and then we ate artichoke dip for dinner and watched the History Channel and as going-away parties go, it certainly could have been worse.

Questions and exercises on the text are on page 214.

AT MUMBAI AIRPORT

BY ANJALI JOSEPH

ANJALI JOSEPH (1978–) was born in Mumbai and studied English at Trinity College Cambridge, England. She has taught English at the Sorbonne and worked as a journalist in Mumbai. This extract is from *Saraswati Park,* her first novel published in 2010 which has earned several awards. Her second novel is entitled *Another Country*.

The fluorescent light hurt his already tired eyes; he slumped, exhausted, on one of the moulded armchairs in the airport. They were upholstered in maroon velour and obviously dated from the 1970s. This would be his first flight, and he couldn't relax. There'd been long queues in the departure halls while he checked in his baggage and got a boarding pass; he'd watched his suitcase disappear behind the lackadaisical, heavy skirt of rubber panels that covered a mysterious opening.

His aunt and uncle waited with him. They had bought passes that allowed them to stay until he had to go through Immigration, and down a rough carpeted slope into unfamiliar territory. It was all so strange, this new landscape; it was another world, that made him sad and afraid. But he was impatient to experience his emotions in peace. If only they would go; he didn't want them to go, but he looked at their patient, tired, excited faces and felt that they didn't belong in this adventure, which wouldn't be able to start until they had left.

'Don't wait, Mohan mama, it'll get late.'

'Passengers for the delayed flight A1130 departing for Dubai at 2.45 are kindly requested to proceed to gate number 37 immediately as the flight is now ready for boarding,' began an announcement.

'Don't be silly,' his aunt said. Her face was a mix of tenderness and tears. 'We're not going to leave you here and go.'

'Passengers for the delayed flight A1130 ...'

'Do you want to eat something?' his uncle asked.

'No, we just had dinner, how can I be hungry.'

'I'll just come,' Mohan said. Lakshmi and Ashish watched him stride into the fluorescent-lit hall. His figure became smaller and the light shone through his hair onto the crown of his head. Bored looking policemen lounged near the barriers at the entrance; they witnessed these separations every day.

Ashish got up and stretched. 'You really don't have to stay,' he repeated to his aunt. To his embarrassment, she looked as if she would cry. She held his hand.

'I know it hasn't been an easy year,' she said. 'But this is your home now, remember that. You can come any time, whether your parents are here or not. Come at Diwali if you like, your cousins will all be here.'

'Okay,' he said. She let go of his hand and he rehoisted the rucksack on his shoulder, uncertain for a moment just which stage in the journey he'd reached.

Mohan mama returned, with a packet of chocolate éclairs, a sweet Ashish had always liked. 'Just in case,' he said, handing them over.

'Thanks,' Ashish muttered. Now he was afraid he'd cry. He'd spotted, out of the corner of his eye, a few other young people, all toting laptops; they must be students too. They were parentless, sitting about and laughing; obviously this wasn't their first year away.

His uncle seemed to read his mood. 'Come,' he said to his wife, 'we'll go now.'

'But there's still time, they said he doesn't have to go yet.'

Mohan put a hand on her shoulder. 'It's time, let him be,' he said.

Ashish's mouth twisted. He dug his nails into his palm. His aunt, then his uncle hugged him. Mohan's embrace was structured, awkward but protective; as ever, it felt like a hug from a well-meaning robot. 'Come back soon,' he said, when he drew away.

Ashish nodded, blurry-eyed. 'Maybe at Diwali,' he said, and a scrap of a smile flew from his face to his aunt's, where it broke out brightly. He stood and watched them go.

He was then excited and desperately lonely after he walked past the immigration counters and towards the darkness that was so close to the windows in the boarding lounge. Here the other passengers' faces had lost their sheen, somewhere in the duty-free shop and the long corridors and stairways between the accessible parts of the terminal and this, the front line of departure.

Another darkness was close. As the time drew nearer, Ashish became choked with tears; his usual, familiar fear returned. It was the one about being alone and abandoned. It was wordless and strong; it pulled him irresistibly. He went to a payphone, put in some change and dialled Narayan's number – he had a powerful urge to tell Narayan that he still loved him – or that he was sorry – something, he couldn't express it. After a few rings he put down the receiver and the coins clinked into the metal tray. Then, again, he looked at the coins in his left palm and put them into the phone. He redialled the number. Nearby, the two girls and a boy he'd seen carrying laptops were sitting together and talking.

'Hello?' That well-known voice, and the soft greeting, slightly bored but inquisitive, that Ashish had so loved. He hesitated.

'Hello?' repeated Narayan, a little less patient.

'H-hello.'

'Yes, hello?'

'It's Ashish.'

'Ashish!' and his heart leapt at the catlike pleasure in Narayan's voice.

'I'm at the airport – I'm leaving a little later. Did I wake you? I'm sorry,' he said with specious formality.

There was an announcement and people began to shove towards the boarding gate now, clutching their passes and their hand luggage and murmuring as though reawakened.

'Is that your flight?' Narayan's voice was sleepy. 'I'm glad you called, Ashish, it's good to hear your voice,' he said.

'It's good to hear yours too,' Ashish whispered. Finally he felt tears running down his face in an unstoppable stream. 'It's just that I'm leaving,' he said nonsensically, and his voice cracked.

There was a small silence. 'I know,' Narayan said.

'I miss you sometimes.'

'I miss you too, Ashish, very often.'

The phone beeped. The money had run out; the line was disconnected. Ashish wiped his face with his hands and joined the boarding queue, which moved through the doors that opened onto the runways. Released once again into the warm, black Bombay night, he smelled the city, its humidity, the scent of rotting flowers, fish, and laundry drying in the breeze; its intimacy.

The little bus took them into the unfamiliar territory of the runway, and he followed the others up the rickety metal staircase to the door of the plane. Inside, the cabin smelled of something minty that caught the back of his throat. He found his seat, stowed his hand luggage in the locker, took out his book, and sat down. When the plane took off half an hour later he was still crying, and remembering the timbre of Narayan's voice.

But he had never taken a flight before, and by the time the 'fasten seat belts' sign was no longer lit, and slender air hostesses handed out small plastic glasses of lemonade, he felt not only better, but like a different person. He hugged the window with his cheek and watched the city, its myriad lights and its pointy sweep into the Arabian Sea. Bombay disappeared behind the plane and they went right into the warm black night; then he relaxed, for everything now was unknown.

Questions and exercises on the text are on page 218.

HEMI'S GIFT

BY T J CORRIGAN

TJ CORRIGAN (1979–) is a Maori writer from Wellington, New Zealand. With her short story *Hemi's Gift* she was one of the finalists for Best Short Story written in English in the 2013 Pikihuia Awards. Her story deals with the theme of "being Maori".

The bus pulls into Auckland station and I grip my bag a little tighter in my hands. There's a line of us waiting to get on, and for the thousandth time I wonder how bad it's going to be when I arrive at the other end.

Two nights ago my dad died, and I am going home to Whāngārei for his tangi.

The driver gets off and tells everyone the bus will be leaving in five minutes. Unfolding his list, he begins ticking off names as people shuffle aboard. I get on and go down to an empty seat near the back. I hope to find solace in being alone.

A Māori man gets on board carrying a battered brown bag and an ancient guitar. He's dressed in old, sloppy clothes. His hair has an overgrown, wild look, like unmown grass, and although he has a big smile on his face, he still looks like the kind of person to disturb the peace.

He strides down the aisle towards the back, towards me, and I shrink into my seat and look away, hoping he'll sit somewhere else. No such luck. He throws himself down on the seat just in front of me and, muttering loudly, begins to pluck at the strings of his guitar.

I shrink lower into my seat, trying to make myself small, and I put a pissed-off look on my face to show everybody on the bus that I am not related to – or associated in any way with – this man.

Up front, a Pākehā couple turn around and look back at the noise he's making, at me sitting behind him, then at each other in a 'typical Māoris' sort of way. That look was exactly why I didn't want him sitting near me. My shoulders slump, and I let my head drop back against the head rest. Now I'm associated with this crazy man just because we both have brown skin – naturally.

The plucking and muttering continues. The bus is permeated by a tense silence that doesn't seem to register with crazy man.

'Me he manu rere ...' he begins to sing. I am annoyed that I have to put up with this noise till Whāngārei, so I rustle around in my bag and pull out my iPod. I make as much noise as possible plugging in the earphones, making a deliberate show of humming and harring my way through playlists. My intent is to shame him into silence. The singing in front of me stops, and suddenly I feel ashamed. But crazy man is looking out the window, at the green hills flying by, seemingly entranced. 'Going home,' he whispers to nobody in particular – least of all me – but I feel the same way.

I remember my laptop, and I pull it out of its bag and stare at it as if I'm waiting for it to answer a question. If I were to fire it up and open Outlook I would see one unread email. It arrived two nights ago, just after I finished watching TV. I saw the blue notification box pop up in the lower right of the screen; and I could tell it was a personal message from Dad because it didn't have one of those stupid 'FWD:' labels on it, and the subject was 'Hi'. I remember thinking that I couldn't be bothered reading some lame message from him at that hour, so I had turned off my laptop and gone to bed – only to be woken three hours later by my tearful mother.

My fingers tap on the edge of the laptop. So do I read the email? Or leave it? What will it say – or what is it that I want it to say? Did he somehow know he was going to have a massive stroke, and wanted to reach out to me, the only child, and tell me one last time that he loved me? That I was the best thing that happened to him and Mum, and all that bullshit every kid secretly longs to hear but cringes when they actually do? Or was it just a quick 'Hello, how's uni? Hope you're looking after yourself'?

I snap my laptop shut and put it away. I notice the trembling in my fingers, and I lean back and close my eyes, squeezing them tight; squeezing the thoughts away and momentarily succeeding. But it doesn't stop the tears.

The bus shudders to a halt. I wake up and look outside. Kaiwaka. Thirty-minute food and toilet break, then off on the last leg home. I get off the bus and search in my bag for my cigarettes.

Shit, I've left them on the fridge in my dorm ... right on top of ... ahh, my wallet! This day just gets better and better. I walk around stretching my legs, and happily I find a stray ciggie at the bottom of my bag. Fag in mouth, I look around for someone with a light. Bugger, crazy man's the only one smoking – typical. I amble over to where he's sitting on the plastic chairs outside the diner.

'Can I borrow a light?'

'Hmm?' He peers up at me through a cloud of smoke, one eye screwed shut and the other bloodshot – figures.

'A light?' I mime the flicking action that people all over the damn world can understand. He smiles at me and laughs, chucking me his lighter, and in an easy tone tells me he thought I said I'd recognised him.

'Me recognise you?' This oughta be good. 'From where?'

Crazy man takes on another persona: 'Jake, hey, Jake! What'chu drinking, bro?' And suddenly I do recognise him, from somewhere. It takes a second, then it clicks; crazy man was in *Once Were Warriors.*

'Me name's Hemi,' says Hemi.

My shoulders relax. I feel relief, like I can trust him now, but I'm not really sure why. I smile. It is the first real smile I've had on my face for days. We sit outside the roadside diner in the small town of Kaiwaka, smoking our cigarettes and looking at the green hills. Cars go by on the main road and the people inside probably just see a couple of horis sucking down tar to make our lungs dark like our skins, but I feel peace in that moment.

'Hey, do you want some food?' Hemi asks me. 'Nah, I don't have any money.'

'You hungry? Come on, I'll buy you food.'

I follow him into the diner and he loads up a tray with sandwiches and cakes.

'You look like you could use a good feed, girl,' he says.

We go outside with the food and eat it in the sun. Afterwards, Hemi reaches into his battered brown bag and hands me a full packet of cigarettes.

'Here, take it. I got a coupla cartons,' he tells me. 'I've just come back from Oz; I been shooting a movie.'

'Really?' I grin.

'Yup; I been shooting with some of those peeps from Ngāti Home and Away.'

'Eh? What are they like?'

'They're all shit.' He laughs like Billy T, and I can't help but join in.

We spark up another ciggie, and I hear Dad's voice asking me if I still smoke. I remember Dad snapping me and my friend smoking cigarettes, in the woodshed when we were fifteen and giving me that look that makes you wither with shame. I remember watching a programme with him when I was ten about a Maori woman who smoked, got lung cancer, lost her hair and died.

I chuck my cigarette away half-smoked, and Hemi looks at me.

A shout erupts from my left as a father pushes his child high in the swing at the diner's playground, and I remember Christmas time when I was about five years old; sitting on my dad's lap in my pyjamas, wearing my brand new jandals, and him reading my new *Henny Penny* book. His hands had looked so big to me, and I remember putting my index finger on top of his and tracing the words on the page. And I remember the look on his face when I told him I was going to uni to get my degree; the first in my family to do so. He didn't say anything. He didn't have to.

INN

‘Come on girl, time to go,’ Hemi says, his voice gentle.

We get back on the bus. Hemi chats to me about working on movie sets with famous actors. He tells me about his family, and what he’s planning on eating when he gets home. I sit there and just listen. Buoyed and supported by his words, I am humbled by this man willing to give a stranger food and company and ask for nothing in return.

In between conversation and silence he strums his guitar and sings. They’re all Māori songs I know, but I don’t join in. I’m happy just to lean back and let myself drift on the sound of Hemi’s voice. I’ve heard Lauren Hill sing at the Logan Campbell Centre with the voice of a thousand angels, and Tina Cross on her knees belting out a flawless solo during *Cats,* but nothing is so memorable to me – feels so soothing – as the melody from Hemi’s guitar mixing with the harmony of his voice.

I lean back in my seat. I close my eyes. And somewhere in the midst of Hemi’s music I grieve for the father I have just lost. In my pain, I am comforted by this gift Hemi has given me, the solace in sound, born from the unexpected meeting between us. The music builds, holds, releases me, until at last the waves of grief subside and, as I open my eyes, Hemi’s voice moans and goes quiet.

‘You’ll be alright, love.’

Questions and exercises on the text are on page 221.

4 CLASSICS

GB

Hamlet, Prince of Denmark

LISTENING **Hamlet, Prince of Denmark cont.**

IRE

Pygmalion

NZ

Sixpence

US

Cat in the Rain

HAMLET, PRINCE OF DENMARK

BY WILLIAM SHAKESPEARE

WILLIAM SHAKESPEARE (1564–1616) Read about William Shakespeare on p. 72. The following extract from Hamlet is a modern prose adaptation of his play.

CAST LIST

HAMLET	son to the former King, nephew to Claudius
HORATIO	friend to Hamlet
THE GHOST OF HAMLET'S FATHER	
OPHELIA	daughter to Polonius
A TROOP OF TRAVELLING PLAYERS	
CLAUDIUS	King of Denmark
GERTRUDE	Queen of Denmark and mother to Hamlet
POLONIUS	Lord Chamberlain
LAERTES	son to Polonius

THE SCENE

Denmark in the thirteenth century

Murder most foul, as in the best it is.
But this most foul, strange, and unnatural.

GHOST OF HAMLET'S FATHER: ACT ONE, SCENE FIVE

Snowflakes twirled in the wind that moaned around the battlements. I turned up the collar of my cloak against the cold, and kept my eyes fixed on the place where the guards had told me they had seen my father's ghost.

Horatio, my oldest friend, was with me. It was Horatio who had brought me the news that my father, the king, was dead – bitten by a snake while he was sleeping in the orchard – and it was Horatio who had stood by my side at my father's funeral. Something in me died too that day, and was sealed up in the Royal Tomb with my father. My grief was so great that it sucked the light and joy out of everything.

From the courtyard below came the sound of drunken laughter.

"Someone is still celebrating the marriage of your mother and your uncle!" Horatio said.

He meant it as a joke, but the joke raised more black thoughts in my mind.

"How could she marry so soon after the funeral?" I said. "How could she forget my father so quickly?"

"You should be happy for her, my lord Hamlet," said Horatio. "She has found new happiness in the midst of sorrow, and your uncle, Claudius, will rule Denmark wisely until you come of age."

I laughed bitterly. I had seen cunning in Claudius's face, but no wisdom. I was about to say so, when midnight began to ring out from the turret above our heads.

And as the last stroke throbbed through the air, the darkness and the falling snow shaped themselves into the spirit of my father, beckoning to me.

Horatio gasped out a warning, but I paid no attention. I ran through the dancing flakes, my heart beating so fast that I thought it would burst.

The ghost was dressed in armour, a circlet of gold gleaming against the black iron of its helm. Its face was my father's face, but twisted in agony, its eyes burning like cold, blue flames. Its voice was a groan of despair that sent shudders down my backbone.

"Hamlet, my son! My spirit cannot find rest until my murder has been avenged."

"Murder?" I cried.

"The serpent who stung me in the orchard was my brother, Claudius," said the ghost. "As I lay asleep, it was he who crept to my side and poured poison in my ear. Claudius took my life, my throne and now my wife. Avenge me, Hamlet!"

Before I could say more, the ghost faded into snowy blackness, and the echoes of its voice became the whistling of the wind.

My mind reeled. Had I really spoken to the ghost of my father, or was it a devil from Hell, sent to trick me into doing evil? I had suspected that Claudius might have had something to do with my father's death, but could I trust the word of a vision from beyond the grave? How could I be sure of the truth? How could I, the Prince of Denmark, not yet twenty years' old, avenge the death of a king?

I turned, and stumbled back to Horatio. His face was grey and he quivered with fear. "Such sights are enough to drive a man mad!" he whispered.

I laughed then, long and hard, because Horatio had unwittingly provided me with an answer.

Who could have more freedom than a mad prince? If I pretended to be mad, I could say whatever I wished and search for the truth without arousing Claudius's suspicion.

* * *

And so my plan took shape. I wore nothing but black. I wandered through the castle, weeping and sighing, seeking out shadowy places to brood. If anyone spoke to me, I answered with the first wild nonsense that came into my head, and all the time I watched Claudius, looking for the slightest sign of guilt. I cut myself off from all friends – except Horatio; I told him everything, for I knew he was the only one I could trust.

A rumour began to spread through the castle that grief had turned my wits. So far, my plan was a success, but it is one thing to invent a plan, and another thing to carry it through. The strain of pretending, of cutting myself off from kindness and good company, was almost too great to bear. There were times when I thought I truly had gone mad, when I felt I could no longer carry the burden of what the ghost had told me. If I avenged my father, my mother's new husband would be revealed as a murderer, and her happiness would be shattered; if I did not, my father's soul was doomed to eternal torment.

Worst of all, I was tortured by doubt. What if Claudius were innocent? What if I had been deceived by an evil spirit? Questions went spinning through my mind, like the stars spinning around the Earth.

Then one day, on a bleak afternoon, alone in my room, I drew my dagger and stared at it. The blade was sharp: if I used it on myself, death would come quickly, and all my doubts and worries would be over – but what then? Would I be sending my soul into an even worse torture? I weighed the dagger in my hand, balancing the fear of what I must do to avenge my father against the fear of what might follow death. It seemed I lacked both the courage to go on with my life, and the courage to end it.

Hearing a knock at my door, I sheathed the dagger and called out, "Come in!" almost relieved at the interruption.

A woman entered. It was Lady Ophelia, her fair hair shining like a candle-flame, her eyes filled with love and concern.

My heart lifted, then sank. Ophelia and I had loved each other since we were children. Before my father's death, I had been certain that she was the one I would marry – but now everything had changed. There was no room in my heart for love.

"Lord Hamlet?" Ophelia said. "My father asks if you will attend the performance of the Royal Players tonight?"

As soon as she mentioned her father, I knew what was happening.

Her father was Polonius, the Royal Chamberlain, a meddling fool who loved gossip and secrets. He had sent Ophelia to try and discover why I was acting so strangely. Ophelia would report everything I said to Polonius, and he would report it to Claudius. I was sickened: the castle of Elsinore was a place where brothers murdered brothers, wives forgot their husbands, and fathers used their daughters as spies.

I laughed carelessly, to hide the ache I felt when I looked at Ophelia's beautiful face. "Tell Lord Polonius that I shall be at the play," I said.

Ophelia turned her head, and I saw a tear fall across her cheek. "My lord," she murmured, "why do you never look at me the way you

used to? There was a time when I believed you loved me, and wished us to marry, but now you seem so cold..."

I longed to tell her how much I loved her, and that my coldness was nothing more than acting, but I did not dare. "*You,* marry me?" I said roughly. "Marry no one, Ophelia! Wives and husbands are all cheats and liars. It would be better for you to join a convent and become a nun!"

At this she ran from the room, her sobs echoing through the corridor, making my heart break.

And then, just as I thought there was no end to my despair, an idea came – first a glimmer, then a gleam, then a burst of light brighter than the sun.

I hurried from my room and went to the Great Hall, where the actors were setting up their stage. I found their leader, a tall man with a look of my uncle about him. After chatting for a few moments, I said casually, "Do you know the play *The Murder of Gonzago?*"

"Certainly, my lord!" came the reply.

I handed the man a purse filled with gold. "Act it tonight," I said. "But I want you to make some changes to the story. Listen carefully..."

I meant to turn the play from an entertainment into a trap – a trap to catch a King.

* * *

That evening, while the audience watched the stage, I watched Claudius. At first he showed little interest in the story, preferring to whisper to my mother and kiss her fingers in a way that filled me with loathing – but gradually the skill of the players won his attention. At the end of the first scene, exactly according to my instructions, the actor playing Duke Gonzago lay down as though asleep and his nephew Lucianus – played by the actor who resembled Claudius – crept up on him and poured poison into his ear.

Even though the light in the hall was dim, I could see the deathly pallor of Claudius's face as he watched this scene. His eyes grew troubled; and he raised a trembling hand towards the stage.

I knew then that I was gazing at the face of a murderer, and that everything the ghost had told me was true.

"No!" Claudius cried out, springing to his feet. "Lights! Bring more lights!"

But all the torches in the world would not light the darkness in his mind. His nerve failed and he hurried from the hall.

Mother made to follow him, but I stopped her at the door. "Do not delay me. I must go to the King!" she said. "Something is wrong."

"And I know what," I told her. "I must talk to you. I will come to your room in an hour. Make sure you are alone, and tell no one of our meeting."

* * *

But I underestimated Claudius's cunning, and the power he had over my mother. When she let me into her room, there was a coldness in her expression and I guessed that she had been speaking to my uncle. Before I could say a word, she said, "Hamlet, you have deeply offended your royal stepfather."

"And you have offended my dead father," I replied.

Mother frowned at me, puzzled. "What do you mean?" she demanded.

"You offended him the day you abandoned your mourning robes in exchange for a wedding gown," I said. "The day you married a liar and a murderer!"

"I won't listen!" Mother shouted. She began to cover her ears with her hands and I caught hold of her wrists to prevent her – she had to hear the truth. Mother screamed in alarm, and then I heard a voice from behind the drawn curtains at her window, calling out, "Help! Murder!"

I was certain it was Claudius – who else would skulk and spy in my mother's bedroom? I drew my sword and plunged it into the curtain, filled with fierce joy that my father was avenged at last...

But it was the body of Lord Polonius that tumbled into the room; I had killed an innocent man.

"You meddling old fool!" I groaned. "What were you doing there?"

"Following my orders," said a voice.

I turned and saw Claudius in the doorway, with two armed guards. A triumphant light glinted in his eyes. "I was afraid you might harm your mother if you were alone with her," Claudius went on. "Your madness has made you violent, Hamlet. You must leave Denmark tonight. I shall send you to friends in England, who will care for you until you are back in your right mind. Guards, take the Prince away!"

Neither my mother nor the guards saw the mocking smile that flickered on his lips, but as soon as I saw it, I knew that Claudius intended me never to return from England. I would be imprisoned, and then secretly murdered.

While I had been trying to trap my uncle, he had been setting a trap for me, and now it had snapped shut.

Questions and exercises on the text are on page 226.

PYGMALION

BY GEORGE BERNARD SHAW

GEORGE BERNARD SHAW (1856–1950) was an Irish playwright who wrote more than 60 plays. Shaw was also an essayist, novelist and short story writer. Most of his writings deal with social issues such as education, marriage, health care, religion and class privilege. *Pygmalion*, a play from 1912, is one of his greatest successes and was also made into a film and the musical *My Fair Lady.* Shaw received the Nobel Prize for Literature in 1925.

In a London street in Covent Garden. Everyone has gone home except the note taker, the gentleman, and the flower girl, who sits arranging her basket, and still pitying herself in murmurs.

THE FLOWER GIRL	Poor girl! Hard enough for her to live without being worrited and chivied.
THE GENTLEMAN	(returning to his former place on the note taker's left) How do you do it, if I may ask?
THE NOTE TAKER	Simply phonetics. The science of speech. That's my profession; also my hobby. Happy is the man who can make a living by his hobby! You can spot an Irishman or a Yorkshireman by his brogue. I can place any man within six miles. I can place him within two miles in London. Sometimes within two streets.
THE FLOWER GIRL	Ought to be ashamed of himself, unmanly coward!
THE GENTLEMAN	But is there a living in that?
THE NOTE TAKER	Oh yes. Quite a fat one. This is an age of upstarts. Men begin in Kentish Town with 80 pounds a year, and end in Park Lane with a hundred thousand. They want to drop Kentish Town; but they give themselves away every time they open their mouths. Now I can teach them –
THE FLOWER GIRL	Let him mind his own business and leave a poor girl –
THE NOTE TAKER	(*explosively*) Woman: cease this detestable boohooing instantly; or else seek the shelter of some other place of worship.

THE FLOWER GIRL (*with feeble defiance*) I've a right to be here if I like, same as you.

THE NOTE TAKER A woman who utters such depressing and disgusting sounds has no right to be anywhere – no right to live. Remember that you are a human being with a soul and the divine gift of articulate speech: that your native language is the language of Shakespeare and Milton and The Bible; and don't sit there crooning like a bilious pigeon.

THE FLOWER GIRL (*quite overwhelmed, and looking up at him in mingled wonder and deprecation without daring to raise her head*) Ah–ah–ah–ow–ow–oo!

THE NOTE TAKER (*whipping out his book*) Heavens! What a sound! (*He writes; then holds out the book and reads, reproducing her vowels exactly*) Ah–ah–ah–ow–ow–oo!

THE FLOWER GIRL (*tickled by the performance, and laughing in spite of herself*) Garn!

THE NOTE TAKER You see this creature with her kerbstone English: the English that will keep her in the gutter to the end of her days. Well, sir, in three months I could pass that girl off as a duchess at an ambassador's garden party. I could even get her a place as lady's maid or shop assistant, which requires better English. That's the sort of thing I do for commercial millionaires. And on the profits of it I do genuine scientific work in phonetics, and a little as a poet on Miltonic lines.

Questions and exercises on the text are on page 230.

SIXPENCE

BY KATHERINE MANSFIELD

KATHERINE MANSFIELD (1888–1923) was born in Wellington, New Zealand. From 1908 she became an expatriate writer in London. *In a German Pension, Bliss and Other Stories* and *The Garden Party and Other Stories* were published during her lifetime. Her short stories depict "a modern woman's engagement with love, art, solitude, impending death and war", according to the New Zealand Book Council. Mansfield led a turbulent life and died at 35 years old from tuberculosis.

Children are unaccountable little creatures. Why should a small boy like Dicky, good as gold as a rule, sensitive, affectionate, obedient, and marvellously sensible for his age, have moods when, without the slightest warning, he suddenly went "mad dog", as his sisters called it, and there was no doing anything with him?

"Dicky, come here! Come here, sir, at once! Do you hear your mother calling you? Dicky!"

But Dicky wouldn't come. Oh, he heard right enough. A clear, ringing little laugh was his only reply. And away he flew; hiding, running through the uncut hay on the lawn, dashing past the woodshed, making a rush for the kitchen garden, and there dodging, peering at his mother from behind the mossy apple trunks, and leaping up and down like a wild Indian.

It had begun at tea-time. While Dicky's mother and Mrs Spears, who was spending the afternoon with her, were quietly sitting over their sewing in the drawing-room, this, according to the servant girl, was what had happened at the children's tea. They were eating their first bread and butter as nicely and quietly as you please, and the servant girl had just poured out the milk and water, when Dicky had suddenly seized the bread plate, put it upside down on his head, and clutched the bread knife.

"Look at me!" he shouted.

His startled sisters looked, and before the servant girl could get there, the bread plate wobbled, slid, flew to the floor, and broke into slivers. At this awful point the little girls lifted up their voices and shrieked their loudest.

"Mother, come and look what he's done!"

"Dicky's broke a great big plate!"

"Come and stop him, mother!"

You can imagine how mother came flying. But she was too late.

Dicky had leapt out of his chair, run through the French windows on to the verandah, and, well – there she stood – popping her thimble on and off, helpless. What could she do? She couldn't chase after the child. She couldn't stalk Dicky among the apples and damsons. That would be too undignified. It was more than annoying, it was exasperating. Especially as Mrs Spears, Mrs Spears of all people, whose two boys were so exemplary, was waiting for her in the drawing-room.

"Very well, Dicky," she cried, "I shall have to think of some way of punishing you."

"I don't care," sounded the high little voice, and again there came that ringing laugh. The child was quite beside himself...

"Oh, Mrs Spears, I don't know how to apologise for leaving you by yourself like this."

"It's quite all right, Mrs Bendall," said Mrs Spears, in her soft, sugary voice, and raising her eyebrows in the way she had. She seemed to smile to herself as she stroked the gathers. "These little things will happen from time to time. I only hope it was nothing serious."

"It was Dicky," said Mrs Bendall, looking rather helplessly for her only fine needle. And she explained the whole affair to Mrs Spears. "And the worst of it is, I don't know how to cure him. Nothing when he's in that mood seems to have the slightest effect on him."

Mrs Spears opened her pale eyes, "Not even a whipping?" said she.

But Mrs Bendall, threading her needle, pursed up her lips. "We never have whipped the children," she said. "The girls never seem to have needed it. And Dicky is such a baby, and the only boy. Somehow ..."

"Oh, my dear," said Mrs Spears, and she laid her sewing down. "I don't wonder Dicky has these little outbreaks. You don't mind my saying so? But I'm sure you make a great mistake in trying to bring up children without whipping them. Nothing really takes its place. And I speak from experience, my dear. I used to try gentler measures" – Mrs Spears drew in her breath with a little, hissing sound – "soaping the boys' tongues, for instance, with yellow soap, or making them stand on the table for the whole of Saturday afternoon. But no, believe me," said Mrs Spears, "there is nothing, there is nothing like handing them over to their father."

Mrs Bendall in her heart of hearts, was dreadfully shocked to hear of that yellow soap. But Mrs Spears seemed to take it so much for granted, that she did too.

"Their father," she said, "Then you don't whip them yourself?"

"Never," Mrs Spears seemed quite shocked at the idea. "I don't think it's the mother's place to whip the children. It's the duty of the father. And, besides, he impresses them so much more."

"Yes, I can imagine that," said Mrs Bendall faintly.

"Now my two boys," Mrs Spears smiled kindly, encouragingly at Mrs Bendall, "would behave just like Dicky if they were not afraid to. As it is..."

"Oh, your boys are perfect little models," cried Mrs Bendall.

They were. Quieter, better-behaved little boys, in the presence of grown-ups, could not be found. In fact, Mrs Spears' callers often made the remark that you never would have known there was a child in the house. There wasn't – very often.

In the front hall, under a large picture of fat, cheery old monks fishing by the riverside, there was a thick, dark horse whip that had belonged to Mr Spears' father. And for some reason the boys preferred to play out of sight of this, behind the dog-kennel or in the tool-house, or round about the dustbin.

"It's such a mistake," sighed Mrs Spears, breathing softly, as she folded her work, "to be weak with children when they are little. It's such a sad mistake, and one so easy to make. It's so unfair to the child. That is what one has to remember. Now Dicky's little escapade this afternoon seemed to me as though he'd done it on purpose. It was the child's way of showing you that he needed a whipping."

"Do you really think so?" Mrs Bendall was a weak little thing and this impressed her very much.

"I do; I feel sure of it. And a sharp reminder now and then," cried Mrs Spears in quite a professional manner, "administered by the father, will save you so much trouble in the future. Believe me, my dear." She put her dry, cold hand over Mrs Bendall's.

"I shall speak to Edward the moment he comes in," said Dicky's mother firmly.

The children had gone to bed before the garden gate banged, and Dicky's father staggered up the steep concrete steps carrying his bicycle. It had been a bad day at the office. He was hot, dusty, tired out.

But by this time Mrs Bendall had become quite excited over the new plan, and she opened the door to him herself.

"Oh, Edward, I'm so thankful you have come home," she cried.

"Why, what's happened?" Edward lowered the bicycle and took off his hat. A red angry pucker showed where the brim had pressed. "What's up?"

"Come – come into the drawing-room," said Mrs. Bendall, speaking very fast. "I simply can't tell you how naughty Dicky has been. You have no idea – you can't have at the office all day – how a child of that age can behave. He's been simply dreadful. I have no control over him – none. I've tried everything, Edward, but it's all no

use. The only thing to do," she finished breathlessly, "is to whip him – is for you to whip him, Edward."

In the corner of the drawing-room there was a what-not, and on the top shelf stood a brown china bear with a painted tongue. It seemed in the shadow to be grinning at Dicky's father, to be saying, "Hooray, this is what you've come home to!"

"But why on earth should I start whipping him?" said Edward, staring at the bear. "We've never done it before."

"Because," said his wife, "don't you see, it's the only thing to do. I can't control the child ..." Her words flew from her lips. They beat round him, beat round his tired head. "We can't possibly afford a nurse. The servant girl has more than enough to do. And his naughtiness is beyond words. You don't understand, Edward; you can't, you're at the office all day."

The bear poked out his tongue. The scolding voice went on. Edward sank into a chair.

"What am I to beat him with?" he said weakly.

"Your slipper, of course," said his wife. And she knelt down to untie his dusty shoes.

"Oh, Edward," she wailed, "you've still got your cycling clips on in the drawing-room. No, really – "

"Here, that's enough." Edward nearly pushed her away. "Give me that slipper." He went up the stairs. He felt like a man in a dark net. And now he wanted to beat Dicky. Yes, damn it, he wanted to beat something. My God, what a life! The dust was still in his hot eyes, his arms felt heavy.

He pushed open the door of Dicky's slip of a room. Dicky was standing in the middle of the floor in his night-shirt. At sight of him Edward's heart gave a warm throb of rage.

"Well, Dicky, you know what I've come for," said Edward.

Dicky made no reply.

"I've come to give you a whipping."

No answer.

"Lift up your night-shirt."

At that Dicky looked up. He flushed a deep pink. "Must I?" he whispered.

"Come on, now. Be quick about it," said Edward, and, grasping the slipper, he gave Dicky three hard slaps.

"There, that'll teach you to behave properly to your mother."

Dicky stood there, hanging his head.

"Look sharp and get into bed," said his father.

Still he did not move. But a shaking voice said, "I've not done my teeth yet, Daddy."

"Eh, what's that?"

Dicky looked up. His lips were quivering, but his eyes were dry. He hadn't made a sound or shed a tear. Only he swallowed and said huskily, "I haven't done my teeth, Daddy."

But at the sight of that little face Edward turned, and, not knowing what he was doing, he bolted from the room, down the stairs, and out into the garden. Good God! What had he done? He strode along and hid in the shadow of the pear tree by the hedge. Whipped Dicky – whipped his little man with a slipper – and what the devil for? He didn't even know. Suddenly he barged into his room – and there was the little chap in his night-shirt. Dicky's father groaned and held on to the hedge. And he didn't cry. Never a tear. If only he'd cried or got angry. But that "Daddy"! And again he heard the quivering whisper. Forgiving like that without a word. But he'd never forgive himself – never. Coward! Fool! Brute! And suddenly he remembered the time when Dicky had fallen off his knee and sprained his wrist while they were playing together. He hadn't cried then, either. And that was the little hero he had just whipped.

Something's got to be done about this, thought Edward. He strode back to the house, up the stairs, into Dicky's room. The little boy was lying in bed. In the half-light his dark head, with the square fringe, showed plain against the pale pillow. He was lying quite still, and even now he wasn't crying. Edward shut the door and leaned against it. What he wanted to do was to kneel down by Dicky's bed and cry himself and beg to be forgiven. But, of course, one can't do that sort of thing. He felt awkward, and his heart was wrung.

"Not asleep yet, Dicky?" he said lightly.

"No, Daddy."

Edward came over and sat on his boy's bed, and Dicky looked at him through his long lashes.

"Nothing the matter, little chap, is there?" said Edward, half whispering.

"No-o, Daddy," came from Dicky.

Edward put out his hand, and carefully he took Dicky's hot little paw.

"You – you mustn't think any more of what happened just now, little man," he said huskily. "See? That's all over now. That's forgotten. That's never going to happen again. See?"

"Yes, Daddy."

"So the thing to do now is to buck up, little chap," said Edward, "and to smile." And he tried himself an extraordinary, trembling apology for a smile. "To forget all about it – to – eh? Little man... Old boy..."

Dicky lay as before. This was terrible. Dicky's father sprang up and went over to the window. It was nearly dark in the garden. The

servant girl had run out, and she was snatching, twitching some white clothes off the bushes and piling them over her arm. But in the boundless sky the evening star shone, and a big gum tree, black against the pale glow, moved its long leaves softly. All this he saw, while he felt in his trouser pocket for his money. Bringing it out, he chose a new sixpence and went back to Dicky.

"Here you are, little chap. Buy yourself something," said Edward softly, laying the sixpence on Dicky's pillow.

But could even that – could even a whole sixpence blot out what had been?

Questions and exercises on the text are on page 233.

CAT IN THE RAIN

BY ERNEST HEMINGWAY

ERNEST HEMINGWAY (1899–1961) was born in Oak Park, Illinois. He volunteered as an ambulance driver for the Red Cross in Italy during the First World War. He also worked as a journalist before becoming a fiction writer. Some famous titles are *The Sun Also Rises, A Farewell to Arms, For Whom the Bell Tolls* and *The Old Man and the Sea*. Hemingway won the Nobel Prize for Literature in 1954.

There were only two Americans stopping at the hotel. They did not know any of the people they passed on the stairs on their way to and from their room. Their room was on the second floor facing the sea. It also faced the public garden and the war monument. There were big palms and green benches in the public garden. In the good weather there was always an artist with his easel. Artists liked the way the palms grew and the bright colors of the hotels facing the gardens and the sea. Italians came from a long way off to look up at the war monument. It was made of bronze and glistened in the rain. It was raining. The rain dripped from the palm trees. Water stood in pools on the gravel paths. The sea broke in a long line in the rain and slipped back down the beach to come up and break again in a long line in the rain. The motor cars were gone from the square by the war monument. Across the square in the doorway of the café a waiter stood looking out at the empty square.

The American wife stood at the window looking out. Outside right under their window a cat was crouched under one of the dripping green tables. The cat was trying to make herself so compact that she would not be dripped on.

"I'm going down and get that kitty," the American wife said.

"I'll do it," her husband offered from the bed.

"No, I'll get it. The poor kitty out trying to keep dry under a table."

The husband went on reading, lying propped up with the two pillows at the foot of the bed.

"Don't get wet," he said.

The wife went downstairs and the hotel owner stood up and bowed to her as she passed the office. His desk was at the far end of the office. He was an old man and very tall.

"Il piove," the wife said. She liked the hotel-keeper.

"Sì, sì, Signora, brutto tempo. It's very bad weather."

He stood behind his desk in the far end of the dim room. The wife liked him. She liked the deadly serious way he received any complaints. She liked his dignity. She liked the way he wanted to serve her. She liked the way he felt about being a hotel-keeper. She liked his old, heavy face and big hands.

Liking him she opened the door and looked out. It was raining harder. A man in a rubber cape was crossing the empty square to the café. The cat would be around to the right. Perhaps she could go along under the eaves. As she stood in the doorway an umbrella opened behind her. It was the maid who looked after their room.

"You must not get wet," she smiled, speaking Italian. Of course, the hotel-keeper had sent her.

With the maid holding the umbrella over her, she walked along the gravel path until she was under their window. The table was there, washed bright green in the rain, but the cat was gone. She was suddenly disappointed. The maid looked up at her.

"*Ha perduto qualche cosa, Signora?*"

"There was a cat," said the American girl.

"A cat?"

"*Sì, il gatto.*"

"A cat?" the maid laughed. "A cat in the rain?"

"Yes," she said, "under the table." Then, "Oh, I wanted it so much. I wanted a kitty."

When she talked English the maid's face tightened.

"Come, Signora," she said. "We must get back inside. You will be wet."

"I suppose so," said the American girl.

They went back along the gravel path and passed in the door. The maid stayed outside to close the umbrella. As the American girl passed the office, the padrone bowed from his desk. Something felt very small and tight inside the girl. The padrone made her feel very small and at the same time really important. She had a momentary feeling of being of supreme importance. She went on up the stairs. She opened the door of the room. George was on the bed, reading.

"Did you get the cat?" he asked, putting the book down.

"It was gone."

"Wonder where it went to," he said, resting his eyes from reading.

She sat down on the bed.

"I wanted it so much," she said. "I don't know why I wanted it so much. I wanted that poor kitty. It isn't any fun to be a poor kitty out in the rain."

George was reading again.

She went over and sat in front of the mirror of the dressing table looking at herself with the hand glass. She studied her profile, first one side and then the other. Then she studied the back of her head and her neck.

"Don't you think it would be a good idea if I let my hair grow out?" she asked, looking at her profile again.

George looked up and saw the back of her neck, clipped close like a boy's.

"I like it the way it is."

"I get so tired of it," she said. "I get so tired of looking like a boy."

George shifted his position in the bed. He hadn't looked away from her since she started to speak.

"You look pretty darn nice," he said.

She laid the mirror down on the dresser and went over to the window and looked out. It was getting dark.

"I want to pull my hair back tight and smooth and make a big knot at the back that I can feel," she said. "I want to have a kitty to sit on my lap and purr when I stroke her."

"Yeah?" George said from the bed.

"And I want to eat at a table with my own silver and I want candles. And I want it to be spring and I want to brush my hair out in front of a mirror and I want a kitty and I want some new clothes."

"Oh, shut up and get something to read," George said. He was reading again.

His wife was looking out of the window. It was quite dark now and still raining in the palm trees.

"Anyway, I want a cat," she said, "I want a cat, I want a cat now. If I can't have long hair or any fun, I can have a cat."

George was not listening. He was reading his book. His wife looked out the window where the light had come on in the square.

Someone knocked at the door.

"Avanti," George said. He looked up from his book.

In the doorway stood the maid. She held a big tortoise-shell cat pressed tight against her and swung down against her body.

"Excuse me," she said, "the padrone asked me to bring this for the Signora."

Questions and exercises on the text are on page 235.

Defoe
Swift
James
Dickens
Trollope

Authors of the English-Speaking World

Classic Authors from Britain and America
A Brief History of English Literature
Contemporary Authors

Classic Authors from Britain and America

VIRGINIA WOOLF 1882-1941

Virginia Woolf was one of the important members of the Bloomsbury Group – a group of writers, artists and intellectuals in London in the early 20th century. Some of her best known books are *Mrs Dalloway, To the Lighthouse* and *Orlando*. In her novels she developed a style of writing called "stream of consciousness" where she describes life moment by moment, focusing more on inner life than on events. In *A Room of One's Own* she deals with the situation of women writers.

CHARLES DICKENS 1812-1870

The Pickwick Papers was first published as monthly episodes in a magazine and was an instant success. Dickens wasn't just a gifted storyteller but he was also a writer with a social conscience. In particular he describes how poverty and corruption affected ordinary people's lives. This can be seen in such classics as *Oliver Twist, David Copperfield* and *Great Expectations*. Dickens had a special talent for giving his characters memorable and appropriate-sounding names, such as Gradgrind, Heep and Bumble.

JANE AUSTEN 1775-1817

Jane Austen led a quiet, middle class life with her family in Hampshire. Her novels are social comedies and the characters are generally from her own class. She observes their adventures and misadventures with affection but also with a critical, sometimes ironic eye. Her best known novels are *Sense and Sensibility, Pride and Prejudice* and *Emma*, all of which have been filmed. Jane Austen never married and died at the age of 42.

WILLIAM SHAKESPEARE 1564-1616

Shakespeare was born and brought up in Stratford-upon-Avon. At the age of 18 he married Anne Hathaway, a local farmer's daughter. Only three years later he left for London to make his way as an actor and playwright. By 1595 he was established and in the following twenty years he wrote and produced more than 30 plays. Some of the best known are: *Romeo and Juliet, A Midsummer Night's Dream, Richard III, King Lear, Hamlet, Much Ado About Nothing, Othello* and *Macbeth*. Shakespeare is also loved for his poetry, especially his many sonnets.

FRANCIS SCOTT KEY FITZGERALD 1896-1940

Francis Scott Key Fitzgerald is regarded as one of the greatest American writers of the 20th century. Four of his novels were published in his lifetime, including *This Side of Paradise*, *The Beautiful and Damned*, and *Tender Is the Night*. However, his most famous work is *The Great Gatsby*, which has been the basis for a number of films. This novel revolves around the wealthy Jay Gatsby whose past is unclear, and who loves the beautiful Daisy Buchanan. The setting is Long Island where Gatsby hosts lavish parties for rich people.

MARK TWAIN 1835-1910

Samuel Langhorne Clemens (Twain's real name) worked as a journalist but also had some experience as a pilot on the Mississippi River, which is depicted in *The Adventures of Huckleberry Finn* where Huck, a young boy and Jim, a slave on the run, sail down south on a raft. Twain was a great humorist and storyteller. His other best known book is *Tom Sawyer*.

EMILY DICKINSON 1830-1886

Emily Dickinson grew up in Amherst and remained at home all her life. In her thirties she withdrew from the outside world, never went out, seeing only her family and some very close friends. Only seven of her poems were published during her lifetime. After her death approximately 1,800 poems were found. Emily Dickinson's last wish had been for all her works to be destroyed. Fortunately it was not carried out.

WALT WHITMAN 1819-1892

Walt Whitman began work as an office boy at the age of only eleven. Later he worked as a printer, a teacher and a journalist. Whitman published his *Leaves of Grass* in 1855. The twelve long poems dealt with freedom and brotherhood and were looked upon as very modern at the time. This was partly because of the content but also because of their free verse form, ignoring the traditional rules of rhyme and rhythm.

The Renaissance (1500–1650)

The Renaissance is sometimes called the 'Revival of Learning' with a new general cultural renewal in Western Europe – in particular, a revived interest in Greek literature. It was at this time that the art of printing was discovered by Johannes Gutenberg and books were printed in their thousands.

In England, the advances made by humanists and early Renaissance writers were interrupted by the turmoil of the Reformation and the despotism of Henry VIII. However, with the accession of Elizabeth I, a literary renaissance was relaunched – especially through the medium of poetry and drama. The greatest writers during this period were Edmund Spencer, Christopher Marlowe and, of course, William Shakespeare.

The Age of Enlightenment (1700)

During this period literary civilization broadened to include more of the middle class, including women. The aristocratic patron gave way to the bookseller. There was now an emphasis on reason and common sense, as opposed to imagination and feeling. Writers began to look for general rather than subjective truths and it was during this period that the novel really flourished.

A well-known writer from this time is Daniel Defoe. He had travelled much and became a 'voyage writer' – a writer who lets you 'see through his eyes'. His most famous book is *Robinson Crusoe* (1719) – the story of a castaway and his struggle for survival on a desert island. Another famous writer of this period is the Irishman Jonathan Swift, probably most famous for his book *Gulliver's Travels* (1726), which is both a satire and a fascinating tale of one man's marvellous adventures.

The Romantic Age (1790–1837)

The Romantic Age was a reaction against the ideals of the Age of Enlightenment. English romantic literature is overwhelmingly a poetic one, with six major poets writing in the first quarter of the 19th century, transforming the literary climate. In the first decade came Blake, Wordsworth and Coleridge, followed later by Byron, Shelley and Keats. The other great literary artist of the period is Jane Austen, whose six novels appeared between 1811 and 1818.

A Brief History of English Literature

The Age of Realism and Naturalism (mid 1800–late 1800)
During this, the Victorian Age, all aspects of society were being scrutinized by writers. There was a huge growth in literature, especially in fiction, practised notably by Charles Dickens, William Makepiece Thackeray, the Brontës, George Eliot, Anthony Trollope, Henry James and Thomas Hardy. Writers during this period aimed at painting a broad picture of life and people and places were described in great detail. Charles Dickens, for example, wrote about the appalling conditions in workhouses and orphanages in his famous novel from this time *Oliver Twist* (1837).

Early Twentieth Century (1900–1927)
During the early part of the 20th century there was a strong desire to experiment with all forms of art. The pre-war years (1901-1913) were rich in good writing of many kinds – old and new, major and minor. Novelists included Rudyard Kipling, John Galsworthy, Arnold Bennett, H. G. Wells and Joseph Conrad.
The writers during the period 1914-1927 are known as 'Modernists' and this period is perhaps the richest in 20th century writing. Two pieces of writing published in 1922 – James Joyce's *Ulysses* and T. S. Eliot's *The Waste Land* differed totally in form from the novels and poems that had preceded them. Other famous writers of this period were Virginia Woolf, D. H. Lawrence, W.B. Yeats and Katherine Mansfield.

Contemporary Authors

CANADA

Michael Ondaatje was born in Colombo, Sri Lanka in 1943 in a family of Dutch-Tamil-Sinhalese-Portuguese origin, and moved to England with his mother in 1954. In 1962 he relocated to Canada where he has lived ever since. He won the Booker Prize for his novel *The English Patient.* His novel *In the Skin of a Lion* is about early immigrant settlers in Toronto. Other works include *Coming Through Slaughter, The Cat's Table* and *Running in the Family.*

Margaret Atwood (1939-) was born in Ottawa but lives in Toronto. She started writing at an early age and is known as a novelist, a poet, a literary critic, an essayist and an environmental activist. In her novels Atwood often writes about women in search of an identity. Among her best-known works are *The Blind Assassin,* which won the Booker Prize, and the trilogy of *Oryx and Crake, The Year of The Flood* and *MaddAddam.*

THE US

Jonathan Safran Foer (1977-) wrote the bestseller *Everything Is Illuminated,* which was named Book of the Year by the Los Angeles Times. His second novel, *Extremely Loud and Incredibly Close* has been made into a film. The story is about nine-year-old Oskar Schell who, when his father is killed in the September 11th attacks on the World Trade Centre, sets out to solve the mystery of a key he discovers in his father´s closet. In *Eating Animals,* Safran Foer's first work of non-fiction, he explores the many reasons we use to justify our eating habits, and looks at the realities of the food industry.

Joyce Carol Oates (1938-) grew up on a farm outside Lockport, New York. Her working class background is often recalled in her fiction, and she is considered to be one of the most outstanding writers in the US today. She has published more than 100 books ranging from literary criticism to poems, plays, young adult fiction and novels, including such titles as *The Falls, The Gravedigger's Daughter* and *The Accursed.* Oates has also written suspense novels under the pseudonyms Rosamond Smith and Lauren Kelly. Since 1978 she has taught Creative Writing at Princeton University, where she has mentored numerous young writers, including Jonathan Safran Foer.

IRELAND

Roddy Doyle (1958-) is one of Ireland's most popular writers. He writes humorously about the ordinary lives of working and middle class Dublin people. His first novel, *The Commitments,* was followed by *The Snapper* and *The Van,* and all three have been made into films. He won the Booker Prize for *Paddy Clark Ha*

Ha Ha in 1993. In his most recent book, *The Guts,* he reintroduces the character Jimmy Rabbitte from his debut novel *The Commitments.*

Marian Keyes (1963–) published her first book, *Watermelon*, in 1995, making her famous worldwide. Her second and third books, *Lucy Sullivan Is Getting Married* and *Rachel's Holiday,* followed quickly after. Keyes draws on her own experiences in her books and is regarded as the pioneer of the chick lit genre. Her stories often depict a strong female character facing problems such as domestic violence, drug abuse, mental illness, divorce and alcoholism. In *Saved by Cake* Keyes describes how she overcame a severe depression by baking cakes.

INDIA

Aravind Adiga was born in Madras in 1974. He grew up first in Mangalore in the south of India and then in Sydney, Australia. He studied literature at Columbia University in New York and Magdalen College, Oxford, before becoming a journalist. His first novel, *The White Tiger,* won the Man Booker Prize for fiction in 2008 and has also been made into a film. In it the reader follows the story of a driver navigating his way through the poverty, corruption and the caste society of modern India. A second novel, *Between the Assassinations* was published in 2008 and *Last Man in Tower* in 2011.

Kiran Desai (1971-), daughter of Anita Desai, was born in India. She lived in New Delhi until she was 14, when her family moved to the US. She studied Creative Writing at Columbia University. Her first novel *Hullabaloo in the Guava Orchard* won the Betty Trask Award in 1998. Her next book, *The Inheritance of Loss* won the 2006 Booker Prize. The novel explores how India's rigid caste system makes people feel trapped and how they dream of escaping it by immigrating to America.

NEW ZEALAND

Lloyd Jones was born in 1955 in Lower Hutt, New Zealand. Since the mid-1980s Jones has written novels, short stories, children's books and non-fiction work. But it was not until his novel, *Mister Pip* (2007), was shortlisted for the Booker Prize that Jones was fully recognized as one of New Zealand's most significant contemporary writers. His most recent work, *A History of Silence: A memoir* was published in 2013. Inspired in part by his thoughts about the devastation caused in Christchurch by the earthquake in 2011, it also deals with how easily we erase stories we find inconvenient.

Fiona Kidman (1940-) has written nearly 30 books in addition to working as a librar-

ian, a radio producer and a scriptwriter. Kidman has been awarded an OBE and DNZM for her services to literature. In much of her fiction she examines how women try to escape from the restriction of social pressures in a conformist society. Among Kidman's latest works are two memoirs, *At the End of Darwin Road* and *Beside the Dark Pool*. In 2013 she published *The Infinite Air*, a biography of the New Zealander Jean Batten who became one of the world's greatest aviators.

ENGLAND

Nick Hornby (1957-) read English at Cambridge University, before working as a journalist. His best-known books are *High Fidelity, About A Boy, How To Be Good, A Long Way Down* and *Juliet, Naked.* His non-fiction books include the football memoir *Fever Pitch.* In his early work in particular, Hornby's male characters, generally in their thirties, are struggling with emotional immaturity and wandering aimlessly in their careers and love lives. Many of his books have been made into films.

Zadie Smith (1975-) was born and grew up in a working class part of London with a Jamaican mother and an English father. Smith is a novelist, essayist and short story writer, as well as a professor at New York University. While still studying English Literature at Cambridge University she wrote her bestselling first novel *White Teeth* that immediately became a bestseller. The novel deals with issues of race and the experience of immigrants in working class and middle class England. Among her other books are *On Beauty* and *NW.*

SOUTH AFRICA

One of South Africa's most distinguished writers is **André Brink** (1935-2015). Although he first wrote in his native Afrikaans, he started writing in English after being censored by the South African government. Among his many novels are *A Dry White Season* (1979), which became a film, and *An Instant in the Wind* (1976), the story of a relationship between a white woman and a black man. His most recent novels are *Praying Mantis* (2005) and *The Blue Door* (2007) and in 2009 he published a memoir, *A Fork in the Road.* Brink's early novels were often concerned with apartheid, but his more recent work deals with new issues raised by life in post-apartheid South Africa.

GHANA

Ama Ata Aidoo (1942-) is a Ghanaian poet, playwright and novelist. Her first novel from 1977, *Our Sister Killjoy* remains one of her most popular works. Other titles by Aidoo include *Changes: a Love Story* and *The Girl Who Can and Other Stories.* In these works she examines the African women's struggle to find her rightful place in a changing society. Her protagonists are strong-willed personalities defying the stereotypical roles of their time. Aidoo has established the Mbaasem Foundation which actively works to promote and support African women writers.

Suggestions for projects start on page 238.

5

SHOP TILL YOU DROP

A GOOD PRICE!

BY RATTAWUT LAPCHAROENSAP

RATTAWUT LAPCHAROENSAP (1979–) was born in Chicago but raised in Bangkok, Thailand. His collection of short stories, *Sightseeing* (2005), won the Asian American Literary Award. These stories are set in contemporary Thailand and provide images far beyond the tourist's exoticized stereotypes. In 2007 *Granta* magazine named him on its list of Best Young American Novelists.

Every Saturday morning, Ma battles the vendors at Chatuchak. Even the most stubborn of vendors have submitted to her entreaties. It is not only charm she exerts upon them, for charm will get you only so far; Ma slashes their prices through an inimitable combination of wit, commonsense economics, high theatrics, and old-fashioned psychological manipulation. That Saturday at the bazaar, a few days before our trip, Ma was at the height of her powers.

The vendor was a young, homely-looking girl. Throngs of people filed past her booth. I stood at a distance as Ma scanned the hundreds of frames neatly laid out on the table. "What do you think?" she asked, putting on the Armanis.

"They look good, Ma."

"Really?"

"Yeah. You look like Jackie Kennedy."

This pleased her. She raised her hand in a fluttering half-gesture, smiling, bending to look at her reflection in the small mirror. "How much?" she finally asked, taking off the glasses with a swift, dramatic gesture. The vendor said twelve hundred. Ma yelped. "They're real, ma'am," the vendor said. "Real Armanis."

"Real or not, that's an awful lot of money."

The girl laughed – a shrill, sheepish sound. A middle-aged Chinese couple walked into the booth, the husband with a vacant look in his eyes. Ma asked for a discount. "I can't, ma'am. Profit margin's small as it is."

"C'mon. Give an old woman a break."

The girl smiled. She said eleven hundred. Ma yelped again.

"I'm not a farang, na? We're all Thai here. Give me the Thai price." The vendor asked Ma to name one. Not eleven hundred, Ma said.

The vendor counteroffered: ten-fifty. Ma put the glasses back on the table. "That's ridiculous," she said, shaking her head, though I could hear that hint of mischief in her voice. Only now, I knew, would

the bargaining begin in earnest. “Let’s go,” Ma said curtly, feigning disappointment. The Chinese couple glanced at us, smiled, and I tried to return the courtesy. The wife went back to browsing and the husband to looking as if he would rather be elsewhere. “Can you believe that?” Ma asked as we made our way toward the aisle, her voice loud enough for the girl to hear. “Twelve hundred for a pair of fake Armanis.”

“Ma –”

“Don’t ‘Ma’ me. You don’t think it’s a little expensive?”

“Well –”

“It’s outrageous.”

There is faith in the way Ma bargains, in the way we started to walk away from the girl. Her faith was substantiated that day. The girl called us back.

“Ma’am! Ma’am!” Ma let go of my arm, turned to face the vendor.

“How’s a thousand, ma’am?” the girl said, getting up from her seat.

“Oh no.” Ma laughed, grabbing my arm again. “Why would I spend that kind of money on a pair of fake Armanis?” Out of the corner of my eye, I saw the Chinese husband snickering softly to himself.

“They’re not fake, ma’am.”

“Oh?”

“No, ma’am. My boyfriend got them from the factory.”

“So they’re stolen?”

“Ma’am!”

“Pirated, then. They’re pirated. You know I could –”

“Ma’am!”

“I’m just teasing. What’s a little teasing?” Ma said. “Don’t take an old woman like me so seriously. Here. Let me look at them again.”

Ma tried them on once more. The girl told her she looked stunning. “I like them,” Ma said, taking off the glasses. “But a thousand? I don’t like them *that* much.” Again, the girl asked Ma to name a price. Ma took out her wallet, handed me the sunglasses, fished out a few bills. “Tell you what. I’ll leave six hundred baht on this table. Then I’ll walk away with those sunglasses.”

“Oi! I can’t do that, ma’am.”

“Of course you can.”

“No, ma’am, that’s impossible.” The girl looked at me. I shrugged. “Okay,” Ma said. “Let me ask you this then: How much did you pay for these glasses?”

“I don’t know, ma’am. My boyfriend was the one –”

“Oh, just tell me. What’s an old woman like me going to do with that kind of information? Your boyfriend’s not here now, is he? How else am I supposed to give you a fair offer?”

“I can’t do that. I’d lose money if I gave it to you for six hundred, though.”

“So six hundred it is then,” Ma said emphatically, laying the money down. The Chinese husband let out a bellowing laugh this time and the girl shot him a look that suggested, suddenly, that she was much older than I had originally assumed. “I can’t let you do that.” The vendor’s voice was strong and curt now, a new pallor on her face.

“Now you’re talking,” Ma teased, smiling. “No need to ‘ma’am’ me all the time. Now we can talk like adults. How much did you pay for these?” The girl shook her head. Six-fifty, Ma offered. The girl shook her head again. Ma took another hundred-baht note from her wallet. Seven-fifty.

“No.”

Ma held the note in her hand, and for a moment they just stood there – the vendor and my mother – locked in a mute battle. I’d seen this type of standoff many times before. I pitied the girl.

“How old are you?” Ma asked suddenly.

“Excuse me?”

“How old are you?”

“I’m twenty-six, ma’am.”

“It’s a good age to be, twenty-six,” Ma said. “You might not think it from the way I look, but it wasn’t so long ago when I was your age. It wasn’t so long ago at all – though you’re far more beautiful than I ever was then.”

The girl just blinked at my mother’s flattery. The Chinese wife, for the first time, looked our way.

“Here’s the situation.” Ma put the hundred-baht note on the table with the other bills, patting the pile of money like a bettor blessing her ante. “I’ll tell you my problem and then you can decide whether or not to give me those glasses for seven-fifty today. Thing is, those glasses aren’t an accessory for me. They’re not an optional luxury. You see, I’m going blind. By this time tomorrow, I might not be able to see a thing. Do you understand what I’m saying? You’re looking at a woman who’s going *blind*. The doctors say those glasses might mean a few more days of sight for me – ask my son if you don’t believe me. Now, you don’t strike me as the type of girl who’d let a woman go blind over a few hundred bahts. But maybe you are. Maybe you’re that type of girl ...”

“Oh come now, child, have a heart.”

It was the Chinese woman, her voice raspy like sandpaper.

Later that day, snaking our way through the aisles of the bazaar, Ma took the bag from my hands, put on the Armanis, and laughed a wild laugh of triumph, turning heads in the hot market.

Questions and exercises on the text are on page 242.

CREATIVE DESTRUCTION

New products are always killing old ones. Think of Polaroid®: The company had a monopoly on instant photography until the digital camera came along. Suddenly, Polaroid's market disappeared because all photography was now instant. Or take DVDs. As soon as they came on the scene, videotapes were worth nothing. No one makes videotapes anymore, and companies that did have been forced to produce something new to stay alive. Joseph Schumpeter called this process creative destruction – when a company creates a new product, improves technology, discovers a better supply source, pioneers a more efficient way to produce, or finds a better method of industrial organization, it can destroy its competition. Unlike traditional economics, which focuses on price competition, this theory focuses on competition from new products or technologies. Creative destruction is driven by entrepreneurs who put new ideas into action. Schumpeter argued that this innovation is the driving force behind long-term economic growth, and called creative destruction 'the essential fact about capitalism.' Ruined companies and disappearing industries are all part of the bigger picture, which is painful, but inevitable – even necessary – as new companies emerge and new jobs get created, setting the stage for economies to grow.

> "The fundamental impulse that sets and keeps the capitalist engine in motion comes from the new consumers, goods, the new methods of production or transportation, the new markets, the new forms of industrial organization that capitalist enterprise creates."
>
> JOSEPH SCHUMPETER

Questions and exercises on the text are on page 248.

SHOPPING, SEDUCTION & MR SELFRIDGE

BY LINDY WOODHEAD

The rise of the department store – or what in Paris were more gracefully called *les grand magasins* – in the second half of the nineteenth century was a phenomenon that encompassed fashion, advertising, entertainment, emergent new technology, architecture and above all, seduction. These forces evolved to merge into businesses that Emile Zola astutely called 'the great cathedrals of shopping', and vast fortunes were made by the men who owned them as they tapped into the female passion for shopping. But arguably no one man grasped the concept of consumption as sensual entertainment better than the maverick American retailer, Harry Gordon Selfridge, who opened his eponymous store on London's Oxford Street in 1909.

In building the West End's first fully fledged department store, he quite literally changed everything about the way Londoners shopped. His visionary, larger-than-life Edwardian building perfectly reflected the character of its founder – the only modest thing about him being his height. It was Harry Gordon Selfridge who positioned the perfume and cosmetics department immediately inside the main entrance; a move that changed the layout – and turnover – of the sales floor for ever more. Selfridge created window-dressing as an art form, pioneered in-store promotions and fashion shows, and offered customer service and facilities previously unheard of in Britain. Above all, he gave his customers fun. At a time when there was no radio or television, when cinema was in its infancy, Selfridge's in Oxford Street offered customers entertainment as fascinating as that at a science museum, with as much glamour as on any music-hall stage. In giving his customers a unique 'day out', Harry Selfridge proudly boasted that after Westminster Abbey and the Tower of London, his store was 'the third biggest tourist attraction in town'. The public could buy much of what they needed at Selfridge's, and much that they never knew they wanted until they were seduced by the tantalizing displays.

Harry Selfridge perfected the art of publicity, spending more money on advertising than any retailer of his era. A consummate

showman, he himself became a celebrity at a time when there were few identifiable, exciting personalities that the public could see at close quarters. When he arrived at work, there was invariably a cluster of customers waiting to meet and greet the 'famous Mr Selfridge'. His ritualistic 'morning tour' of the store, where his staff of thousands lined up anxiously by their counters in eager anticipation of a personal nod of approval from their boss, was the curtain-raiser to the daily show at Selfridge's – the only difference being that for his audience, entrance was free.

There was no shortage of shops or stores in London and many other wealthy provincial cities in Britain when – after twenty-five years working at the celebrated store Marshall Field & Co. in Chicago

– Selfridge masterminded his grand plan to open in the imperial capital. The industrial transformation that had occurred in Britain had created a new spending population who were proud to show off their wealth by acquiring consumer goods, and retailers scrambled to cope with an almost insatiable demand. The new rich had large houses to equip, a prodigious number of children – not to mention an army of servants – to dress, and their own position in society to promote. Happily for retailers, conspicuous consumption, always so crucial in defining wealth and status, had found itself a much larger market. [...]

The great stores acted as a catalyst for change in women's lives. For the first time women were able to 'cross the line', venturing out in public to buy goods for themselves, to experience shopping and be observed doing it without in any way jeopardizing their reputations. Not all stores were the size of cathedrals, but certainly fashionable women in London, Manchester and Newcastle, and further afield in Paris, New York, Philadelphia and Chicago, were spending a lot more time shopping, than going to church. Small wonder when the stores were light, bright, warm and enticing. Neither did these stores cater exclusively for the carriage trade. The department store was the anchor in a rapidly expanding egalitarian, urban society, drawing its customer base from a mix of old and new money, and able to offer not just fixed prices but also sale bargains. For many people these stores were infinitely more glamorous and comfortable than their own homes. In 1880s Chicago, Harry Selfridge had pioneered the policy of browsing, making Marshall Field's an ideal location for those who were 'just looking', and opened a 'Bargain Basement' for those on a budget. He had also introduced a restaurant, a reading-room, a crèche and a ladies' rest-room complete with nurse, and so could justifiably claim to have helped emancipate women: 'I came along just at the time when women wanted to step out on their own. They came to the store and realized some of their dreams.'

Questions and exercises on the text are on page 250.

6 THE ARTS

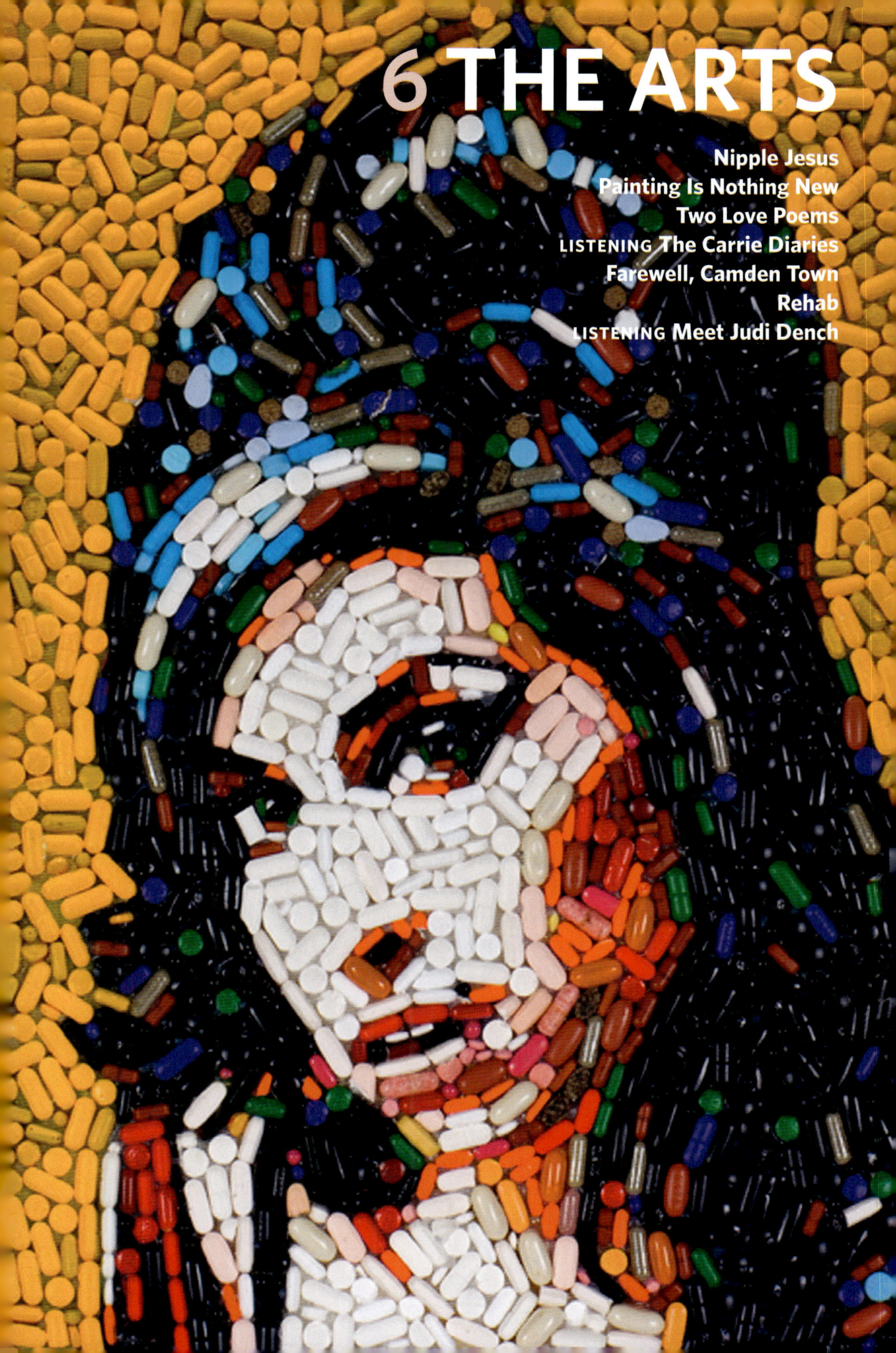

NIPPLE JESUS

BY NICK HORNBY

NICK HORNBY (1957–) is an English journalist, novelist, essayist, lyricist and screenwriter. He is best known for his novels *High Fidelity, About a Boy* and *How to Be Good*. He has received numerous literary awards for his books, of which several have been filmed.

Dave had got a job in an art gallery guarding a very special picture.

It was off to the side, in a room all of its own, and there was a curtain across the entrance, so it was separate from the others. Outside, there was a sign that said: 'WARNING! This room contains an exhibit of a controversial nature. Please do not enter if you feel you might be offended. Over 18s only'. The woman didn't say anything about that. She just ignored it – never asked me if *I* might be offended.

'You're in here,' she said. 'Watch out. We're expecting trouble.' And then she went off.

I went behind the curtain, and there on the far wall was this massive picture of Jesus. I'd say it was probably ten feet high, five or six feet wide, something like that. It's kind of like the pictures you've seen before – eyes closed, the old crown of thorns on his head. That was when he was on the cross, wasn't it? It's sort of a close-up, head and shoulders, so you only see a bit of the cross, but what this picture has that the normal ones don't – not to me they don't, anyway – is that you can really tell just how much it must have fucking hurt, being nailed up. Usually, it looks like he's having a kip, but this one, his face is all screwed up in agony. You really wouldn't want to be in his shoes, I'll tell you. So the first thing I thought was, bloody hell, that's a good picture. Because it makes you think, and I don't often think about things like that. I haven't been anywhere near Jesus since Lisa's sister got married, three years ago.

And the second thing I thought – I'd forgotten about the sign and the curtain and all that for a moment – was, who the fuck would get offended by that? Because you can go into any church and see the same sort of thing. Not so realistic, maybe, a bit more PG than R, but, you know, basically the same sort of stuff: moustache and beard, crown of thorns, sad. Because you can't tell how it's done from a distance, see. When you step behind the curtain, you just see the picture, and the face. You have to get quite close up to see anything else. So I couldn't

understand it, why there was all the fuss. I just thought: religious people. Nutters. 'Cos they are, most of them, aren't they? I mean, to each his own and everything, but you wouldn't want to marry one, would you?

There's a chair in front of the picture, and I walked towards it to have a sit-down. And as I got closer, I could see that the picture was made up of hundreds – thousands, maybe millions – of little squares, like the mosaics I pinched from the Roman ruins. And when I got really close, I could see that these millions of little squares were actually little pictures, and every single little picture had at least one female breast in it. So ... you know those pictures that are made up of dots? Well, that's how this Jesus picture was done, except all the dots are nipples. And that's what the picture's called – *Nipple Jesus.* There were big breasts and small breasts, and big nipples and small nipples, and black breasts and white breasts. And some of the pictures had as many as four breasts in them, and I could see then that all of the pictures were stills from porn mags, and he'd cut them all up and stuck them on. Must have taken him years. So now I understood what the sign was about.

I hated the picture then. Two minutes ago I'd liked it, now I hated it. And I hated the bloke who'd done it, too. Wanker. I went to have a look at the name of the artist, and it turned out to be a woman. Martha Marsham. How can you be a woman and do that? I thought. I could have understood some bloke doing it, some bloke with too many dirty magazines and no girlfriend. But a bird? And I hoped that someone did manage to fuck the picture up somehow, and if they did, I said to myself, I wouldn't try to stop them. I might even give them a hand. Because that is offensive, isn't it, a Jesus made out of nipples? That's out of order.

One thing I forgot to say before: this was about six o'clock in the evening, and the exhibition hadn't opened to the public yet. It was opening the next day, but we'd been called in to do the first-night party. I was actually still looking at all the little pictures when the first people came in, holding wine glasses. I felt a bit of a tosser, like I'd been caught looking at dirty pictures, which is actually what I was doing, if you think about it. Or even if you don't. I stopped looking, quick, and stood by the chair with my hands behind my back, looking straight ahead, like I was on sentry duty, while these two people, a man and a woman, looked at the picture.

'It's rather lovely, isn't it?' said the woman. She was about my age; short hair, quite posh.

'Is it?' The bloke didn't seem too sure, so I decided I liked him more than her, even though he had floppy hair and braces and a suit.

'Don't you think?'

He shrugged, and they left the room. There was none of that stuff, the stuff they take the piss out of in TV comedies, where they stroke their chins and talk bollocks. (There never is, in my experience, which has now lasted two days. Most people don't say anything much. They look and they go. If you ask me they're scared of talking bollocks, which pisses me off, because, once I was sat here for a while I wanted the bollocks. Something to laugh at. But there isn't any.) The next couple were younger, early twenties, studenty types, and they were more interested in me than the picture.

'Fucking hell,' said the bloke.

'What?'

'Look at him.'

And the girl looked at me, and laughed. It was like I was part of the exhibition, and I couldn't hear what they were saying.

'Well,' she said. 'Can you blame them?'

And then they went, too. By this stage, I was starting to feel a bit sorry for this Martha woman. I mean, you spend fucking who knows how long doing this thing and people come in here, look at me, laugh, and then fuck off again. I might ask her for half her royalties; or whatever it is she gets.

Questions and exercises on the text are on page 257.

PAINTING IS NOTHING NEW

BY KEITH HARING

KEITH HARING (1958–1990) was an American artist and during a brief but intensive career that spanned the 1980s, Haring's work was featured in over 100 solo and group exhibitions. Keith Haring died of AIDS at the age of 31 and since his death, he has been the subject of several international retrospectives. The work of Keith Haring can be seen today in the exhibitions and collections of major museums around the world.

Painting is nothing new. People have been drawing since the Stone Age. In every culture people have attempted to depict their world as they see it and feel it. Images have been drawn, scratched, sprayed, carved, baked or painted in whatever materials were available to that culture at that particular time. Man-made images have always been important and necessary elements in this ritual we call "life." They have adorned our shelters, tools, clothing, monuments, vessels, bodies, temples and the land itself. Different cultures have attributed to them greater or lesser value and designated to them different degrees of meaning and purpose. But they are always there in one form or another. It is part of mankind's way of reaffirming and celebrating its existence.

In the last 100 years we have seen the invention of telecommunications, radio, automobiles, television, air and space travel, computers, genetic science, satellites, lasers, and on and on. In short, our experience of life has been drastically altered. The role of the image maker cannot be seen as the same as it was 100 years ago, or even 10 years ago. The rate of change is accelerating at an increasingly rapid speed and the artist has to change with it. Contemporary artists cannot ignore the existence of media and technology and at the same time cannot abandon ritual and popular culture. The image maker may be more important now than at any other time in the history of man because he possesses qualities that are uniquely human. The human imagination cannot be programmed by a computer. Our imagination is our greatest hope for survival.

Questions and exercises on the text are on page 259.

TWO LOVE POEMS

One half of me is yours, the other half yours
Mine own, I would say; but if mine, then yours,
And so all yours

BY WILLIAM SHAKESPEARE, FROM THE MERCHANT OF VENICE

YOU FIT INTO ME

you fit into me
like a hook into an eye
a fish hook
an open eye

BY MARGARET ATWOOD

Questions and exercises on the text are on page 261.

FAREWELL, CAMDEN TOWN

BY MITCH WINEHOUSE

I arrived back at Heathrow airport on the morning of Sunday, 24 July. My friend Hayden picked me up and drove me to his house in north London where Jane was waiting for me. We cried and cried until it seemed there were no tears left.

We went to Janis's house not far away and we all cried some more. Alex and Riva were already there and people continued to arrive throughout the day. I was in a daze and I don't really remember much of what went on. Things were happening around me and I felt removed from the scene, as if I was watching a movie.

I kept asking myself, how could this have happened?

I had seen Amy the day before I flew to New York and she was fine. Janis, Richard and Reg had seen her the next day and she was fine. And she was still fine later that night – although, according to Andrew, she was 'tipsy'. When Andrew checked on her a bit later, she was singing and playing drums in her room. He had checked on her again in the morning and thought she was asleep. Then he checked a few hours later and realized she wasn't asleep. Immediately he had raised the alarm.

A lot of people believe that Amy's life was in turmoil during her last eighteen months. But nothing could be further from the truth. Yes, she had lapses back into alcoholism, but those lapses had been gradually getting further and further apart. There was no doubt in those around her that her life was going in the right direction. I always equated Amy's neatness, or lack of it, to how well-ordered her mind was at any particular time. During those last eighteen months the clothes in her wardrobes were neat and tidy, her books and CDs were organized alphabetically and her sketchbooks numbered.

I knew that Amy couldn't have died from a drug overdose, as she had been drug-free since 2008. But although she had been so brave and had fought so hard in her recovery from alcoholism, I knew she must have lapsed once again. I thought that Amy hadn't had a drink for three weeks. But she had actually started drinking at Dionne's Roundhouse gig the previous Wednesday. I didn't know that at the time.

The following morning Janis, Jane, Richard Collins (Janis's fiancé), Raye, Reg and I went to St Pancras mortuary to officially identify Amy. Alex couldn't bring himself to go, which I fully understood. When we arrived there were loads of paps outside the court, but they were all very respectful. We were shown into a room and saw Amy behind a window. She looked very, very peaceful, as if she was just asleep, which in a way made it a lot harder. She looked lovely. There was a slight red blotchiness to her skin, which was why, at the time, I thought she might have had a seizure: she looked as she had done when she had had seizures in the past.

Eventually the others left Janis and me to say goodbye to Amy by ourselves. We were with her for about fifteen minutes. We put our hands on the glass partition and spoke to her. We told her that Mummy and Daddy were with her and that we would always love her.

I can't express what it was like. It was the worst feeling in the world.

Then we went to Camden Square, where we were joined by Alex and Riva. The police were still investigating the possibility of foul play, so we weren't allowed inside the house. But hundreds of fans were there and they had turned the square into a shrine. We gathered together and looked at the tributes left at the edge of the police cordons. I thanked the reporters and fans for coming, and shook hands with many of them, fighting back the tears. There were drinks and cigarettes, some beautiful notes and lovely artwork, soft toys, flowers and candles. It was very touching and comforting to know how much Amy was loved. Eventually I broke down and couldn't stop crying.

After that we went back to Janis's house where our friends and other members of the family were waiting. I told them what had come into my mind during the bleak hours over the Atlantic as I'd flown home. 'I started thinking of a Foundation,' I said. 'Amy's Foundation. So that disadvantaged young people dealing with addiction, ill health or homelessness can be supported.'

I hadn't thought much more than that but the idea was out there now. Gradually others started adding to it, and it grew.

The post-mortem examination was inconclusive. The Metropolitan Police said, 'It did not establish a formal cause of death,' and that they were awaiting the results of further toxicology tests, which were not expected for two to four weeks. In the meantime, the police treated Amy's death as unexplained.

An inquest was opened and adjourned until 26 October to allow us to make the funeral arrangements.

In the Jewish tradition a funeral must take place at the earliest opportunity and, since the coroner had released the body, the funeral could take place the following day, 26 July. Certain branches of Judaism do not permit cremation, but my mother had been cremated and we thought that was what Amy would have wanted for herself when she was to be reunited with her Nan Cynthia. There was so much to do and my marvellous friends rallied round us to ensure that everything that had to be done was done, in time for the service and cremation. I started to write Amy's eulogy.

Questions and exercises on the text are on page 264.

REHAB

BY AMY WINEHOUSE

They tried to make me go to rehab
but I said, "No, no, no"
Yes, I've been black but when I come back
you'll know, know, know
I ain't got the time
and if my daddy thinks I'm fine
He's tried to make me go to rehab,
I won't go, go, go

I'd rather be at home with Ray*
I ain't got seventy days
'Cause there's nothing, there's nothing you
can teach me
That I can't learn from Mr. Hathaway**

Didn't get a lot in class
But I know it don't come in a shot glass

They tried to make me go to rehab
but I said, "No, no, no"
Yes, I've been black but when I come back
you'll know know know
I ain't got the time
and if my daddy thinks I'm fine
He's tried to make me go to rehab,
I won't go, go, go

*Ray Charles, legendary American musician, singer and composer
**Donny Hathaway, American soul music artist in the 60s and 70s

The man said, "Why do you think you here?"
I said, "I got no idea
I'm gonna, I'm gonna lose my baby
So I always keep a bottle near"
He said, "I just think you're depressed"
Kiss me, "Yeah baby, and the rest"

They tried to make me go to rehab,
I said, "No, no, no"
Yes, I've been black but when I come back
you'll know, know, know

I don't ever wanna drink again
I just, ooh, I just need a friend
I'm not gonna spend ten weeks
Have everyone think I'm on the mend

And it's not just my pride
It's just 'til these tears have dried

They tried to make me go to rehab,
I said, "No, no, no"
Yes, I've been black but when I come back
you'll know, know, know
I ain't got the time
and if my daddy thinks I'm fine
He's tried to make me go to rehab,
I won't go, go, go

Questions and exercises on the text are on page 267.

SW1
Silver Cross
Downstairs Bar
TELEPHONE
BUS STOP

7 GLIMPSES OF ENGLAND

TORN ON THE PLATFORM

BY JACK PEÑATE

Once more just before I'm leaving
Torn on the platform
Once more just before I'm leaving
Torn on the platform

'Cause I miss you and I love you
And I know this is over for now
'Cause I miss you, oh, how I miss you
You're not my girl you're my town

A weekend away, leave the city today
Don't want the big smoke to leave me behind
The train leaves at 2, Platform 3 Waterloo
50p to the tramp makes me feel kind

I get a good seat with a window
My feet are up on the one in front everyone stares
But why do they care? Like there's feelings in chairs
Stuck for 3 hours until I get there

My eyes, eyes, eyes are not dry, dry, dry
As I realize-lize-lize
That in a few minutes this train will be gone
Sighs, sighs, sighs, city flies, flies, flies
Wonder why, why, why
Would anyone want to leave where I come from?

I'm torn on the platform
I'm torn on the platform
I'm torn on the platform

It's 1:58, wish that I had been late
And missed the train and given them an excuse
But what is the use? I've less slack than a noose
Do or die, stay or go, what should I choose?

'Cause my eyes, eyes, eyes are not dry, dry, dry
As I realize-lize-lize
That in a few minutes this train will be gone
Sighs, sighs, sighs, city flies, flies, flies
Wonder why, why, why
Would anyone want to leave where I come from?

I'm torn on the platform
I'm torn on the platform
I'm torn on the platform

Like in a film the motion starts to slow
As the beeping carriage doors begin to close
Momentarily I'm standing froze
Then I jump between the gap, land on the platform flat

I'm not torn on the platform
I'm torn on the platform
I'm torn on the platform

Questions and exercises on the text are on page 275.

A LION WITH A PRICE TAG

BY ANTHONY BOURKE AND JOHN RENDALL

A lion cub with a price tag was not an easy thought to assimilate. The cubs were proving to be a successful drawcard for the Christmas shoppers, with the prospect of becoming the Christmas present for the person who already had everything.

We had not thought about lions before. Of course we had seen them in zoos, but that was as far as our interest and knowledge extended. Neither of us had even read Joy Adamson's 1960 book *Born Free,* the story of Elsa the lioness which had been found as a cub, raised and rehabilitated back into the wild by Joy and her husband George Adamson, who was a game warden with the Kenyan Wildlife Department.

We sympathized with the cubs, for despite the efforts of the staff they were incessantly disturbed by intrigued shoppers, yet we had

to restrain the same urge within ourselves. Each person demanded a response. The female snarled in an alarming manner and people were satisfied, but her brother pretended none of us existed. He was irresistible, and we sat, enchanted, beside their cage for hours.

John: 'Why don't we buy him?'

Ace: 'I've already named him Christian.'

We found out much later that the staff had named him Marcus, a handsome masculine name, but Christian seemed to suit him, and we liked the irony of Christians being fed to the lions in Roman times, which was also a reminder of the danger to which we could be exposing ourselves, and the people around us.

We intuitively knew that we were both serious, and a curious excitement began to grow. Even if it was only for a couple of months, surely we could offer him a better life than this, and try to ensure a better future for him? Or was it that we just wanted to take Christian away from everyone else, and have him to ourselves? Neither of us had ever fantasized about or dreamed of owning an exotic pet, but he was completely irresistible.

Suddenly our lives were to be incomplete without a lion cub. An impractical idea for two young Australians visiting Europe, but at least we could allow ourselves the luxury of investigating the possibility of buying him. We enquired if he was still for sale. The female had been sold, but the male was still available, for two hundred and fifty guineas, equivalent in 2009 to three thousand five hundred English pounds. This was a vast sum to us, but, undaunted, we nonchalantly agreed that it seemed a very reasonable price. The assistant at the zoo suggested we speak to the Harrods buyer. He was, she pointedly warned us, interviewing any prospective purchasers very thoroughly, as Harrods believed it was important the lions did not fall into irresponsible hands.

We returned the next morning looking far more respectable, with our hair skilfully flattened, and wearing the tweed sports coats our parents, very perceptively, had insisted would be useful abroad, but which until now had been lying untouched at the bottom of our suitcases. We succeeded, with the help of few tiny white lies and our enthusiasm, in convincing Roy Hazle, the buyer for Harrods, that we would be responsible guardians/foster parents for a lion. Now, when Harrods was prepared to part with him, we had the first option to buy Christian.

Questions and exercises on the text are on page 276.

THE ROAD TO WIGAN PIER

BY GEORGE ORWELL

ERIC ARTHUR BLAIR (1903–1950), better known by his pen name George Orwell, was an English novelist, essayist, journalist and critic. He is considered one of the most influential English writers of the 20th century. He is best known for his dystopian novel *1984* and for *Animal Farm*, his allegory on a totalitarian state. In *1984* he coined the term Big Brother as a way to describe the authorities' constant control of the citiziens.

> Every miner of long standing that I have talked to had either been in a fairly serious accident himself or had seen some of his mates killed, and in every mining family they tell you tales of fathers, brothers, or uncles killed at work.

The most obviously understandable cause of accidents is explosions of gas, which is always more or less present in the atmosphere of the pit. There is a special lamp which is used to test the air for gas, and when it is present in at all large quantities it can be detected by the flame of an ordinary Davy lamp burning blue. If the wick can be turned up to its full extent and the flame is still blue, the proportion of gas is dangerously high; it is, nevertheless, difficult to detect, because it does not distribute itself evenly throughout the atmosphere but hangs about in cracks and crevices. Before starting work a miner often tests for gas by poking his lamp into all the corners. The gas may be touched off by a spark during blasting operations, or by a pick striking a spark from a stone, or by a defective lamp, or by 'gob fires' – spontaneously generated fires which smoulder in the coal dust and are very hard to put out. The great mining disasters which happen from time to time, in which several hundred men are killed, are usually caused by explosions; hence one tends to think of explosions as the chief danger of mining. Actually, the great majority of accidents are due to the normal every-day dangers of the pit; in particular, to falls of roof. There are, for instance, 'pot-holes' – circular holes from which a lump of stone big enough to kill a man shoots out with the promptitude of a bullet. With, so far as I can remember, only one exception, all the miners I have talked to declared that the new machinery, and

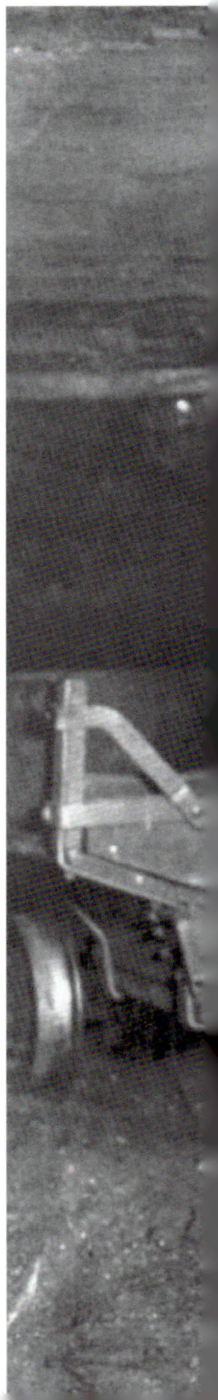

'speeding up' generally, have made the work more dangerous. This may be partly due to conservatism, but they can give plenty of reasons. To begin with, the speed at which the coal is now extracted means that for hours at a time a dangerously large stretch of roof remains unpropped. Then there is the vibration, which tends to shake everything loose, and the noise, which makes it harder to detect signs of danger. One must remember that a miner's safety underground depends largely on his own care and skill. An experienced miner claims to know by a sort of instinct when the roof is unsafe; the way he puts it is that he 'can feel the weight on him'. He can, for instance, hear the faint creaking of the props. The reason why wooden props are still generally preferred to iron girders is that a wooden prop which is about to collapse gives warning by creaking, whereas a girder flies out unexpectedly. The devastating noise of the machines makes it impossible to hear anything else, and thus the danger is increased.

When a miner is hurt it is of course impossible to attend to him immediately. He lies crushed under several hundredweight of stone

in some dreadful cranny underground, and even after he has been extricated it is necessary to drag his body a mile or more, perhaps, through galleries where nobody can stand upright. Usually when you talk to a man who has been injured you find that it was a couple of hours or so before they got him to the surface. Sometimes, of course, there are accidents to the cage. The cage is shooting several yards up or down at the speed of an express train, and it is operated by somebody on the surface who cannot see what is happening. He has very delicate indicators to tell him how far the cage has got, but it is possible for him to make a mistake, and there have been cases of the cage crashing into the pit-bottom at its very maximum speed. This seems to me a dreadful way to die. For as that tiny steel box whizzes through the blankness there must come a moment when the ten men who are locked inside it *know* that something has gone wrong; and the remaining seconds before they are smashed to pieces hardly bear thinking about. A miner told me he was once in a cage in which something went wrong. It did not slow up when it should have done, and they thought the cable must have snapped. As it happened they got to the bottom safely, but when he stepped out he found that he had broken a tooth; he had been clenching his teeth so hard in expectation of that frightful crash.

Questions and exercises on the text are on page 281.

NO BOUNDARIES

BY STEPHEN HAWKING

STEPHEN HAWKING (1942–) is an English theoretical physicist and author. His current title is Director of Research at the Centre for Theoretical Cosmology at Cambridge University. He was diagnosed with ALS shortly after his 21st birthday and spends his time in a wheelchair, speaking with a computerized voice. In spite of these difficulties he has combined family life, research, writing and travel.

I was born on January 8, 1942, exactly three hundred years after the death of Galileo. I estimate, however, that about two hundred thousand other babies were also born that day. I don't know whether any of them was later interested in astronomy. I was born in Oxford, even though my parents were living in London. This was because during World War II, the Germans had an agreement that they would not bomb Oxford and Cambridge, in return for the British not bombing Heidelberg and Göttingen. It is a pity that this civilized sort of arrangement couldn't have been extended to more cities.

When I was twenty-one and contracted ALS, I felt it was very unfair. Why should this happen to me? At the time, I thought my life was over and that I would never realize the potential I felt I had. But now, fifty years later, I can be quietly satisfied with my life. I have been married twice and have three beautiful and accomplished children. I have been successful in my scientific career: I think most theoretical physicists would agree that my prediction of quantum emission from black holes is correct, though it has not so far earned me a Nobel Prize because it is very difficult to verify experimentally. On the other hand, I won the even more valuable Fundamental Physics Prize, awarded for the theoretical significance of the discovery despite the fact that it has not been confirmed by experiment.

My disability has not been a serious handicap in my scientific work. In fact, in some ways I guess it has been an asset: I haven't had to lecture or teach undergraduates, and I haven't had to sit on tedious and time-consuming committees. So I have been able to devote myself completely to research.

To my colleagues, I'm just another physicist, but to the wider public, I became possibly the best-known scientist in the world.

This is partly because scientists, apart from Einstein, are not widely known rock stars, and partly because I fit the stereotype of a disabled genius. I can't disguise myself with a wig and dark glasses – the wheelchair gives me away.

Being well known and easily recognizable has its pluses and minuses. The minuses are that it can be difficult to do ordinary things such as shopping without being besieged by people wanting photographs, and that in the past the press has taken an unhealthy interest in my private life. But the minuses are more than outweighed by the pluses. People seem genuinely pleased to see me. I even had my biggest-ever audience when I was the anchor for the Paralympic Games in London in 2012.

I have had a full and satisfying life. I believe that disabled people should concentrate on things that their handicap doesn't prevent them from doing and not regret those they can't do. In my case, I have managed to do most things I wanted. I have traveled widely. I visited the Soviet Union seven times. The first time I went with a student party in which one member, a Baptist, wished to distribute Russian-language Bibles and asked us to smuggle them in. We managed this undetected, but by the time we were on our way out the authorities had discovered what we had done and detained us for a while. However, to charge us with smuggling Bibles would have caused an international incident and unfavorable publicity, so they let us go after a few hours. The other six visits were to see Russian scientists who at the time were not allowed to travel to the West. After the end of the Soviet Union in 1990, many of the best scientists left for the West, so I have not been to Russia since then.

I have also visited Japan six times, China three times, and every continent, including Antarctica, with the exception of Australia. I have met the presidents of South Korea, China, India, Ireland, Chile, and the United States. I have lectured in the Great Hall of the People in Beijing and in the White House. I have been under the sea in a submarine and up in a hot air balloon and a zero-gravity flight, and I'm booked to go into space with Virgin Galactic.

My early work showed that classical general relativity broke down at singularities in the Big Bang and black holes. My later work has shown how quantum theory can predict what happens at the beginning and end of time. It has been a glorious time to be alive and doing research in theoretical physics. I'm happy if I have added something to our understanding of the universe.

Questions and exercises on the text are on page 283.

THE PEOPLE YOU NEVER HEAR FROM

BY CAITLIN MORAN

Caitlin Moran (1975–) is an English broadcaster, TV critic and columnist for *The Times,* where she writes three columns a week. Caitlin Moran has won several prizes among others the 2011 Galaxy Book of the Year Award for her debut book *How to Be a Woman.*

A third of the people in this country are dependent on benefits.

Of course, you wouldn't know that was the figure from television, media or literature. Judging by the lives of our popular fictional characters, you'd presume that if a third of the country *were* anything, it would be either a) maverick coppers, b) high-class call girls, c) pairs of whimsical post-grad kidults in urban flat-shares, or d) Jamie Oliver – not people signing on. You never really see people on benefits. You never really hear about them – apart from as statistics in newspaper reports, or as cast members of *Shameless.*

Perhaps due to the odd, ongoing mysteriousness about the bedrock of this country's class system, writing about benefits prompts a very mixed, and often confused, response.

Two weeks ago, I wrote about my friend Richey – a schizophrenic whose Housing Benefit is being cut, in May. I wrote about how this means he must leave Brighton – where his friends, family and support system is – pick another, cheaper town at random, and begin his life again.

The comments, emails and letters I received were intriguing. By and large, people who were sympathetic to Richey's situation were people who had experience of a similar situation – either personally, or with a loved one.

Those who were unsympathetic; meanwhile, tended to be speaking theoretically – discussing figures and reports that they'd read, rather than actual people they knew.

For the unsympathetic, one idea seemed paramount – encapsulated in: 'If I were a well-paid columnist, I would help [Richey] out – instead of taking to my column and whining about it.'

The presumption here is that there's only about six poor people in Britain – and if all their broadsheet columnist friends just bailed them out, we could dismantle the welfare system tomorrow. And for those who are genuinely worried, let me assure you: I've bailed out as many as I can. I am like Bob Geldof with a typewriter, except with much better hair. I have thrown UNICEF bags of grain and powdered milk at every troubled friend I know.

But the problem with this solution – let's call it MoranAid – is that a) I don't personally know everyone who needs financial help, and b) many of the people who need help aren't as charming and accidentally well connected as Richey. Let's face it – a lot of disabled/mentally ill/poor people are grumpy, or charmless, or shy, or friendless. Probably the same proportion as in 'normal' society. They just aren't going to persuade nearby people to support them, financially, unfailingly, until they die.

That's why I like the Welfare State – which helps everyone: even people with terrible personalities, or who don't know broadsheet columnists – rather than the Big Society, which is wholly optional and ad hoc, i.e., the situation we had right up until 1945 – paupers' graves, workhouses, parish handouts and all.

From a purely selfish point of view, as a British citizen, one of the things I particularly like about the Welfare State is the lack of admin: instead of seeking out local, winsome widows and pressing bread into their grateful hands, I pay my tax bill, get someone else to source needful widows, and use the time now freed up to watch *Masterchef*, or give the kids a bath.

I guess if I were a bit richer, I could hire a PA, and get *her* to do it –that would be my only hope at contributing to the Big Society. Using a PA – but in the meantime, I'm pretty happy with the way the DSS does it.

I had a similar kind of postbag a few months ago, when I wrote about how me and my eight siblings were brought up on benefits – how poor we were, and our constant terror that these benefits would be taken away.

Again, several people asked why their taxes should have been used to pay for my parents' decision to have eight children 'that they couldn't afford'.

Well, I can't speak for my parents now – just as I couldn't alter their decisions then. What I *do* know, and can say, is that the principle of the welfare system was that I should not suffer from the decisions, or fortunes, of my parents. That as soon as I was born, the State stepped in, and acted like the well-paid columnist our social circle so sorely lacked, in Wolverhampton, in 1986 – bailing me and all my siblings out.

It clothed me and fed me, and gave me glasses when I squinted, and opened a library where we all read so much, we all subsequently went to university, and now pay taxes of our own, that bail out other children – who, in turn, will bail out other children, with equally unfortunate parents.

In this respect, at its best, the Welfare State is like some fabulous Electric Boogaloo – the current passing from one citizen to another, making us all body-pop joyfully into education, and up the class system.

And when we get here – onto pages like this, into newspapers like this – we can, finally, tell people about it.

So the country hears a little bit more about how one third of us live our lives.

Questions and exercises on the text are on page 285.

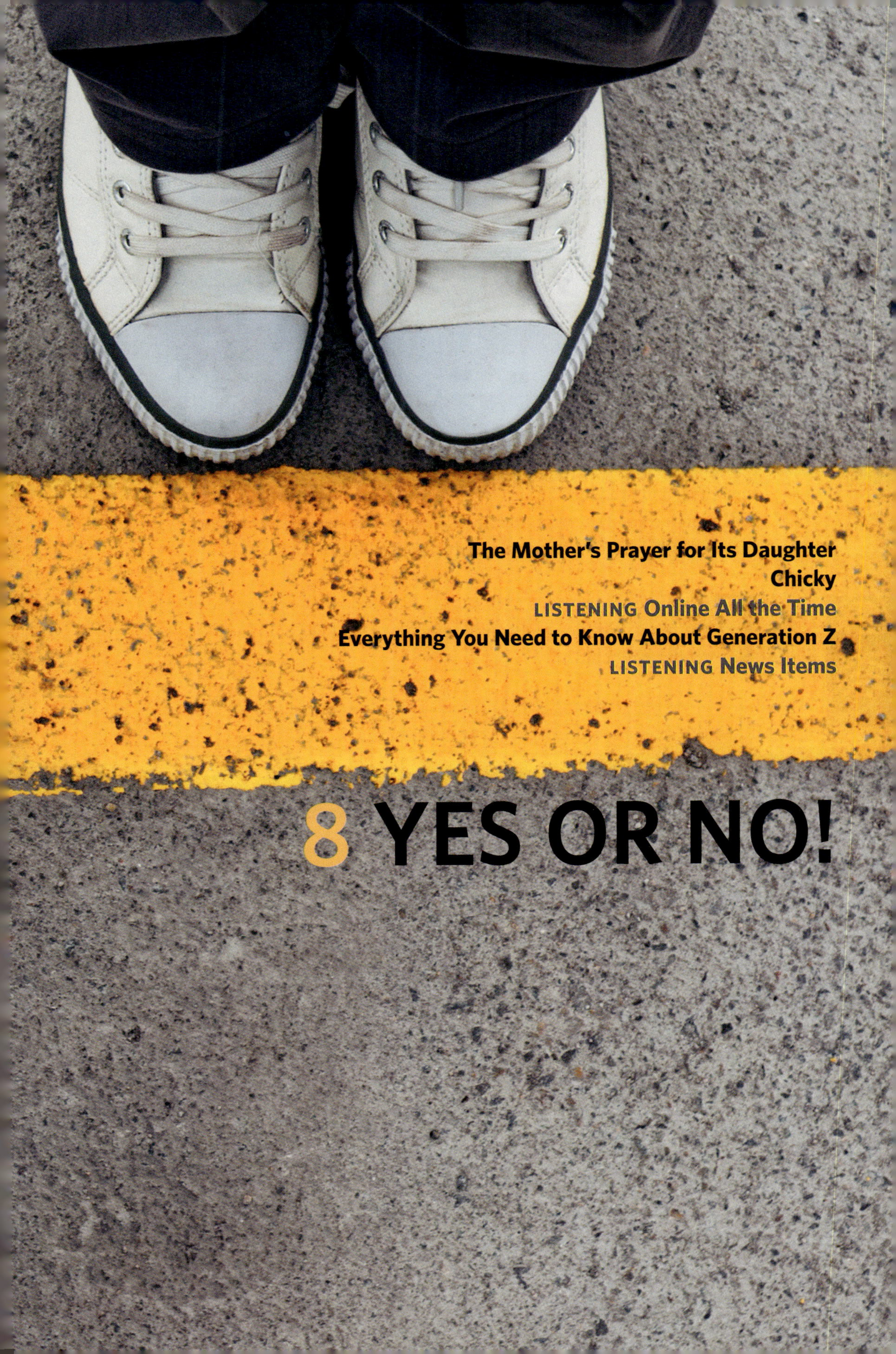

8 YES OR NO!

THE MOTHER'S PRAYER FOR ITS DAUGHTER

BY TINA FEY

ELIZABETH STAMATINA "TINA" FEY (1970–) is an American actress, comedian, and producer, known for among other work her part in the NBC sketch comedy series *Saturday Night Live.* She has also written an autobiography entitled *Bossypants,* which was published in 2011.

First, Lord: No tattoos. May neither the Chinese symbol for truth nor Winnie-the-Pooh holding the FSU logo stain her tender haunches.

May she be Beautiful but not Damaged, for it's the Damage that draws the creepy soccer coach's eye, not the Beauty.

When the Crystal Meth is offered,
May she remember the parents who cut her grapes in half
And stick with Beer.

Guide her, protect her
When crossing the street, stepping onto boats, swimming in the ocean, swimming in pools, walking near pools, standing on the subway platform, crossing 86th Street, stepping off of boats, using mall restrooms, getting on and off escalators, driving on country roads while arguing, leaning on large windows, walking in parking lots, riding Ferris wheels, roller-coasters, log flumes, or anything called "Hell Drop," "Tower of Torture," or "The Death Spiral Rock 'N Zero G Roll featuring Aerosmith," and standing on any kind of balcony ever; anywhere, at any age.

Lead her away from Acting but not all the way to Finance.
Something where she can make her own hours but still feel

intellectually fulfilled and get outside sometimes
And not have to wear high heels.

What would that be, Lord? Architecture? Midwifery? Golf course design? I'm asking You, because if I knew, I'd be doing it, Youdammit.

May she play the Drums to the fiery rhythm of her Own Heart with the sinewy strength of her Own Arms, so she need Not Lie With Drummers.

Grant her a Rough Patch from twelve to seventeen.
Let her draw horses and be interested in Barbies for much too long,
For Childhood is short – a Tiger Flower blooming Magenta for one day –
And Adulthood is long and Dry-Humping in Cars will wait.

O Lord, break the Internet forever,
That she may be spared the misspelled invective of her peers
And the online marketing campaign for Rape Hostel V: Girls Just Wanna Get Stabbed.

And when she one day turns on me and calls me a Bitch in front of Hollister,
Give me the strength, Lord, to yank her directly into a cab in front of her friends,
For I will not have that Shit. I will not have it.

And should she choose to be a Mother one day, be my eyes, Lord,
That I may see her, lying on a blanket on the floor at 4:50 A.M., all-at-once exhausted, bored, and in love with the little creature whose poop is leaking up its back.
"My mother did this for me once," she will realize as she cleans feces off her baby's neck. "My mother did this for me," And the delayed gratitude will wash over her as it does each generation and she will make a Mental Note to call me. And she will forget.
But I'll know, because I peeped it with Your God eyes.

Amen

Questions and exercises on the text are on page 290.

CHICKY

BY MAEVE BINCHY

MAEVE BINCHY (1940–2012) was an Irish writer and her works, which were often set in Ireland, have been translated into 37 languages. They include *The Lilac Bus* as well as *Tara Road* and *Circle of Friends*, which were both adapted for the screen.

Everyone had their own job to do on the Ryans' farm in Stoneybridge. The boys helped their father in the fields, mending fences, bringing the cows back to be milked, digging drills of potatoes; Mary fed the calves, Kathleen baked the bread and Geraldine did the hens.

Not that they ever called her Geraldine, she was Chicky as far back as anyone could remember. A serious little girl pouring out meal for the baby chickens or collecting the fresh eggs each day, always saying 'chuck, chuck, chuck' soothingly into the feathers as she worked. Chicky had names for all the hens, and no one could tell her when one had been taken to provide a Sunday lunch. They always pretended it was a Shop Chicken, but Chicky always knew.

Stoneybridge was a West of Ireland paradise for children during the summer, but the summer was short and most of the time it was wet and wild and lonely on the Atlantic coast. Still, there were caves to explore, cliffs to climb, birds' nests to discover and wild sheep with great curly horns to investigate. And then there was Stone House. Chicky loved to play in the huge overgrown garden. Sometimes the Miss Sheedys, three sisters who owned the house, and were ancient, let her play at dressing up in their old clothes.

Chicky watched as Kathleen went off to train to be a nurse in a big hospital in Wales, and then Mary got a job in an insurance office. Neither of those jobs appealed to Chicky at all, but she would have to do something. The land wouldn't support the whole Ryan family. Two of the boys had gone to serve their time in business in big towns in the West. Only Brian would work with his father.

Chicky's mother was always tired and her father always worried. They were relieved when Chicky got a job in the knitting factory. Not as a machinist or home knitter but in the office. She was in charge of sending out the finished garments to customers and keeping the books. It wasn't a *great* job but it did mean that she could stay at home, which was what she wanted. She had plenty of friends around the place, and each summer she fell in love with a different O'Hara boy but nothing ever came of it.

Then one day Walter Starr, a young American, wandered into the knitting factory wanting to buy an Aran sweater. Chicky was instructed to explain to him that it was not a retail outlet, they only made up sweaters for stores or mail order.

'Well you're missing a trick then,' Walter Starr said. 'People come to this wild place and they *need* an Aran sweater, and they need it now, not in a few weeks' time.'

He was very handsome. He reminded her of how Jack and Bobby Kennedy had looked when they were boys, same flashing smile and good teeth. He was suntanned and very different to the boys from round Stoneybridge. She didn't want him to leave the knitting factory and he didn't seem to want to go either.

Chicky remembered a sweater they had in stock which they had used to be photographed. Perhaps Walter Starr might like to buy that one – it wasn't exactly new but it was nearly new.

He said it would be perfect.

He invited her to go for a walk on the beach and he told her this was one of the most beautiful places on earth.

Imagine! He had been to California *and* Italy and yet he thought Stoneybridge was beautiful.

And he thought Chicky was beautiful too. He said she was just so cute with her dark curly hair and her big blue eyes. They spent every possible moment together. He had only intended to stay a day or two but now he found it hard to go on anywhere else. Unless she would come with him, of course.

Chicky laughed out loud at the idea that she should pack in her job at the knitting factory and tell her mother and father that she was going around Ireland hitchhiking with an American that she had just met! It would have been more acceptable to suggest flying to the moon.

Walter found her horror at the idea touching and almost endearing.

'We only have one life, Chicky. *They* can't live it for us. We have to live it ourselves. Do you think *my* parents want me out here in the wilds of nowhere, having a good time? No, they want me in the Country Club playing tennis with the daughters of nice families, but hey, this is where I want to be. It's as simple as that.'

Walter Starr lived in a world where everything was simple. They loved each other, so what was more natural than to make love? They each knew the other was right so why complicate it by what other people would say or think or do? A kindly God understood love. Father Johnson, who had taken a vow never to fall in love, didn't. They didn't need any stupid contracts or certificates, did they?

And after six glorious weeks, when Walter had to think of going back to the States, Chicky was ready to go with him. It involved an

immense amount of rows and dramas and enormous upset in the Ryan household. But Walter was unaware of any of this.

Chicky's father was more worried than ever now because everyone would say that he had brought up a tramp who was no better than she should be.

Chicky's mother looked more tired and disappointed than ever, and said only God and his sainted mother knew what she had done wrong in bringing Chicky up to be such a scourge to them all.

Kathleen said that it was just as well she had an engagement ring on her finger because no man would have her if he knew the kind of family she came from.

Mary, who worked in the insurance office and was walking out with one of the O'Haras, said that the days of *her* romance were now numbered, thanks to Chicky. The O'Haras were a very respectable family in the town and they wouldn't think kindly about all this behaviour at all.

Her brother Brian kept his head down and said nothing at all. When Chicky asked him what he thought, Brian said he didn't think. He didn't have time to think.

Chicky's friends, Peggy, who also worked in the knitting factory, and Nuala, who was a maid for the three Miss Sheedys, said it was the most exciting, reckless thing they had ever heard of, and wasn't it great that she had a passport already from that school trip to Lourdes.

Walter Starr said they would stay in New York with friends of his. He was going to drop out of law school, it wasn't really right for him. If we had several lives, well then, yes, maybe, but since we only have one life it wasn't worth spending it studying law.

The night before she left, Chicky tried to make her parents understand this. She was twenty, she had her whole life to live, she wanted to love her family and for them to love her in spite of their disappointment.

Her father's face was tight and hard. She would never be welcome in this house again, she had brought shame on them all.

Her mother was bitter. She said that Chicky was being very, very foolish. It wouldn't last, it couldn't last. It was not love, it was infatuation. If this Walter really loved her then he would wait for her and provide her with a home and his name and a future instead of all this nonsense.

You could cut the atmosphere in the Ryan household with a knife.

Chicky's sisters were no support. But she was adamant. *They* hadn't known real love. She was not going to change her plans. She had her passport. She was going to go to America.

'Wish me well,' she had begged them the night before she left, but they had turned their faces away.

'Don't let me go away with the memory of you being so cold.' Chicky had tears running down her face.

Her mother sighed a great sigh. 'It would be cold if we just said, "Go ahead, enjoy yourself." We are trying to do our best for you. To help you make the best of your life. This is not love, it's only some sort of infatuation. You can't have our blessing. It's just not there for you. There's no use pretending.'

So Chicky left without it.

At Shannon airport there were crowds waving goodbye to their children setting out for a new life in the United States. There was nobody to wave Chicky goodbye, but she and Walter didn't care. They had their whole life ahead of them.

No rules, no doing the right thing to please the neighbours and relations.

They would be free – free to work where they wanted and at what they wanted.

No trying to fulfil other people's hopes – marry a rich farmer in Chicky's case, or become a top lawyer, which was what Walter's family had in mind for him.

Questions and exercises on the text are on page 290.

EVERYTHING YOU NEED TO KNOW ABOUT GENERATION Z

Facebook? Of course. Books? Definitely not. Video games? For sure. Sport? No way. Speed? Yes. Patience? Not so much.

This, in a nutshell, is the life of the "Generation Z" -- independent, stubborn, pragmatic and always in a rush.

These youngsters, born after 1995 and unaware of a world without Internet, live a life that seems a million miles removed from the hopes, dreams and morals of previous generations.

They are so hooked into the digital world that some academics have nicknamed them "the mutants".

Here are a few of the habits of Generation Z:

DAILY LIFE

They want everything, everywhere and immediately. They surf on two screens simultaneously. They don't mind paying through the nose for the latest smart phone but turn up their nose at paying for a film or a song when you can get that for free online.

Aged 13 to 20, they get all the latest trends from social media and find the morals of their elders out-of-date.

Their fashions are those found worldwide over the web: they watch American blockbusters like "Hunger Games" or "Divergent", listen to Korean K-pop and, when they dance, they "twerk".

When they speak, their vocabulary is peppered with acronyms, incomprehensible to those not in the know. "Swag" is the new "cool".

And their new idols are Internet stars, like PewDiePie, who has the world's most subscribed YouTube channel.

THEIR FRIENDS

People from Generation Z find it easier to talk online than in person. Their friends on social media are as important to them as their friends in real life but sometimes they do actually meet up in person with these "virtual" pals.

More than eight out of 10 are hooked on social networks and more than half of them think that this is where their real social life takes place.

They are on dating websites from the age of 16 -- sometimes before.

WHAT THEY KNOW

Even as young as they are, they have already seen so many technologies become obsolete. For this reason, they have become the ultimate "self-educators", learning how to use new stuff via self-help videos on YouTube.

As for the web, violence, porn, they've already seen it all.

WHAT THEY WATCH

According to US consultancy Sparks and Honey, the average Generation Z-er spends more than three hours a day in front of a screen.

They live in constant "FOMO", fear of missing out. They can't stand the idea of not being in the loop when something new and exciting comes out.

Facebook is their main poison, despite its flagging popularity among some Americans. Photos on Instagram, quick messages on Snapchat. Twitter and Tumblr are omnipresent.

But it's not all passive: Generation Z are also putting themselves out there on YouTube or "Vlogging" (video blogging), hoping to become the next "Fred" (Lucas Cruikshank), who made his name at the grand old age of 13.

Everyone surfs the web while watching the TV and they think that everything is possible with technology. But, they have a short attention span and tend to skim-read rather than read properly, which can lead to difficulty at school.

GENERATION Z AT WORK

This is a generation that wants to create their own company -- between 50 percent and 72 percent want to run their own start-up.

The idea of "business" brings up negative responses: "complicated", "brutal", "a jungle".

They believe success comes from their "network" rather than from qualifications and they prefer a flat organisation to a hierarchy at work.

They want to succeed and achieve, with 76 percent aiming to make their hobby their job.

THE FUTURE OF GENERATION Z

These are children of the crisis and it shows in their outlook. Most of them say they are "stressed out" by what they see as a bleak future, especially in terms of economy and environment.

Given the same pay, 25 percent of the Generation Z in France would choose the most "fun" company, 22 percent the most innovative and 21 percent the most ethical.

But like any idealistic generation, they want to change the world and love the idea of volunteer work, which a quarter of Americans in their late teens are already doing.

Questions and exercises on the text are on page 296.

9
OUTLOOK ON THE US

QUIET STRENGTH

BY SUSAN CAIN

Montgomery, Alabama. December 1, 1955. Early evening. A public bus pulls to a stop and a sensibly dressed woman in her forties gets on. She carries herself erectly, despite having spent the day bent over an ironing board in a dingy basement tailor shop at the Montgomery Fair department store. Her feet are swollen, her shoulders ache. She sits in the first row of the Colored section and watches quietly as the bus fills with riders. Until the driver orders her to give her seat to a white passenger.

The woman utters a single word that ignites one of the most important civil rights protests of the twentieth century, one word that helps America find its better self.

The word is "No."

The driver threatens to have her arrested.

"You may do that," says Rosa Parks.

A police officer arrives. He asks Parks why she won't move.

"Why do you all push us around?" she answers simply.

"I don't know," he says. "But the law is the law, and you're under arrest."

On the afternoon of her trial and conviction for disorderly conduct, the Montgomery Improvement Association holds a rally for Parks at the Holt Street Baptist Church, in the poorest section of town. Five thousand gather to support Parks's lonely act of courage. They squeeze inside the church until its pews can hold no more. The rest wait patiently outside, listening through loudspeakers. The Reverend Martin Luther King Jr. addresses the crowd. "There comes a time that people get tired of being trampled over by the iron feet of oppression," he tells them. "There comes a time when people get tired of being pushed out of the glittering sunlight of life's July and left standing amidst the piercing chill of an Alpine November."

He praises Parks's bravery and hugs her. She stands silently, her mere presence enough to galvanize the crowd. The association launches a citywide bus boycott that lasts 381 days. The people trudge miles to work. They carpool with strangers. They change the course of American history.

I had always imagined Rosa Parks as a stately woman with a bold temperament, someone who could easily stand up to a busload of glowering passengers. But when she died in 2005 at the age of ninety-two, the flood of obituaries recalled her as soft-spoken, sweet, and small in stature. They said she was "timid and shy" but had "the courage of a lion." They were full of phrases like "radical humility" and "quiet fortitude." What does it mean to be quiet *and* have fortitude? these descriptions asked implicitly. How could you be shy *and* courageous?

Parks herself seemed aware of this paradox, calling her autobiography *Quiet Strength* – a title that challenges us to question our assumptions. Why *shouldn't* quiet be strong? And what else can quiet do that we don't give it credit for?

Questions and exercises on the text are on page 307.

THE NEGRO MOTHER

BY LANGSTON HUGHES

LANGSTON HUGHES (1902–1967) was an American poet, social activist, novelist, playwright, and columnist. Hughes is particularly known for his insightful, colorful portrayals of black life in America from the twenties to the sixties. He wrote novels, short stories and plays, as well as poetry.

Children, I come back today
To tell you a story of the long dark way
That I had to climb, that I had to know
In order that the race might live and grow.
Look at my face – dark as the night –
Yet shining like the sun with love's true light.
I am the child they stole from the sand
Three hundred years ago in Africa's land.
I am the dark girl who crossed the wide sea
Carrying in my body the seed of the free.
I am the woman who worked in the field
Bringing the cotton and the corn to yield.
I am the one who labored as a slave,
Beaten and mistreated for the work that I gave–
Children sold away from me, husband sold, too.
No safety, no love, no respect was I due.
Three hundred years in the deepest South:
But God put a song and a prayer in my mouth.
God put a dream like steel in my soul.
Now, through my children, I'm reaching the goal.
Now, through my children, young and free,
I realize the blessings denied to me.
I couldn't read then. I couldn't write.
I had nothing, back there in the night.
Sometimes, the valley was filled with tears,
But I kept trudging on through the lonely years.
Sometimes, the road was hot with sun,
But I had to keep on till my work was done:
I *had* to keep on! No stopping for me –
I was the seed of the coming Free.

I nourished the dream that nothing could smother
Deep in my breast – the Negro mother.
I had only hope then, but now through you,
Dark ones of today, my dreams must come true:
All you dark children in the world out there,
Remember my sweat, my pain, my despair.
Remember my years, heavy with sorrow –
And make of those years a torch for tomorrow.
Make of my past a road to the light
Out of the darkness, the ignorance, the night.
Lift high my banner out of the dust.
Stand like free men supporting my trust.
Believe in the right, let none push you back.
Remember the whip and the slaver's track.
Remember how the strong in struggle and strife
Still bar you the way, and deny you life –
But march ever forward, breaking down bars.
Look ever upward at the sun and the stars.
Oh, my dark children, may my dreams and my prayers
Impel you forever up the great stairs –
For I will be with you till no white brother
Dares keep down the children of the Negro mother.

Questions and exercises on the text are on page 309.

WE ARE THE FUTURE

BY THOMAS L. FRIEDMAN AND MICHAEL MANDELBAUM

In March 2010, a large gala dinner was held at the National Building Museum in Washington, D.C. – black ties, long dresses. But this was no ordinary dinner. There were forty guests of honor. So here's our brainteaser for readers: We will give you the names of most of the honorees, and you tell us what dinner they were attending. Ready?

Linda Zhou, Alice Wei Zhao, Lori Ying, Angela Yu-Yun Yeung, Lynnelle Lin Ye, Kevin Young Xu, Benjamen Chang Sun, Jane Yoonhae Suh, Katheryn Cheng Shi, Sunanda Sharma, Sarine Gayaneh Shahmirian, Arjun Ranganath Puranik, Raman Venkat Nelakanti, Akhil Mathew, Paul Masih Das, David Chienyun Liu, Elisa Bisi Lin, Yifan Li, Lanair Amaad Lett, Ruoyi Jiang, Otana Agape Jakpor, Peter Danming Hu, Yale Wang Fan, Yuval Yaacov Calev, Levent Alpoge, John Vincenzo Capodilupo, and Namrata Anand.

Sorry, wrong, it was not a dinner of the China-India Friendship Association. Give up? All these honorees were American high school students. They were the vast majority of the forty finalists in the 2010 Intel Science Talent Search, which, through a national contest, identifies and honors the top math and science high school students in America, based on their solutions to scientific problems. As the list of names makes clear, most finalists hailed from immigrant families, largely from Asia.

If you need any convincing about the virtues of immigration, attend the Intel science finals. We need to keep a constant flow of legal immigrants into our country, whether they wear blue collars or

lab coats. It is a part of our formula that very few countries can copy. When all of these energetic, high-aspiring people are mixed together with a democratic system and free markets, magic happens. If we want to keep that magic, we need immigration reform that guarantees that we will always attract and retain, in a legal, orderly fashion, the world's first-round aspirational and intellectual draft choices.

The overall winner of the 2010 Intel contest – a $100,000 award for the best project out of the forty – was Erika Alden DeBenedictis of New Mexico, who developed a software navigation system that would enable spacecraft to "travel through the solar system" more efficiently. To close the evening, Alice Wei Zhao of North High School in Sheboygan, Wisconsin, was chosen by her fellow finalists to speak for them. She told the audience: "Don't sweat about the problems our generation will have to deal with. Believe me, our future is in good hands."

Questions and exercises on the text are on page 311.

THE AGE OF EXCITEMENT

BY BILL BRYSON

BILL BRYSON (1951–) was born in the US but settled in England in 1977. He is famous for his travel books such as *The Lost Continent*, and *Neither Here Nor There*, an account of his first trip around Europe. Bill Bryson has also written several books on the English language, including *Mother Tongue* and *Made in America*.

I don't know how they managed it, but the people responsible for the 1950s made a world in which pretty much everything was good for you. Drinks before dinner? The more the better! Smoke? You bet! Cigarettes actually made you healthier, by soothing jangly nerves and sharpening jaded minds, according to advertisements. 'Just what the doctor ordered!' read ads for L&M cigarettes, some of them in the *Journal of the American Medical Association* where cigarette ads were gladly accepted right up to the 1960s. X-rays were so benign that shoe stores installed special machines that used them to measure foot sizes, sending penetrating rays up through the soles of your feet and right out the top of your head. There wasn't a particle of tissue within you that wasn't bathed in their magical glow. No wonder you felt energized and ready for a new pair of Keds when you stepped down.

Happily, we were indestructible. We didn't need seat belts, airbags, smoke detectors, bottled water or the Heimlich manoeuvre. We didn't require child safety caps on our medicines. We didn't need helmets when we rode our bikes or pads for our knees and elbows when we went skating. We knew without written reminding that bleach was not a refreshing drink and that gasoline when exposed to a match had a tendency to combust. We didn't have to worry about what we ate because nearly all foods were good for us: sugar gave us energy, red meat made us strong, ice cream gave us healthy bones, coffee kept us alert and purring productively.

Every week brought exciting news of things becoming better, swifter, more convenient. Nothing was too preposterous to try. 'Mail Is Delivered by Guided Missile', the *Des Moines Register* reported with a clear touch of excitement and pride on the morning of 8 June 1959, after the US Postal Service launched a Regulus I rocket carrying three thousand first-class letters from a submarine in the Atlantic Ocean on to an airbase in Mayport, Florida, one hundred miles away.

Soon, the article assured us, rockets loaded with mail would be streaking across the nation's skies. Special delivery letters, one supposed, would be thudding nosecone-first into our back yards practically hourly.

'I believe we will see missile mail developed to a significant degree,' promised Postmaster General Arthur Summerfield at the celebrations that followed. In fact, nothing more was heard of missile mail.

Perhaps it occurred to someone that incoming rockets might have an unfortunate tendency to miss their targets and crash through the roofs of factories or hospitals, or that they might blow up in flight, or take out passing aircraft, or that every launch would cost tens of thousands of dollars to deliver a payload worth a maximum of $120 at prevailing postal rates.

The fact was that rocket mail was not for one moment a realistic proposition, and that every penny of the million or so dollars spent on the experiment was wasted. No matter. The important thing was knowing that we could send mail by rocket if we *wanted* to. This was an age for dreaming, after all.

Looking back now, it's almost impossible to find anything that wasn't at least a little bit exciting at the time. Even haircuts could give unusual amounts of pleasure. In 1955, my father and brother went to the barber and came back with every hair on their heads standing to attention and sheared off in a perfect horizontal plane. This arresting style was known as a flat-top. They spent most of the rest of the decade looking as if they were prepared in emergencies to provide landing spots for some very small experimental aircraft, or perhaps special delivery messages sent by miniature missile. Never have people looked so ridiculous and so happy at the same time.

There was a certain endearing innocence about the age, too. On 3 April 1956, according to news reports, a Mrs Julia Chase of Hagerstown, Maryland, while on a tour of the White House, slipped away from her tour group and vanished into the heart of the building. For four and a half hours, Mrs Chase, who was described later as 'dishevelled, vague and not quite lucid', wandered through the White House, setting small fires – five in all. That's how tight security was in those days: a not-quite-lucid woman was able to roam unnoticed through the Executive Mansion for more than half a working day. You can imagine the response if anyone tried anything like that now: the instantaneous alarms, the scrambled Air Force jets, the SWAT teams dropping from panels in the ceiling, the tanks rolling across the lawns, the ninety minutes of sustained gunfire pouring into the target area, the lavish awarding of medals of bravery afterwards, including posthumously to the seventy-six people in Virginia and eastern Maryland killed by friendly fire. In 1956, Mrs Chase, when found, was taken to the staff kitchen, given a cup of tea and released into the custody of her family, and no one ever heard from her again.

Questions and exercises on the text are on page 316.

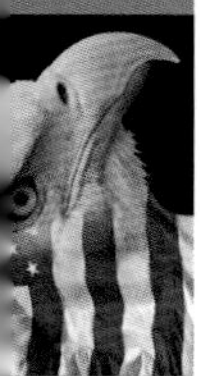

THE BIRTH OF HELA

BY REBECCA SKLOOT

On February 5, 1951, after Jones got Henrietta's biopsy report back from the lab, he called and told her it was malignant. Henrietta didn't tell anyone what Jones said, and no one asked. She simply went on with her day as if nothing had happened, which was just like her – no sense upsetting anyone over something she could deal with herself.

That night Henrietta told her husband, "Day, I need to go back to the doctor tomorrow. He wants to do some tests, give me some medicine." The next morning she climbed from the Buick outside Hopkins again, telling Day and the children not to worry.

"Ain't nothin serious wrong," she said. "Doctor's gonna fix me right up."

Henrietta went straight to the admissions desk and told the receptionist she was there for her treatment. Then she signed a form with the words operation permit at the top of the page. It said:

> I hereby give consent to the staff of The Johns Hopkins Hospital to perform any operative procedures and under any anaesthetic either local or general that they may deem necessary in the proper surgical care and treatment of: ________________________________

Henrietta printed her name in the blank space. A witness with illegible handwriting signed a line at the bottom of the form, and Henrietta signed another.

Then she followed a nurse down a long hallway into the ward for colored women, where Howard Jones and several other white physicians ran more tests than she'd had in her entire life. They checked her urine, her blood, her lungs. They stuck tubes in her bladder and nose.

On her second night at the hospital, the nurse on duty fed Henrietta an early dinner so her stomach would be empty the next morning, when a doctor put her under anesthetic for her first cancer treatment. Henrietta's tumor was the invasive type, and like hospitals nationwide, Hopkins treated all invasive cervical carcinomas with radium, a white radioactive metal that glows an eerie blue.

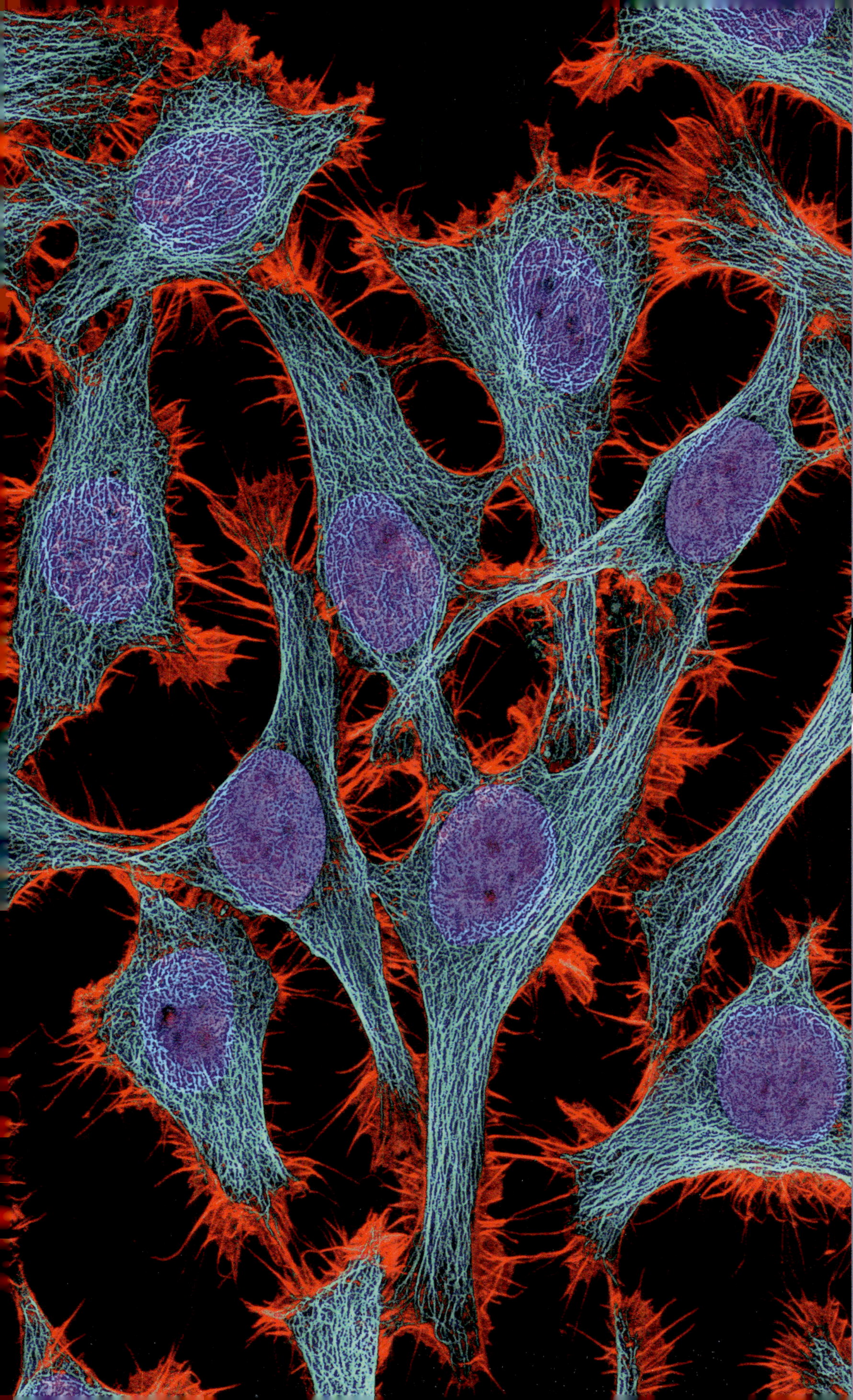

When radium was first discovered in the late 1800s, headlines nationwide hailed it as "a substitute for gas, electricity, and a positive cure for every disease." Watchmakers added it to paint to make watch dials glow, and doctors administered it in powdered form to treat everything from seasickness to ear infections. But radium destroys any cells it encounters, and patients who'd taken it for trivial problems began dying. Radium causes mutations, that can turn into cancer, and at high doses it can burn the skin off a person's body. But it also kills cancer cells.

Hopkins had been using radium to treat cervical cancer since the early 1900s, when a surgeon named Howard Kelly visited Marie and Pierre Curie, the couple in France who'd discovered radium and its ability to destroy cancer cells. Without realizing the danger of contact with radium, Kelly brought some back to the United States in his pockets and regularly traveled the world collecting more. By the 1940s, several studies – one of them conducted by Howard Jones, Henrietta's physician – showed that radium was safer and more effective than surgery for treating invasive cervical cancer.

The morning of Henrietta's first treatment, a taxi driver picked up a doctor's bag filled with thin glass tubes of radium from a clinic across town. The tubes were tucked into individual slots inside small canvas pouches hand-sewn by a local Baltimore woman. The pouches were called Brack plaques, after the Hopkins doctor who invented them and oversaw Henrietta's radium treatment. He would later die of cancer, most likely caused by his regular exposure to radium, as would a resident who traveled with Kelly and also transported radium in his pockets.

One nurse placed the Brack plaques on a stainless-steel tray. Another wheeled Henrietta into the small colored-only operating room on the second floor, with stainless-steel tables, huge glaring lights, and an all-white medical staff dressed in white gowns, hats, masks, and gloves.

With Henrietta unconscious on the operating table in the center of the room, her feet in stirrups, the surgeon on duty, Dr. Lawrence Wharton Jr., sat on a stool between her legs. He peered inside Henrietta, dilated her cervix, and prepared to treat her tumor. But first – though no one had told Henrietta that TeLinde was collecting samples or asked if she wanted to be a donor – Wharton picked up a sharp knife and shaved two dime-sized pieces of tissue from Henrietta's cervix: one from her tumor, and one from the healthy cervical tissue nearby. Then he placed the samples in a glass dish.

Wharton slipped a tube filled with radium inside Henrietta's cervix, and sewed it in place. He sewed a plaque filled with radium to the outer surface of her cervix and packed another plaque against it.

He slid several rolls of gauze inside her vagina to help keep the radium in place, then threaded a catheter into her bladder so she could urinate without disturbing the treatment.

When Wharton finished, a nurse wheeled Henrietta back into the ward, and Wharton wrote in her chart, "The patient tolerated the procedure well and left the operating room in good condition." On a separate page he wrote, "Henrietta Lacks... Biopsy of cervical tissue... Tissue given to Dr. George Gey."

A resident took the dish with the samples to Gey's lab, as he'd done many times before. Gey still got excited at moments like this, but everyone else in his lab saw Henrietta's sample as something tedious – the latest of what felt like countless samples that scientists and lab technicians had been trying and failing to grow for years. They were sure Henrietta's cells would die just like all the others. [...]

Henrietta spent the next two days in the hospital, recovering from her first radium treatment. Doctors examined her inside and out, pressing on her stomach, inserting new catheters into her bladder, fingers into her vagina and anus, needles into her veins. They wrote notes in her chart saying, "30 year-old colored female lying quietly in no evident distress," and "Patient feels quite well tonight. Morale is good and she is ready to go home."

Before Henrietta left the hospital, a doctor put her feet in the stirrups again and removed the radium. He sent her home with instructions to call the clinic if she had problems, and to come back for a second dose of radium in two and a half weeks.

Meanwhile, each morning after putting Henrietta's cells in culture, Mary started her days with the usual sterilization drill. She peered into the tubes, laughing to herself and thinking, *Nothing's happening. Big surprise.* Then, two days after Henrietta went home from the hospital, Mary saw what looked like little rings of fried egg white around the clots at the bottoms of each tube. The cells were growing, but Mary didn't think much of it – other cells had survived for a while in the lab.

But Henrietta's cells weren't merely surviving, they were growing with mythological intensity. By the next morning they'd doubled. Mary divided the contents of each tube into two, giving them room to grow, and within twenty-four hours, they'd doubled again. Soon she was dividing them into four tubes, then six. Henrietta's cells grew to fill as much space as Mary gave them.

Still, Gey wasn't ready to celebrate. "The cells could die any minute," he told Mary.

But they didn't. They kept growing like nothing anyone had seen, doubling their numbers every twenty-four hours, stacking hundreds

on top of hundreds, accumulating by the millions. "Spreading like crabgrass!" Margaret said. They grew twenty times faster than Henrietta's normal cells, which died only a few days after Mary put them in culture. As long as they had food and warmth, Henrietta's cancer cells seemed unstoppable.

Soon, George told a few of his closest colleagues that he thought his lab might have grown the first immortal human cells.

To which they replied, Can I have some? And George said yes.

Questions and exercises on the text are on page 318.

RESOURCE SECTION

Welcome to the Resource Section of Solid Gold. It's here to help you improve the way you learn and use English. It will help you build your vocabulary and sharpen up your grammar, as well as showing you ways to get better at understanding, speaking, reading and writing in English. There's no need to read the whole Resource Section from start to finish – just go straight to the section you need as you work through the book.

Three keys are the letters S, L and P:

Strategies. Don't just do your homework, think about the way you study and decide how to improve your spoken English and your ability to understand when other people speak English. Decide on ways to get better at writing.

Logbook. Keep a logbook and write down how you're progressing. Write a date next to each entry. Get into the habit of reflecting on how you learn. Keep a note of the different strategies you use and how well you think they work for you.

Portfolio gives you solid proof of what you've achieved. Tests, papers, recordings – anything you've produced in English should be kept in your portfolio. You'll be surprised how much you've collected at the end of the year.

Follow these links:

1. **On Studying**
2. **On Critical Reading**
3. **Genres and the Rhetorical Process**
4. **On Speaking**
5. **On Writing**
6. **On Language**
7. **Pick and Choose**

1 ON STUDYING

Strategies to Improve Your Language Skills

Read more about how you can improve your reading, listening and speaking skills.

Using mind maps for taking notes

What is the best way of taking notes? The obvious way, and the one most people use is to write them down one line at a time – so-called 'linear' notes. Unfortunately, the brain does not work that way. It does not store information in neat lines and columns. The brain works primarily with key concepts in an interlinked and integrated manner, where information is stored by pattern and association. So it might help your mind to store and recall the information if you were to take your notes in the way the brain works.

Here is an example of a mind map showing the various parts and functions of this book.

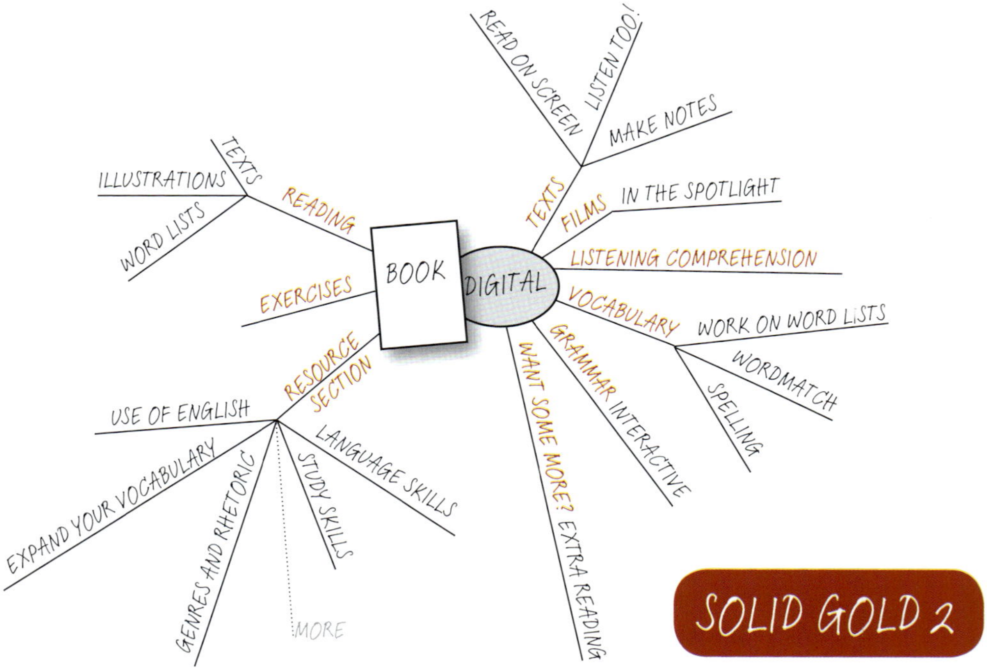

1 Start in the centre – with the main topic in big letters – preferably with a symbol or drawing. Then draw branches spreading out from it.
2 Words should be printed in capital letters. When reading back later, a printed map is far easier to take in. The printed words should be on lines, and each line should be connected to other lines.
3 Put any related points on the same main branches, each one shooting off like a new sub-branch. Again one word per line.

4 Use different coloured pencils or pens for related topics.
5 Draw as many pictures or symbols as you can.
6 When you have completed each main branch, enclose it in a different coloured border.
7 Add to each map regularly as you learn more about each subject. The more artistic and distinctive you can make your mind maps, the better. The right brain responds to colour and artistry and it also likes to have an overall picture. So by making your mind maps you will be involving both sides of your brain in the learning task and improving your learning and creativity.

Learning Log

Keeping a learning log is a good way to track of your progress in English.
Use the questions below as a checklist after each unit as part of a learning log.

Your use of English

1 How do you feel when expressing yourself in English? What can be done to improve the situation? Would you like to work more often in small groups? More whole-class discussions? Some other alternatives?
2 Have you used mind maps when taking notes and structuring information? How did it turn out?
3 What written work have you done in this unit? How did it turn out?
4 Do you feel that your vocabulary has increased? Which words were easy to remember? What methods do you use when learning new words?
5 Has your understanding of English grammar improved? What have you been working on lately? What do you need more information about?
6 How have you prepared your homework? Are you satisfied with your efforts?
7 How often do you look up the meaning of words?
8 Can you suggest any ways of making the course more efficient and/or more enjoyable?

Assessment

Assessment is necessary in order to keep a record of your progress. Use the following questions when you need some feedback.

Name ______________________________ Date ______________

I think this statement matches my level of English. Choose 0–4.

0=not at all 1=a little 2=fairly well 3=very well 4=perfectly

I can understand both the whole and details of English spoken at a rapid pace. ☐

I can understand English in more formal contexts. ☐

I can take part in discussions and comment on general content and details. ☐

I can choose and use different strategies to solve problems and improve my interaction in English. ☐

I can discuss, comment and draw conclusions when reading a text. ☐

I can read and understand different genres of English. ☐

I can adjust my written and spoken production to the situation, the recipient and to the context as required. ☐

I can express myself orally and in writing in a clear, coherent and structured way using appropriate genres. ☐

I can discuss and comment on the content of written material. ☐

I can improve my own writing. ☐

I can choose material from different media and use it in my own written production as well as in oral interaction. ☐

I can check and critically evaluate spoken as well as written sources. ☐

I can discuss cultural differences in various contexts and make comparisons with my own knowledge and experiences. ☐

2 ON CRITICAL READING

When you look for information – especially on the Internet – it's very important that you evaluate the sources you intend to use. Anyone can publish articles on the net, as you know, and therefore it's very important to pay attention to the work you're referring to.

When you're looking for information you usually have an assignment that you're working on and finding facts is a big part of the working process which could be described as:

- Defining the assignment and finding research questions.
- Finding information. Where can it be found?
- Searching for information from different sources.
- Evaluating and analysing the information.
- Compiling a text.
- Reporting.

Critical reading and reviewing of sources

Who is the author?
Is it a well-known person? Someone who is an expert in the field? Does he or she have a title? Is there a presentation of this person to be found anywhere? Does the author represent a particular standpoint or opinion?

Who lies behind the web page?
Is it an organization which is well-known within this field?

Can you tell when the text was published and how up-to-date the information is?
It's important to check when the web page was last updated and, if possible, when the information you're looking at was first published.

What is pure fact? And what are opinions or value statements?
You need to practise, preferably with a group of other students, your ability to tell facts from values and opinions. This done, you can of course refer to what people think – their opinions – but you need to be clear about the difference and it isn't always easy to do.

Are the facts consistent with information from other sources?
It's always useful to compare different sources to be on the safe side – to make sure that what you're using is credible. Be sure to discuss with classmates whether your material is credible.

For more information see Skolverket
www.skolverket.se/skolutveckling/resurser-for-larande/kollakallan/in_english

Click on the links to read more about newspapers and advertising

On Newspapers

On Advertising

3 GENRES

When you speak or write you tend to adapt what you say or write according to who you're addressing, what you're speaking or writing about and to the situation you find yourself in. These different ways of speaking or writing are known as different genres or different text types.

Purpose

Every genre has a specific purpose. The purpose determines how the genre is constructed. Instructions, for example, are meant to explain a process and are constructed so that the information is given step by step.

Structure

Every genre has its own structure. A set of instructions starts by stating the goal – for example: How to make a delicious fudge cake. This is then followed by a list of ingredients and step-by-step instructions showing how to make the cake.

A news program can also be considered as a genre and has its own structure, often starting with the day's headlines, followed by details of the major news items, moving on to smaller news items and ending with the weather report. You would probably be surprised if it started with the weather report and ended with major international news.

Language

Every genre has a specific use of language. For example, many newspaper articles are reporting something in the past tense, while a set of instructions will require action verbs in the imperative form.

When writing in a particular genre you need to know how to structure the text and what type of language is required. In this course you'll learn how to write **speeches, formal letters, a job application with a CV, a discussion essay, an argumentative essay and a book review.** These different genres will mean differences in the grammar and vocabulary to be used. The above are examples of written genres. But we also speak in different genres. For example, you may need to inform someone or discuss a matter of great importance.

The Rhetorical Process

When you're writing or preparing a speech you can make use of something called the rhetorical process. It helps you work in a more structured and methodical way. It will help you to understand the aim or purpose of the text, who you should address your writing to and the context, i.e. when, where and how the text is to be used.

1 Understand the aim and the context

Before writing a text or putting together a speech, start by asking yourself:

What's the aim? What do I want to achieve? What does the context demand? If you tackle the following questions first it'll be easier to write your paper, letter, news item or speech:
What's the purpose? Do I want to write a story, an instruction, a review or what?
Who's the recipient? Friends of yours? Complete strangers? A potential employer?
Where's your text to be published? On Facebook, in a letter of application, as a paper, as a speech to be given?
How do I best convey the message? What's required for the genre I've chosen – formal/informal, step-by-step instructions, interest, suspense?
Why this means of communication? Is there a better way?

2 Find, collect and evaluate material

Find and collect ideas from books, the Internet, magazines, newspapers, radio/TV, etc. Go through the material and make a note of the sources. Remember to be a critical reader (see page 151). What can you use? Pick out what you need. Structure your material, i.e. see how different items can go together and decide what order to put things in.

3 Plan and write your essay

Make a plan before you start to write an article or a speech. It will make your assignment much easier. Think of your work as having three parts:

Introduction Here your aim is to catch the reader's or listener's attention. Ask a question, make a statement or give a brief presentation of the subject. For example if you're going to write about the importance of recycling you can start by explaining *why* it's important. It's very important since a good opening paragraph will immediately capture the interest of your readers so that, hopefully, they'll want to go on reading it until the end. There are various means that writers use to 'hook' their readers. These include:

- beginning with an amusing or interesting anecdote
- beginning with a question
- beginning with a quotation
- beginning with a startling or paradoxical statement

Body This is where the main part of the subject is presented. Supporting paragraphs make up the main body of your essay and their purpose is to support and develop the main idea of your essay (your thesis statement).
Generally speaking, the body should consist of three or more paragraphs, each one dealing with a new idea, argument, etc.

A good paragraph should consist of the following:

1 A topic or opening sentence which states the main idea of the paragraph.
2 Supporting sentences which develop the paragraph topic and contain facts or examples relating to the topic sentence.
3 A summary sentence which rounds off the paragraph.

To connect your supporting paragraphs (and supporting sentences within paragraphs) you should make use of certain linking words such as First, Second, Finally, In addition, On the other hand. (See pages 176–179 for a full list.)

Conclusion Finish your text by explaining your conclusions or by summing up the text. The concluding paragraph should not contain any new material. Instead, it should summarize or restate the main idea of the essay so that the reader will be left with the feeling that your essay is complete. So you should:

1 Restate the strongest points of your essay that support your main idea.
2 Conclude your essay by restating the main idea (the thesis sentence) in different words.
3 Give your personal opinion or suggest a plan for action.
4 In your final sentence, sum up your argument very briefly, linking it to the title. Like the introduction, the conclusion should only be a small part of the essay.

4 Language check
Go through what you've written. Have you made the right choices of formal or informal language? Did you use words and phrases that suit your purpose? When you've checked your work it's always a good idea to ask someone else to read through what you've written and to offer feedback.

5 And when giving a speech ... memorize and act it out. **See On Speaking** pages 157–159 for more advice!

CHECKLIST FOR WRITING

When you've finished working on your text, check it one last time – to see if there's anything you should or would like to change. Use the following as a guide.

1 Read the text to yourself. Does it make sense or is there anything missing?
2 Have you divided the text into separate paragraphs?
3 Is there an introduction, a thesis (the main body of the text) and a conclusion?
4 Does the title or heading match the text?
5 Do the structure and choice of vocabulary match the genre?
6 What does your text require – formal or informal language? Make sure not to mix the two.
7 Check the use of linking words. For example: *To begin with ..., In addition ..., In conclusion ...*
8 Check the use of verbs. For example, the -s form, the use of tenses.
9 Check punctuation and capital letters.
10 Check spelling.
11 Check overall grammar. For example, the use of tenses, articles, prepositions, pronouns and adverbs.

Peer response – writing

Before you get peer response it's important that you check your own text and that you analyze it in order to make it better.

DISCUSS THE TEXT WITH THESE QUESTIONS AS A GUIDE:

1 What's the purpose of the text?
2 Does the message come across? How can you summarize the message?
3 Does the headline correspond to the text?
4 What genre is this? Is it well chosen?
5 How is the text structured? Does the introduction link with the conclusion?
6 What kind of linking words are used?
7 Does the choice of vocabulary and grammar correspond to the genre?
8 Is there a good variation of words?
9 Are the sentences grammatically correct?
10 What about paragraphing, spelling, punctuation?
11 Does anything need to be changed?
12 How can the text be improved? Make a few suggestions.

4 ON SPEAKING

Advice on giving talks and presentations

Research has shown that speaking in front of others is one of the things that people fear most. Even the most experienced speakers, including politicians and TV presenters can feel nervous before they face an audience.
But you can speak effectively and confidently in spite of your nerves by preparing correctly beforehand and by following the right techniques in delivering your speech.

Key features of speaking

When giving a talk or making a presentation, it's vital that you think about the following.

1. Your topic – what you're saying, both in general and in detail.
2. Your purpose – why you're speaking.
3. Your audience – how you're going to make your subject interesting.

You therefore need to plan carefully what you say so that you:

1. include all the necessary information (topic).
2. present ideas in a logical order (purpose).
3. speak in a way that suits the people in front of you (audience).

How to organize your speech

There are different types of speeches depending on the aim of your speech. Do you want to discuss an important matter, persuade your audience to share your opinion or just report on a book you've read? For further information how to use these genres when writing a speech see On Writing page 160. Also see the Rhetorical Process on p. 153 for more information.

Most good pieces of writing must have an outline and a structure and a good speech is no exception. Your speech must have an introduction, a body and a conclusion, providing a solid foundation for a successful speech.

Introduction

The introduction is probably the most important part of your speech. It's now that you have to get the attention of your audience, to engage their interest in what you intend to say. You can do this in several ways: Raise a thought-provoking question, make an interesting or controversial statement, use a quotation or even tell a joke.

Body

The body is the largest part of your speech. Now your audience have been introduced to the subject of your speech and are ready to hear your arguments, your thoughts or your discussion.

A good way to outline the body of your speech is to formulate a series of points that you would like to highlight. A point could be a statement about a product, a discussion about healthy habits or, in a eulogy, a nice memory you have of the person.

Organize things so that related points follow one another and that each point builds upon the previous one. This gives your speech a logical progression. Don't include too many points as your listeners may lose interest.

Conclusion

Conclude strongly. You may:

- summarize the main points of your speech
- make some predictions about the future (related to the speech)
- end with a final reflection
- wish someone the best of luck (in a speech addressed to a person)

At the very end indicate that your speech is over by saying *Thanks for listening* showing you are grateful for the attention of the audience.

Giving the talk

Learn these five tricks.

1 Use notes

You should never read a speech. Reading a speech is not giving a talk – it's reading aloud, and that's quite a different activity. In addition, while reading you're not looking at your audience.

Instead, get into the habit of making brief notes, preferably with bullet points of your main ideas, on cards, rather than A4 sheets of paper, so that you don't forget what to say. Practise using notes so that you don't get lost. (You can practise at home in front of a mirror.) Also, number the cards in case they fall on the floor and get scattered!

2 Use body language

If all the audience has got to look at is you, make yourself look interesting. Use your hands to emphasize a point, make an occasional gesture, or even move around a little, from time to time. Above all, relax and remember to change your tone of voice occasionally. Create variety. A dull, monotonous voice is only effective if you're training to be a hypnotist!

3 Keep contact with your audience

Do this with your eyes. Divide the audience into three sections – left, middle and right. Find one friendly face in each section. Take it in turns to direct your speech at them. And smile!

4 Keep it simple
Audiences can't take in a lot at one sitting. Just think what you feel like in a lesson where the teacher just drones on and on with fact after fact, boring you rigid. Similarly, if your talk is too long, complicated, detailed, or full of statistics, your audience will get bored and might even fall asleep!

A good talk should be reasonably brief – 5–8 minutes is reasonable. Follow a clear structure so that the audience knows where it is at any given time – either at the beginning, in the middle or coming to the end. Another tip – it's not a good idea to pass visual props or hand-outs around the audience while you're talking. They'll be too interested in examining whatever's being passed round and they won't listen to you.

5 Use humour and drama
Finally, spice up a talk with a joke or anecdote or two – everyone loves jokes or a good story and they also give the impression that you're confident.

Peer response - speaking

For most people, making a speech in front of a group usually means feeling both anxious and nervous. It's therefore important that you, as a listener, do all you can to **encourage the speaker**. The speaker needs to get feedback but speaking in front of a group can be an awkward situation and the speaker may feel they're being criticized rather than helped. So giving your response in writing might be a better idea.

CHECKLIST WHEN RESPONDING TO A SPEECH

1. What was the purpose of the speech? Did it come across?
2. How did the speaker adjust his or her speech to the audience?
3. Did the speaker make good contact with the audience?
4. Did the opening of the speech link to the ending?
5. Did the speaker use any props, like pictures? How did that work out?
6. Did the person speak without a script?
7. Was it easy to understand? Was the speech clear, and loud enough to hear?
8. Comment on the use of body language.
9. What could be improved?
10. What were the best things about the speech?

Click on the links to read more about self-assessment and debating.

Self-assessment

On Debating

5 ON WRITING

A letter written to a business, a college, or anyone not considered a friend or a family member should be written in a formal style. An essay is also a formal piece of writing and the language you use should reflect this. You should avoid:

* shortened forms (it's, don't, they're, etc.),
* colloquial English, such as phrasal verbs (break up, call off, etc.) and idioms (kill two birds with one stone, and slang (cheesed off, etc.)

Instead, your writing should:

1 consist of fairly long and fairly complex sentences.
2 use long forms (it is, they are, do not, etc.).
3 have a wide range of vocabulary.
4 make greater use of the passive tense than in more informal writing (It is found..., Research has shown... etc.).
5 be divided into paragraphs.

Click on the links to read more about a formal letter and a letter to the editor.

Writing a formal letter

Writing a letter to the editor

Writing a letter of complaint

A letter of complaint is a formal letter. Here is an example. Note the way it is laid out.

❶ 8 Poplar Lane
Manchester MN11 3SR

Magaluf Holidays ❷
24 High Street
Manchester MN1 4AP

2 September, 20XX ❸

Dear Sir, ❹

Re: Holiday No HT43: Hotel Don Carlos, Magaluf ❺

❻ I am writing to complain about the accommodation provided for my wife and me at the Hotel Don Carlos, Magaluf from 13th-26th August 20XX
I booked the above holiday at your office on March 18th. At that time I was told we would be given an air-conditioned room with a balcony and en-suite bathroom. This was confirmed in writing by Mr Perkins on 21st March 20XX, along with other details about the holiday.

However, when we arrived at the hotel we were shown to a room lacking all these amenities. We immediately complained to your courier, Amanda Borrow. After negotiations, she informed us that the hotel had made a mistake over the booking and very much regretted that no other room was available.

The standard of accommodation which we were forced to accept detracted considerably from our enjoyment of the holiday. Also, your company will have paid less for this room than for the one we originally booked.

I therefore expect an appropriate rebate on the sum paid, plus some form of compensation for our 'less-than-enjoyable' holiday experience with your company.

I look forward to hearing from you soon.

Yours faithfully, ❼

James Baker
James Baker ❽

1 Put your address on the right.

2 Put the address of the person/company you are writing to on the left.

3 Put the date under your address. You can write it three ways:
January 3 2015
3 January 2015
3/1/15
Nowadays people tend to use '3, 12, 21', etc rather than '3rd, 12th' or '21st' and don't forget that you should never write the date as 03-01-15 when writing to English-speaking people. In American English, the date is written with the month first, namely 1/3/15.

4 Begin as follows:
Dear Sir, (If you don't know the name of the person you're writing to but know it's a man.)
Dear Madam, (If you don't know the name of the person you're writing to but know it's a woman.)
Dear Sir/Madam, (If you don't know the name or the gender of the person you're writing to.)
Dear Mr/Mrs/Ms .... (If you know the surname of the person you are writing to.)
NOTE: In a formal letter you should never address anyone by their first name unless you know them socially.

5 If you have a reference include it after the salutation, so the person reading it will know at a glance what the letter is about. It is normal to preface it with 'Re:' (= regarding, or reference).

6 Set out your letter in brief paragraphs using fairly formal English. Avoid using slang!

7 End as follows:
Yours faithfully, (If you start your letter 'Dear Sir' or 'Dear Madam')
Yours sincerely, (If you start your letter Dear Mr/Mrs/Ms...)

8 Sign your full name, then type it out underneath.

Writing a job application

When applying for a job you send your CV together with a letter of application. Most of the information about you is to be found in your CV. The main purpose of the letter is to explain why you are interested in the job.

Samantha Lewis
45 Milton Road
Brixton
London SW2 3JD

Cate Magazine Ltd.
Company Address
City & postcode

6 January, 20XX

Dear Sir/Madam,

I wish to apply for the post of fashion editor at Cate Magazine, as advertised in the *Daily News* on 6 September.

As you will see from my enclosed CV, I have worked as a journalist and a fashion editor since graduating with a first class degree in media at the University of Wales. I was honoured to be awarded the Young Journalist of the Year prize in 2012 for my work at Women's World magazine.

I am fast and efficient with a keen eye for fashion and design. My communicative skills facilitate both internal teamwork and working with external writers and designers. Fluency in both French and Spanish allows me to stay informed on the latest European trends.

Working for a new and cutting-edge magazine like Cate Magazine has always been a dream of mine, and I hope to be given the chance to show how my enthusiasm and determination can lead to even more success for the magazine.

Thank you for taking the time to consider this application and I look forward to hearing from you.

Yours faithfully,

Samantha Lewis

Samantha Lewis

Writing a CV

When you apply for a job in Britain, you'll almost certainly be asked to send in a CV (Curriculum Vitae, which is Latin for 'an account of your life'). This is a short written description of your education, qualifications, previous employment and sometimes also your personal interests. It's usually the first thing a prospective employer will see from you. It's important, therefore, to make your CV as clear as possible. You should ensure that it's printed on good quality paper and that it's as free from errors as possible. You'll find a typical CV on the next page.

Samantha Lewis
45 Milton Road, London SW2 3JD
Tel: 0978 3562 32177
Email: Samantha@cvmail.magazine.com

PROFESSIONAL EXPERIENCE

2013– Present ***Women's World***, London, England.
Fashion Editor. Responsible for in-house journalists and a large pool of freelance writers and designers.
Young Journalist of the Year Award, 2013. Increased writers' output by 1000 words/week/writer.

2011–2013 ***Vanity*** magazine, Manchester, England.
Journalist, and Arts and Reviews Editor.
Established new efficient reviewing policy, and re-styled the features sections.

2009–2011 ***One Break*** magazine, London, England.
Journalist (internship). Shadowed the senior journalists, gaining insight into the different departments of the magazine. Published first article three weeks into the internship.

EDUCATION

2006–2009 ***University of Wales***, Cardiff, Wales. BA (Hons) Media. First Class Honours.

1999–2006 ***Hampton High School***, Basingstoke, England.
A-levels: Spanish (A), English (B), Psychology (A)
GCSEs: English Language, English Literature, Mathematics, Core Science, History, Geography, Spanish, Art and Design, ICT, Religious Studies.

OTHER SKILLS

Fluent in Spanish and French. Full driving licence. Experienced Windows, Mac, Office, Photoshop and InDesign user.

INTERESTS

Photography, film, theatre, skiing and squash.

Writing a discussion essay

A discussion essay presents and discusses issues surrounding a particular topic–usually one that is debatable and open to argument. It should provide a well-rounded understanding of the issues before the writer presents his/her personal opinions and conclusions. Its main function is to answer the questions posed in the introduction. Preparing for a discussion essay is a step-by-step job.

1. Choose your discussion essay topic. Make sure the topic is one that you're interested in personally since it'll be easier for you to write. Find information that gives good views of different angels of your topic.
2. Outline your discussion essay. Your goal at this point is to get your thoughts on the discussion essay topic organized and in place.
3. Write your introduction. The goal in the introduction of your discussion essay is to introduce the issues relating to the topic and to provide your reader with important background information.
4. Write the body of your discussion essay. You should present each issue individually.
5. Write your discussion essay conclusion. Your goal with your conclusion is to summarize the overall information from the discussion essay body.

Why do so many people have an unhealthy lifestyle? ❶

"The greatest wealth is health." – Virgil ❷ A healthy lifestyle means maintaining a balanced and nutritious diet as well as engaging in sports or other fitness related activities. But according to the World Health Organization, only one in ten people exercise regularly and most people do not follow a healthy diet. Overweight and obese people suffer from many health complications such as diabetes, high blood pressure, high cholesterol and even cancer. ❸ In this discussion I will attempt to give an overview of some reasons behind unhealthy lifestyles.

The first aspect to be discussed is the need for good habits. A healthy lifestyle does not always start when children are young. Not all parents encourage their children to eat vegetables, fruits, wholemeal and wholegrain foods. Many parents, due to lack of time sometimes find the easy way out by chosing the fast food alternative. This could be the starting point for an unhealthy lifestyle for those children. ❹

School canteens do not always offer healthy food, and there may be vending machines selling soft drinks and candy on the school premises. Schoolchildren are thereby exposed to unhealthy eating.

A further aspect to be considered is the unhealthy food often found at fast food outlets. Eating out at pizzerias and hamburger places is common, because of the cheap prices which attract many people. Unfortunately, it is mostly deep fried and greasy foods that are available at these restaurants. Once a pattern of unhealthy eating is established, it is difficult to break. ❺

Not everybody takes daily exercise. Firstly, many schools only offer PE classes twice a week. Secondly, many students prefer to concentrate on their studies and often consider indulging in physical activities a waste of time. Thirdly, many adults do not allocate time for physical activity because they work long hours. When they get home late in the evening, there is no time for physical activity. They not only deprive themsleves of exercise but they are also poor role models to their children. 6

In short, leading an unhealthy lifestyle can depend on many reasons, such as lack of time and the establishment of bad habits in childhood. 7

1 The headline poses a question for the writer to clarify in the essay.
2 Opening with a quote can attract the interest of the reader.
3 In this paragraph, the writer indicates the importance of the topic and gives a statement of what will be discussed in the essay.
4 This is the first main paragraph. Here the writer focuses on the aspect of good habits. Notice the use of the topic sentence: "The first aspect to be discussed is the need for good habits." This provides a key to the content of the paragraph.
5 The second main paragraph concerns the habit of eating out. Notice again that here, the writer groups all the ideas into a single paragraph, and that there is a topic sentence at the start of the paragraph: "A further aspect to be considered is…"
6 This paragraph now moves on to consider the lack of physical activity. Several aspects are mentioned. Notice how sequencers are used: "firstly…", "secondly…", thirdly...",.
7 This paragraph provides a brief conclusion to the writing. The conclusion only needs to be brief – there is no need to restate everything that has been said before.

To sum up

1 Start by a using a headline showing the intent of your paper.
2 Write a background to your discussion.
3 Present your issue.
4 Finally briefly conclude your findings.
5 Use linking words.
6 Paragraph your text.

Writing an argumentative essay or speech

In an argumentative essay you want to convince others about a belief, a point of view or an opinion. You take a clear stand and support your opinions with various arguments.

Step by step

1 You may be given a topic such as *Abolish the Monarchy* or choose one of your own. Start by finding and reading articles on the subject to find useful arguments.
2 Make an outline of your essay. Effective planning e.g. with a mind map will help you structure your arguments logically. Decide in which order you are going to present your arguments.
3 Start with your *introduction*. Here it is vital to capture the attention of your reader or listener. Give some background information and present your *thesis statement,* in this case *Say No to Smoking!* The thesis statement should consist of one or two sentences.

4 Continue with the main body of text where it is essential to support your viewpoint with examples and facts. Refer to current research if possible. Related arguments should be grouped into paragraphs of their own. Use linking words to connect the paragraphs. Rhetorical questions and repetition can be used for emphasis.
5 Your conclusion should be short and memorable. It should tie up any loose ends, and summarize what you have said. You may also suggest some kind of action.

Example speech (or essay)

Say No to Smoking! ❶

Did you know that more and more young people now smoke? ❷ There seems to be a trend today among young people to smoke. Some decades ago there were many more campaigns to encourage young people to say no to smoking, and consequently fewer started smoking. ❸ Now, once again, there is a need to help teens say no to smoking. ❹

There are many reasons why young people should not smoke. First of all, smoking can lead to addiction, just like drugs or alcohol. A cigarette contains more than 4,000 chemical compounds and at least 400 toxic substances. The nicotine is absorbed into a smoker's bloodstream and quickly reaches the brain, where it releases adrenaline, creating a feeling of pleasure and energy. The constant desire for this feeling of pleasure and energy can lead to addiction. Research shows that children and teens may be especially sensitive to nicotine, making them more likely to become addicted. Tobacco companies use additives and chemicals to make cigarettes more addictive. That is their way of keeping their customers. Imagine being in the power of the tobacco industry because of your addiction, always needing cigarettes close to hand and being dependent on them. According to the Swedish Cancer Society (SCS), as many as forty-five young people start smoking in Sweden every day, amounting to 16,000 young people a year. ❺

Secondly, smoking is expensive. Smoking 10 cigarettes a day costs 836 crowns a month, or 10,038 crowns a year, if the cost remains at 55 crowns per packet. That is money that could be spent on a holiday abroad or paying for a driving license. Instead this money literally goes up in smoke. Furthermore, there are also the public costs of medical care to treat people who have contracted various smoking-related diseases. These costs have to be paid for by our taxes. It is estimated by the Swedish Cancer Society that smoking costs society thirty billion crowns annually. That money could be used to improve schools and hospitals instead. ❻

Finally, smoking affects how long you will live. Research has shown that life expectancy is reduced by seven to eight years, i.e. roughly eleven minutes per cigarette, for people who smoke about fifteen cigarettes a day. Smokers are more likely to suffer from lung cancer, heart attacks, strokes and other smoking-related diseases. Every other smoker will die of a smoking-related disease. Young people might hear that smoking helps people relax and even helps to improve concentration. Some believe that smokers are more efficient, become more creative and think more clearly. However, there is no scientific research to prove this. In other words, while there is evidence to prove the negative aspects of smoking, the counter-arguments have never been proven. ❼

In conclusion, smoking is an addictive habit that makes the tobacco companies rich while having a bad effect on health. Young people have to decide for themselves what is important for their future. Is it better to live a life without addiction and be able to spend money on useful things that will not harm your body? Those who already are smokers can receive medical help to quit. Anyone who wants to learn more about the dangers of smoking should contact an organization such as A Non-Smoking Generation, which has worked for the prevention of smoking among children and teens since 1979, and can offer useful information.

Let us hope for a better future where everyone will say no to smoking! 8

1 Give the thesis statement in the title.
2 Catch the attention of the listener/reader with a rhetorical question.
3 Give some brief background information.
4 Clarify the thesis statement that will be argued in the essay.
5 This is the first main paragraph, in which the addictive substances in cigarettes are presented. The reference to SCS makes your arguments more trustworthy.
6 The second main paragraph concerns the effects of smoking on personal economy and public spending on health care. Notice the use of linking words such as .. *secondly... furthermore.* Again there is a reference to the Swedish Cancer Society to back up the statement *"smoking costs society thirty billion yearly"*.
7 This paragraph now moves on to consider the bad effects of smoking on health. The opposing arguments that smoking has some positive effects are dismissed because they are not backed up by evidence. The writer could also have chosen to refute (disprove) them.
8 This paragraph provides a brief conclusion. Here some kind of action is suggested, either to give up smoking or find out more about the dangers of smoking.

To sum up

- Start with a heading showing the thesis statement of your essay.
- The introduction should contain a short background and your thesis statement.
- The body text should consist of at least three supporting paragraphs where the arguments are presented.
- Remember to divide the text into paragraphs.
- Make use of linking words, especially between paragraphs.
- Try to counter arguments from the opposing side.
- Sum up and suggest some kind of action.

Writing a project

Your task is to look closer at a subject area related to your education, to society, working life, cultural conditions, current issues or ethical issues.
Decide on a subject to investigate and what questions to answer. When using library books and encyclopedias or information from the Internet, use only sources in English. Your project should consist of three parts: introduction, body and conclusion.

Use Times New Roman 12, spacing 1.5.

General outline

Title page

- The title of the project, your name and class.

Introduction

- State your subject and explain why you chose it.
- State the aim of your investigation. What you intend to do. What do you mean by this? What questions do you intend to answer?
- Keep this introduction short – maximum half a page.

Body

- What are your findings? No personal opinions in this part but only facts that you have found.
- The body of the project should be about 1½ pages.

Conclusion

- Discuss and draw some conclusions when summing up your project. Here you may comment and give your personal views on the result.
- Half a page is sufficient.

References

- List the sources you have used.

Some advice when writing

Gather information

- Look for information from reliable sources. Use only sources in English.
- Look for useful information. Remember to list your sources for future reference. Be critical and compare different sources. (See p. 151.)
- Look up any words you don't understand.
- Write down keywords and/or make a mindmap of your project.

Start writing

- Make a timetable showing when you'll have time to write and check your text. This will help you to meet your deadline.
- Use the general outline as you write your project.
- Don't 'copy paste'. Make sure you don't use or copy text from another writer. If you

wish to quote another writer, show this by using quotation marks.

- Remember to structure your text using linking words! (See pp. 176–179.)
- *Remember to hand in your project in good time.*

Analyzing and discussing a novel

Consider the following points when you're discussing a novel.

1 Plot

What is the story about? Is the basic storyline interesting, exciting, moving? Do the different elements in the book link together well? Is the story original? How are the various elements of the plot handled? Is there a sub-plot? If so, how is it related to the main plot?

2 Structure

How is the book structured? Does it follow a chronological time line or does it use flashback, etc? Does the main climax lead to a satisfactory ending?

3 Setting

Where and when does the story take place? Briefly describe the setting and comment on it. Is it real or imaginary? Does it play a significant role in the work? Is a sense of atmosphere evoked? If so, how? Does the setting influence the main characters and/or the plot?

4 Characters

Who are the main characters? Are they well-drawn? Are they realistic? Do they change? Who was your favourite character? Why?

5 Theme

What is the main theme (love, hatred, revenge, hope)? How is it revealed and developed? Is the theme traditional and familiar or new and original? Is it well handled?

6 Style

What are the intellectual, emotional and aesthetic qualities of the writing, e.g. simplicity, humour, satire, harmony? How effective is dialogue? What message, if any, do you think the writer wants to convey to his/her readers?

7 Target audience/genre

At what group or kind of person is this book aimed? Will it interest them? What genre does this book belong to (science-fiction, thriller, romantic novel, historical novel, fantasy, crime novel, etc.)?

8 Personal response

Did you like the book? Why? Why not? What was your favourite/least favourite part of the book? How does this book compare with other books by the same author or with other books of a similar type? Would you recommend it to others to read?

Sample texts

Americanah

"You can't write an honest novel about race in this country," insists one character in Americanah. "If you write about how people are really affected by race, it'll be too obvious. Black writers…have two choices, they can do precious or they can do pretentious. When you do neither, nobody knows what to do with you."

Well, this book proves that's not true. MacArthur "genius grant" winner Chimamanda Ngozi Adichie has written a brutally honest novel about race in this country, and it's not precious or pretentious. It's gripping.

As the author of 2006's *Half of a Yellow Sun*, which took readers inside Nigeria's civil war, Adichie always gives a voice to characters that many Westerners haven't heard. And *Americanah* is no different.

The story follows childhood sweethearts Ifemulu and Obinze from their early years in Nigeria to their search for better lives in the U.S. and England. But the love story is mostly an excuse for Adichie to let them rail about what it's like to be Nigerians in a strange land, and their observations are devastating.

Ifemulu notices that students at her American college expect her to talk about "the black experience," even though that would mean speaking on behalf of Jamaicans and African-Americans who have nothing in common with her. She argues with her Senegalese hairdresser about whether "natural" hair shows pride or laziness. She wonders if black women love Obama just because he married a dark-skinned woman.

And she rants about these experiences on her blog, laying waste to political correctness, getting her friends to weigh in. Their opinions might surprise you. Your own might too — if this book doesn't make you rethink them.

Americanah isn't just another novel that's meant to make people feel better about racism. It's a conversation starter, one that will have you debating with yourself long after you've turned the last page.

David Annand, *The Daily Telegraph*

Writing a review

After reading and discussing your novel the task is to write a review. You will find the guidelines in the digital material.

Click on the link to read more about writing a review.

Writing a review

6 ON LANGUAGE

The language of literary criticism

Narrative

antagonist	In drama or fiction the antagonist opposes the hero or protagonist.
anti-hero	The anti-hero is a type who is incompetent, unlucky, tactless, clumsy, cack-handed, stupid – in other words, a bit of a loser.
denouement	The explanation at the end of a book or play in which everything is explained or settled. This is especially common in mystery or detective stories.
fable	A traditional short story that teaches a moral lesson.
fiction	A general term for such things as novels and short stories about imaginary people and events.
genre	A French word for a kind, a literary type or class. When it comes to novels, typical genres are: adventure novel, children's novel, crime/detective novel, fantasy novel, Gothic novel, historical novel, romantic novel, science-fiction novel, thriller, western, whodunit.
narrative	Something that is told as a story.
narrator	The 'person' who tells the story in a novel, short story, drama or film. This is either a first-person narrator, who is a character in the story or there may be a third-person or omniscient narrator, who relates what happens to all the characters in the third person.
non-fiction	Books or articles about real facts or events, not imaginary ones.
novel	An extended piece of prose fiction, usually at least 50,000 words long.
plot	The sequence of events in which a story is told in a novel, short story, film or play.
prose	Written language in its usual form, such as short stories, novels or newspaper articles, as opposed to poetry.
protagonist	The main character or hero of a play, film or story.
pulp fiction	Novels written for the mass market, intended to be 'a good read'.

satire	Satire makes great use of irony, exaggeration, ridicule and several other techniques to criticize people or society.
setting	The place or time that the action of a book, film, etc. takes place.
short story	A short written story, usually containing only a few characters and events.
stream of consciousness	A way of showing the continuous flow of a character's thoughts and feelings without using the usual methods of description or conversation.
style	How a particular writer says things, such as the writer's choice of words, his/her figures of speech, the length of his/her sentences, etc.
sub-plot	A subordinate or minor collection of events in a novel or drama.
theme	The main subject or idea in a piece of writing. What the writing is "about".

Drama

character	A person in a book, play or film.
climax	The most exciting or important part of a story/play usually comes near the end.
comedy	A play that is intended to entertain people and make them laugh.
drama	In general any work of fiction to be performed for the theatre, television or radio.
farce	A funny play (or film), in which the characters are involved in complicated and silly situations.
fringe theatre	Drama presented on small stages or at festivals. The plays are often by new writers, and experimental in style or subject matter.
one-act play	A play of only one act which is usually between 15 and 40 minutes long.
parody	A piece of writing or music that copies a particular well-known style in an amusing way.
sketch	A short humorous scene on stage or television that is usually part of a larger show.
soliloquy	A speech in a play for one character who is alone on stage and speaks his/her thoughts out loud. This often gives an insight into

the mind and psychology of a character. A well-known soliloquy is Hamlet's *To be or not to be, that is the question.*

tragedy — A serious play that ends sadly, especially with the death of the main character. Hamlet is one of Shakespeare's best known tragedies.

Figurative language

allegory — A story with a double meaning, e.g. *Animal Farm* by George Orwell.

euphemism — Using a mild or less negative word or phrase for a more direct one – usually to avoid shocking or upsetting people, e.g. to pass away instead of 'to die'.

metaphor — A way of describing something by comparing it to something else, without using 'like' or 'as', e.g. *The rain came down in buckets. The city is a jungle.*

personification — Sometimes a poet writes of an object as if it is a person. DH Lawrence does this in his poem *End of Another Home Holiday, when he personifies house roofs: And all the little roofs of the village bow low, pitiful, beseeching, resigned.*

simile — An expression that describes something by comparing it with something else, using 'as' or 'like', e.g. *As white as snow. Like a bull in a china shop.*

Useful phrases for discussion

Here are some useful phrases you can use when discussing things in English.

To give your opinion

In my opinion, …
I believe/feel that …
Well, as I see it, …
The way I see things …
Personally, I feel that …
If you ask me, …
It's my experience that …

To ask someone else for their opinion

What's your opinion, (Jake)?
(Jake), what's your feeling about …?
What do you think, (Maria)?
(Maria), what do you think about/of …?

To agree with an opinion

Yes, I agree with you.
Yes, you're right.
That's what I think too.
I agree with (Anna).

Use these phrases when you agree strongly.
Absolutely!
Exactly!
I quite agree!
That's exactly how I feel.
I agree with you completely!
I couldn't agree more!

To agree with an opinion, but with reservations

I agree in a way, but …
I see your point, but …
I see/know what you mean, but …
I see/know/understand what you're saying, but …
I see/know where you're coming from, but …
You have a point there, but …
I'm not entirely sure about that.

To disagree with an opinion

No, I disagree.
I'm sorry, I don't agree with you there.
I'm not so sure about that.
I take a slightly different view on that.
No, I think you're wrong.

Use these phrases when you disagree strongly.
Come off it!
That's rubbish!
What a load of crap! (very informal)

To say you can't hear or understand what someone is saying

(Sorry,) I missed that.
(Sorry,) I didn't catch that.
(I'm sorry,) could you repeat that, please?
I'm sorry, could you explain that again, please?
I'm not sure Iunderstand what you mean (by) …
I'm afraid I don't follow you.
I'm sorry, you've lost me.

To interrupt a discussion
Could I just stop you there!
Hold on a second.
Do you mind if I say something?
Can I just make a point here!
Can I get a word in, please! (slightly ironic)

To say that others have misunderstood you
That's not quite what I meant.
I think you've misunderstood me.
Perhaps I didn't explain this very clearly.

To talk again about something that's been said
If I could just go back to something (Jake) said/mentioned earlier …
Going back to what (Jake) said/mentioned earlier …
As (Maria) said earlier …

To show interest in what someone is saying
(Yes,) that's true.
That's very true.
That's a point!
Good point!

Linking words

Linking words are essential for your writing to be natural and clear. They help you to connect ideas and sentences, so that people can follow your ideas. A piece of writing without linking words reads like a series of unrelated statements with no flow.

Linking words can be used to:
- link the flow of ideas in your writing.
- guide your reader towards the next stage of your argument.
- link paragraphs together.

Sample text
The words in **bold** in the following text are called linking words. When looking at the text you can see that the text would work without these linking words. Why use them? Well, the reason is that it helps the text to flow better, since one sentence naturally leads onto the next rather than having a text where sentences are simply piled one upon the other.

Paragraph one
Most families nowadays have a car **not only** for going back and forth to work **but also** for taking the children to and from various after school activities. **That is**, a car has become a necessity for most people **and** few can imagine life without one as it gives them freedom of

movement. This freedom of movement, **however**, has its negative side as more and more people spend increasing amounts of time being stuck in traffic jams and getting nowhere. **In other words**, this freedom has come at a great price and the situation is deteriorating year after year.

Paragraph 2

So what can we do about it? **Firstly**, we need to make it less attractive for people to drive to work or into cities. **For example**, a congestion charge could be introduced, as in London, making people pay to enter the city centre between certain hours of the day. **In addition**, cars could be banned from entering city centres at peak times unless they have four people in them. This would have the effect of encouraging car sharing **rather than** having streams of cars with only one person in them.

Paragraph 3

Another possibility is to encourage people to use public transport or to cycle to work. **For instance**, in London there are thousands of cycles to hire all over the city and it has been a resounding success.

Paragraph 4

To sum up, we cannot continue to use cars in the way we do now. Something has to change. **In reality**, it's unlikely that people will voluntarily give up their cars. **Furthermore**, there are very few politicians brave enough to pass such laws. **To put it simply**, the car and growing congestion are here to stay whether we like it or not.
Here's a selection of words used to link ideas, depending on the direction of your argument.

1 Adding more to a point already made

Also, Moreover, Furthermore, Again, What is more, In addition
Besides (that), Above all, As well as that, ...
Not only... but, Similarly, In the same way, Likewise
In fact, In reality, It is found that...
As for, As to, With respect to, Regarding
Taking cannabis regularly can be addictive. *Furthermore/In addition/Moreover* it can lead to taking harder drugs such as heroin.

2 Writing in lists

Firstly, Second(ly), Third(ly)
Another, Yet another, In addition
To begin with, In the second place
Moreover, Additionally, In addition, Also
Next, Then, After that
And to conclude, Lastly, Finally
Too much caffeine is bad for your health. *Firstly/To begin* with, it is very addictive. *Secondly/In addition* it can lead to high blood pressure.

3 Putting the same idea in a different way
In other words, Rather, In that case
To put it (more) simply ...
In view of this, With this in mind
To look at this another way, ...
Dogs are cuddly, loving, loyal and fun – *in other words*, perfect pets.

4 Introducing examples
That is (to say), In other words
For example, For instance, Namely, An example of this is ...
As follows, As in the following examples, Such as, Including
Especially, Particularly, In particular, Specifically, Mainly, Mostly, Generally, Usually
There are many different ways of getting rich – *for example/for instance*, you could win £1 million on the National Lottery.

5 Introducing an alternative viewpoint
By contrast, Another way of viewing this is ..., Alternatively
One alternative is..., Another possibility is ...
On the one hand..., On the other hand ...
Conversely, In comparison, On the contrary, Though, Although
'Are you in favour of fox hunting?'
'No. *On the contrary*, I believe it's cruel, barbaric and should be banned.'
On the one hand, people want a high standard of education and medical care, but *on the other hand* they aren't ready to pay for it through higher taxes.

6 Returning to emphasize your earlier viewpoint
However, Nonetheless, Nevertheless, Despite this fact, Although, Though, At the same time, On the other hand, All the same, Even if X is true, ...
A lot of money has already been spent on education. *However/Nevertheless*, a lot more will need to be spent in the future.
New Zealand is a very small country. *Nonetheless/Despite this fact*, it has produced a large number of world class sportsmen and sportswomen.

7 Showing the results of something
Therefore, Accordingly, As a result
So, it can be seen that ...
The result is ..., The consequence is ..., And that is way
Resulting from this, Consequently, As a consequence
We can see that ..., It is evident that ...
Because of this, Thus, For this/that reason, Owing/Due to X ...
This suggests that …, It follows that …
He didn't work hard enough at university, and *consequently/as a result* failed his final exams.
The job meant moving to Canada for three years. *For that reason/Because of this*, she turned it down.

Our roads are getting increasingly congested. The government, *therefore/accordingly*, needs to do something to persuade more and more people to use public transport.
James was out fishing for the day on September 11 2001. *Thus/Therefore* he didn't know about the terrorist attack on the World Trade Center in New York until he got home later that evening.

8 Summing up or concluding

Therefore, So, My conclusion is ...
In short, In conclusion, To conclude, On the whole
To summarize, To sum up briefly, In brief, Thus, we can see that ...
In conclusion, there can be no doubt that smoking causes lung cancer and other respiratory diseases.

Word-building

Common prefixes

Here are some common prefixes used in English plus their meanings. Try learning these meanings as knowing them can often help to work out what a word means.

	Prefix	Meaning	Examples
1	ab	away, from	*abnormal, abscond*
2	ad-	to	*adverb, admire*
3	anti-	opposed to/against	*antisocial, antibiotic*
4	auto-	of or by oneself	*automatic, automobile*
5	bi-	twice, double	*bicycle, biannual*
6	con-	with; together	*connect, congress*
7	de-	from, off, down	*depart, detract*
8	dis-	not (negative)	*dislike, disinherit*
9	ex-	out, or former	*ex-husband, exterior*
10	in-	not; in	*incapable, incoherent*
11	inter-	between, among	*interbreed, interpret*
12	micro-	extremely small	*microchip, microscope*
13	mis-	bad(ly), wrong(ly)	*mishap, mistake*
14	mono-	one, single	*monogamous, monopoly*
15	multi-	more than one, many	*multitude, multiplication*
16	over-	too much	*overenthusiastic, overcharge*
17	pre-	before	*predict, preview*
18	post-	after	*postgraduate, posterity*
19	pro-	for	*propose, propel*
20	re-	again, or back	*regain, recede*
21	sub-	under	*submarine, subway*
22	super-	over, extra	*superman, superior*
23	trans-	across, over	*transatlantic, transcend*
24	un-	not (negative)	*unhappy, unsure*
25	under-	little, beneath	*underground, underestimate*

Common suffixes

A Noun suffixes

The most common noun suffixes are the following:

-er/or	Common suffix for jobs or for people who do an activity. *teacher, gardener, shopper, administrator, advisor.*
-ist/-ism	You use -ist when talking about people (their beliefs or jobs or people who play musical instruments) and -ism when talking about people's beliefs, ideologies, etc. *optimist, economist, atheist, pianist, Buddhism*
-ness	This is used to make nouns from adjectives. *brightness, emptiness, darkness, nervousness, happiness*
-tion/-ion	This is usually used to make nouns from verbs. *abortion, accommodation, civilization, punctuation, decision*

Others

-ance	*appearance, tolerance, maintenance*
-hood	*childhood, adulthood, falsehood*
-ity	*ability, charity, prosperity*
-ment	*agreement, compliment, imprisonment*
-ship	*censorship, leadership, ownership*

B Adjective suffixes

-able/-ible	This is usually used to change verbs into adjectives. It means 'can be done'. advisable, dependable, suggestible, edible, memorable

Others

-al	*musical, critical, medical*
-ful	*beautiful, awful, wonderful*
-ive	*addictive, effective, responsive*
-less	*careless, pointless, hopeless*
-ous	*poisonous, generous, jealous*

Proverbs

Here are some common British proverbs that are worth learning.

Absence makes the heart grow fonder.

Actions speak louder than words.

A friend in need is a friend indeed.

A rolling stone gathers no moss.

A stitch in time saves nine.

All that glitters is not gold.
All's fair in love and war.
All's well that ends well.
Appearances are deceptive.
As you make your bed so you must lie in it.
Beauty is only skin deep.
Beggars can't be choosers.
Better late than never.
Better safe than sorry.
Blood is thicker than water.
Charity begins at home.
Cut your coat according to your cloth.
Don't count your chickens before they're hatched.
Don't put all your eggs in one basket.
Easy come, easy go.
First come, first served.
Honesty is the best policy.
If you can't beat them, join them.
It's no use crying over spilt milk.
Let bygones be bygones.
Let sleeping dogs lie.
Like father, like son.
Live and let live.
Look before you leap.
Many hands make light work.
More haste, less speed.
Necessity is the mother of invention.
No gain without pain.
Once bitten, twice shy.
One good turn deserves another.
One man's meat is another man's poison.
Out of sight, out of mind.
Practice makes perfect.
Rome wasn't built in a day.
Speech is silver, silence is golden.
Still waters run deep.
The end justifies the means.
The early bird catches the worm.
The proof of the pudding is in the eating.
There's no place like home.
Too many cooks spoil the broth.
Two wrongs don't make a right.
United we stand, divided we fall.
Variety is the spice of life.

Waste not, want not.
When in Rome do as the Romans do.
When the cat's away, the mice will play.
Where there's a will there's a way.
You can't have your cake and eat it.
You can't teach on old dog new tricks.
You can't judge a book by its cover.
You scratch my back and I'll scratch yours.

7 PICK AND CHOOSE - EXERCISES FOR EXTRA READING

Discussion/Writing - general questions on fact and fiction

1 What's the title of the text?
2 Who wrote it?
3 Who's the main character? Describe him/her.
4 Are there any other people in the story/text? Describe them.
5 Where and when does the story take place?
6 What can you say about the type of language used?
7 Does the story/text have a message? If so, what is it?
8 Did you like the story/text? Give reasons.
9 What reflections did you make when reading the story/text?

Speaking/Acting

- Write down some key words and retell the text to a friend.
- Invite one of the characters to your "talk show". Prepare questions and interview him/her about his/her life.
- If the text has lots of dialogue, then try rewriting parts of it as a play. Then act it out with others.
- Make a presentation by using facts from a text you've read.

Writing

- One of the main characters is tweeting about something that's happened. What does he/she write?
- Write an email to one of the characters who perhaps has a problem, giving them advice on what to do.
- Continue writing the story. What happens after the end of it? Use your imagination!
- If you didn't like the end of the story, then try rewriting it with your own ending.
- Write a newspaper article based on facts from the text.
- Write an instruction on how to deal with a certain situation.
- Write a summary of the text.

Focus on language

- Look up any words you didn't understand.
- Write down useful phrases that would be good to know when speaking or writing.
- Were there any idioms or proverbs in the text? If so find out what they mean.
- Pick out 8–10 words and try to find synonyms or definitions for these words or try writing your own sentences using these words.

Find out more

- Find facts about the writer of the story.
- If you enjoyed the story, why not read a complete book by that author.
- Use *Suggested Links* to search the Internet for more information on a topic.
- Watch a film or a TV programme dealing with the topic you've studied.

1 GO-AHEAD

CRACKING THE CODE

☐ Learning English
☐ Starter
☐ Textwork
☐ Vocabulary: Definitions
☐ Interact
☐ Activity
☐ Pair work: Small talk
☐ Focus on verbs to do with speaking and listening
☐ Check your English

LETTER TO A FUNERAL PARLOR

☐ Starter
☐ Interact
☐ Pre-writing
☐ Writing

WSM: IX

☐ Interact

WE BEAT THE STREET

☐ Starter
☐ Textwork
☐ Vocabulary: Words of similar meaning
☐ Interact
☐ Writing
☐ Expand your vocabulary: British and American English

LISTENING: WE BEAT THE STREET CONT.

☐ Starter
☐ Listen and recall
☐ Interact

WSM: TEACHERS URGED TO 'GET TOUGH' ON BAD BEHAVIOUR

☐ Use of English: Sentence-changing 1
☐ Sum up and comment
☐ Books to read and enjoy

CRACKING THE CODE (page 10)

001 **Learning English**

Work in groups of 3–4. Read and discuss the following.

1 What are your feelings about the English language? What are your reasons for studying it?
2 What do you think is a) the easiest b) the most difficult thing about learning English?
3 Which of the four language skills do you find most difficult in English: Listening, speaking, reading or writing?
4 English is a "Please" and "Thank you" language. Why are these words so important to use?

Assess your English in Resource Section on page 149. What do you need to focus on?

Before starting your studies in this course read through the following pages and discuss them. *Strategies to improve your language skills.*

002 **Starter**

What is important when communicating apart from words? Give examples.

003 **Textwork**

Show that you have understood the text *Cracking the Code* on pages 10–12 by completing the statements below with information from the text. Sometimes one or two words are enough.

1 A complete command of a language does not __________ successful communication.
2 Sometimes, even in your native language you can experience __________ and can feel that you're unable to __________.
3 *That's not what I meant* is a book intended for __________ in English.
4 When it comes to communication, the words you use, compared to other factors, are not __________.
5 According to the 7-38-55 rule, 55% of the impact of our communication is __________.
6 We are now able to increase our means of communicating internationally thanks largely to __________.
7 One example of success with international communication is that __________.
8 One example of failure with international communication is that __________.
9 Deborah Tannen has defined five areas that need to be developed to succeed at communication. Decide which area these sentences belong to.

1 = Language skills 2 = Intercultural skills 3 = Communication skills
4 = Personal skills 5 = Small talk skills

a) You need to be completely focused on what you're doing. ________
b) You need to understand what sort of people you're speaking to. ________
c) Choose language that's persuasive and gets your message across. ________
d) This will help to warm up relationships. ________
e) You need to know how much emotion to show. ________

Practise the vocabulary in Wordmatch/Spelling

004 Vocabulary: Definitions

Here are definitions of eight words from the text. Can you work out what they are? To help you, the first and last letter of each missing word is given.

1 A period of ten years. d________e
2 How high or low a sound is, especially a musical note. p________h
3 A principle or idea, e.g. the _____ of free speech. c________t
4 All the workers employed in an organization. s________f
5 Your _____ is what you intend or plan to do; your aim. i________n
6 Someone who's paid to work for someone else. e________e
7 Feeling sure about your own ability to do things and be successful. c________t
8 To make something to become larger in amount or size. i________e

005 Interact

1 Were you surprised at the 7–38–55 per cent rule? What else did you learn from the text?
2 Why are intercultural skills so important in communication?
3 What kind of misunderstandings in communication have you experienced?
4 What language skills will your future career demand?

006 Activity

Imagine you're a Martian anthropologist with no understanding of human practises. Try to think up explanations for what humans do in the following situations:

a) Eating at McDonalds
b) Checking in at an airport
c) Working out in a gym
d) Going to the hairdresser
e) Fishing on the river bank

007 **Pair work: Small talk**

Work in pairs. Imagine you're at a restaurant for lunch but there's only one spare seat free – next to someone who's already eating. You decide to sit there.

Here are the opening words of a dialogue. See if you can continue it using "small talk".

A: Excuse me, do you mind if I sit here?
B: No, of course not.
A: Thank you. It's very crowded today isn't it?
B: Yes, there are a lot more people here than usual.

008 **Focus on verbs to do with speaking and listening**

Complete the definitions below with a suitable verb. Choose from the following: (Use a dictionary if necessary.)

announce	discuss	gossip	natter	scold	waffle
bug	eavesdrop	lisp	overhear	snap at	
chat up	go on about	mumble	patronize	stammer	

1 To __________ someone is to criticize them angrily because they've done something wrong.
2 To __________ someone __________ is to talk in a friendly way to someone you're sexually attracted to.
3 To __________ is to talk too much about other people's private lives.
4 To __________ is to hear, especially by accident, a conversation in which you're not involved.
5 To __________ is to talk a lot but without saying anything relevant or important.
6 To __________ something is to tell people officially about a decision, plans, etc.
7 People who __________ pronounce the 's' sound as 'th'. So they'd say 'What a thweet baby' instead of 'What a sweet baby'.
8 To __________ is to speak or say something in a quiet voice in a way that's not clear.
9 To __________ is to listen secretly to what other people are saying.
10 To __________ someone is to talk to them as if they were stupid when in fact they're not or as if you were better or superior to them in some way.
11 To __________ someone is to talk to them quickly in an angry way because you're annoyed with them.
12 To __________ is to talk about a subject with someone and tell each other your ideas or opinions.
13 To __________ is to speak with difficulty, repeating sounds or words and often stopping, before saying things correctly. For example, "Wh-wh-when can we g-g-go?"
14 To __________ is to talk for a long time, especially about unimportant things.
15 To __________ is to talk too much about a particular subject, so that the people you're talking to become annoyed or bored.
16 To __________ a room is to put a special device somewhere in order to listen secretly to other people's conversations.

009 **Check your English**

No two people are at exactly the same level of English, so here's a chance to see how much English you already know – especially English vocabulary. Work in groups of 3–4. Your teacher will give you more information.

LETTER TO A FUNERAL PARLOR (page 13)

010 **Starter**

Work in small groups. Here are some 'new' words that have come into the English language in recent years. Try and guess what they mean. The first one has been done for you.

cremains	The cremated remains of a dead person. (A person's ashes.)
bestie	______________________
beatboxing	______________________
phablet	______________________
flexitarian	______________________
chatbot	______________________
photobomb	______________________

Are there any other 'new' words like these you've heard of?

011 **Interact**

1. Do you think the person who wrote the letter was being oversensitive about the word 'cremains'? Why?/Why not?
2. The writer would prefer the word 'ashes' to 'cremains'. Do you agree?
3. The writer of the letter says that 'cremains' and 'brunch' are known as portmanteau words. A portmanteau is a large heavy suitcase that opens into two parts. Can you explain the connection?

Here are some other common 'portmanteau' words. Can you work out which two words have been combined in each?

1. motel ______________ + ______________
2. shopaholic ______________ + ______________
3. brunch ______________ + ______________
4. camcorder ______________ + ______________
5. fanzine ______________ + ______________
6. Oxbridge ______________ + ______________
7. smog ______________ + ______________

Practise the vocabulary in Wordmatch/Spelling

Vocabulary: Choose the word

012 **Pre-writing**

Before you start writing make sure you all have read and discussed the text about Genres and The Rhetorical Process in Resource Section on pages 153–155.

013 **Writing**

Imagine you're the owner of the funeral parlor. Write a letter in reply to the one you received. Use 150–180 words.

Remember to start your letter with Dear Madam/Sir and end with Yours faithfully. Don't forget to sign the letter with your full name.

For more advice on how to write a formal letter see Resource Section on page 160.

WSM: IX

The following poem is taken from *Twelve Songs* by W. H. Auden. It was made famous through the film *Four Weddings and a Funeral* where it was read out at a funeral scene by the dead person's gay lover. (W. H. Auden was himself gay.)

Stop all the clocks, cut off the telephone,
Prevent the dog from barking with a juicy bone,
Silence the pianos, and with muffled drum
Bring out the coffin, let the mourners come.

Let aeroplanes circle moaning overhead
Scribbling on the sky the message He is Dead,
Put crêpe bows round the white necks of the public doves,
Let the traffic policemen wear black cotton gloves.

He was my North, my South, my East and West,
My working week and my Sunday rest,
My noon, my midnight, my talk, my song:
I thought that love would last for ever: I was wrong.

The stars are not wanted now: put out every one;
Pack up the moon and dismantle the sun,
Pour away the ocean and sweep up the wood,
For nothing now can ever come to any good.

014 **Interact**

1 How is his lover described?
2 How does the mourner want the world to react?

WE BEAT THE STREET (page 15)

015 **Starter**

Work in pairs.

They say that young people need role models. Do you agree? Working together write down 5 suitable role models for young people today. Try to think of the reason you chose them.

1 ______________________________
2 ______________________________
3 ______________________________
4 ______________________________
5 ______________________________

Now find another pair. Compare and discuss your choices.

016 **Textwork**

Read through the text *We Beat the Street* and decide which of the four alternatives (A, B, C or D) you think is correct. Sometimes two answers are correct.

1 What do we learn about the three doctors?
   A ☐ They were the toughest kids in their neighborhood.
   B ☐ They wouldn't have become doctors without each other.
   C ☐ They now work in a much nicer part of New York.
   D ☐ They believe there's a need for strong role models for young people.

2 What do they want to show young people?
   A ☐ That struggles and obstacles can lead to success.
   B ☐ That it's easy to avoid getting involved in dangerous situations.
   C ☐ That it's good to be impulsive.
   D ☐ That having a dream doesn't usually lead to success.

3 Why was Rameck upset with his history teacher?
   A ☐ Because she wasn't black.
   B ☐ Because he didn't think that the history taught was culturally diverse.
   C ☐ Because the textbook about American history featured mainly white people.
   D ☐ Because Martin Luther King was only mentioned briefly.

4 What did the USO plan to do?

A ☐ To find ways to get lots of money.

B ☐ To cause a lot of trouble for the authorities.

C ☐ To get the teachers to join in their protest.

D ☐ To organize a walkout at as many schools in Newark as possible.

5 What happened when the students reached the Board of Education headquarters?

A ☐ They demanded to speak to the superintendent.

B ☐ Lots of students were arrested by the police.

C ☐ They entered the lobby of the building and refused to move.

D ☐ Hassan was interviewed by a TV camera crew.

6 What was the final result of their protest?

A ☐ Rameck got into a lot of trouble with the authorities.

B ☐ Rameck was asked to join a committee to develop a new curriculum.

C ☐ The curriculum was changed to include African-American and Hispanic history.

D ☐ Rameck became a school hero.

Practise the vocabulary in Wordmatch/Spelling

---

017 Vocabulary: Words of similar meaning

Complete the pairs of words below with another word that is similar in meaning. Choose from the following words, all taken from the text.

accomplish	diverse	obstacle	scurry
daunting	emphasize	outspoken	
deserve	grab	remarkable	

1 clutch, seize, ___________

2 merit, warrant, ___________

3 extraordinary, noteworthy, ___________

4 achieve, attain, ___________

5 accentuate, highlight, ___________

6 blunt, candid, ___________

7 difficulty, stumbling block, ___________

8 dart, scamper, ___________

9 discouraging, disheartening, ___________

10 assorted, varied, ___________

018 **Interact**

Work in pairs. Take turns to ask and answer the following questions.

1 What do you think of this way of protesting? What methods would you use to achieve change?

2 Are you happy with your own school? Would you change anything? Are there any subjects that you don't really see the point of studying? If so, why not?

3 Is education a life-long activity? Do you see yourself learning for the rest of your life? What would you love to learn?

019 **Writing**

Write a formal letter (180–200 words) to your country's education minister about how the Swedish education system could be improved. Make general comments or focus on one area that you think needs to be changed.

Remember to start your letter with *Dear Sir/Madam* and end with *Yours faithfully*. Don't forget to sign the letter with your full name.

For more advice on how to write a formal letter see Resource Section on page 160.

020 **Expand your vocabulary: British and American English**

In *Solid Gold 1*, you built up a basic vocabulary. In *Solid Gold 2*, you'll concentrate on more specific vocabulary items which will expand your vocabulary further. We'll start with some of the differences between British and American English.

There are many words in British English and American English that are different. It's important to know the most common ones.

Complete the sentences below with the correct British word. Choose from the following. The American word is in brackets after each sentence.

bonnet   crisps   jam   plaster   trainers

1 "Do you like my new pair of ___________?" (sneakers)
2 "I'd like a packet of ___________, please." (potato chips)
3 He lifted up the ___________ to check the engine. (hood)
4 I always put ___________ on my toast. (jelly)
5 "I've cut my finger! Pass me a ___________." (band-aid)

Now go to the Expand your vocabulary section of the book and do the exercise *British and American English* on page 324.

LISTENING: WE BEAT THE STREET CONT.

021 Starter

Work in small groups. Look at these two photos.

Describe the photos. Where do you think the schools are?

022 Listen and recall

Listen to the rest of the extract from *We Beat the Street* and then answer the questions below by completing the sentences. Before you start, read through the questions below.

1 Rameck was asked why he wrote on both sides of the paper? What was his reply?
That he was ___________.
2 What did Rameck say about the answers he'd written?
That they ___________.
3 The teacher refused to grade his paper. How did Rameck react?
He crumpled up ___________.
4 What did Rameck take from the seventh-grade boy?
He took ___________.
5 What did he do to his biology teacher?
He ___________.
6 How did the class she was teaching react?
They ___________.
7 Rameck had to go and see the principal. What was the result of the interview?
Rameck ___________.
8 At the final hearing what did Rameck say to the biology teacher?
He apologized and asked her to ___________.
9 How did the biology teacher reply?
She asked the superintendent of Newark schools ___________.

Practise the vocabulary in Wordmatch/Spelling

023 **Interact**

1 The biology teacher gives Rameck a second chance. Is she making the right or wrong decision? Give arguments for your opinions.
2 What kind of rules should apply in your school. Give suggestions and arguments.

Assessment and strategies. Evaluate your spoken English! Use the Assessment in Resource Section page 149 and Speaking strategies in the digital part.

WSM: TEACHERS URGED TO 'GET TOUGH' ON BAD BEHAVIOUR

024 **Use of English: Sentence-changing 1**

In Solid Gold 2 all the grammar exercises are in Grammar in Action 3 in the digital material. Here in the book there is a section called Use of English where in order to complete the exercises, a good knowledge of grammar is needed. These are the types of exercises found in the Cambridge First Certificate (FCE) and the Certificate of Advanced English (CAE) exams.

The first type of exercise is on sentence-changing.

Complete the second sentence so that it has a similar meaning to the first sentence, using the words given. *Do not change the word given.* You must use between three and six words, including the word given.

1 Why wouldn't he give you his email address?
REFUSE
Why __________ you his email address?
2 Can you give me a lift into town tomorrow?
ABLE
Will __________ me a lift into town tomorrow?
3 The lecturer didn't speak loudly enough for the students at the back to hear.
QUIETLY
The lecturer spoke __________ the students at the back to hear.

Now go to the Use of English section of the book and do the exercise *Sentence-changing 1* on pages 348–349.

025 **Sum up and comment**

1 What have you learnt about communication that you didn't know before?
2 What are you hoping this course will give you? What are your goals?
3 How can the use of assessment in combination with strategies help you improve your English?
4 Write in your learning log, see Resource Section page 149, and comment on three questions of your own choice.

026 **Books to read and enjoy**

Davis, Lydia: *The Collected Stories*
Diaz, Junot: *The Brief Wondrous Life of Oscar Wao*
Lodge, David: *Changing Places*
Oates, Joyce Carol: *I'll Take You There*
Smith, Zadie: *On Beauty*
The Three Doctors: *We Beat the Street*

2 CHALLENGES

I AM MALALA

☐ Starter
☐ Textwork
☐ Vocabulary: What does it mean?
☐ Vocabulary: Choose the word
☐ Interact
☐ Focus on verbs to do with looking

WSM: MALALA YOUSAFZAI'S SPEECH AT THE UNITED NATIONS

LISTENING: INDIRA GANDHI ON EDUCATION

☐ Starter
☐ Listen and recall
☐ Vocabulary: Fill in the gaps
☐ Pre-speaking
☐ Speaking/Writing
☐ Expand your vocabulary: Pairs of words that are easily confused

FRIDAY 4TH APRIL

☐ Starter
☐ Textwork
☐ Vocabulary: Definitions
☐ Interact
☐ Looking at words to do with family and relationships

WSM: SOME INTERESTING FACTS ABOUT IRELAND AND IRISH PEOPLE

FOR A LAUGH

☐ Starter: Sort out the riddles
☐ Textwork
☐ Interact
☐ Vocabulary: Choose the word
☐ Let's talk! What if ...?

NO PLANS AT ALL

☐ Starter
☐ Interact
☐ Vocabulary: Right or wrong?
☐ Creating a situation from a dialogue
☐ Use of English: Sentence-changing 2

☐ Sum up and comment
☐ Books to read and enjoy

I AM MALALA (page 20 ⧉)

027 Starter

Work in pairs or small groups.
Look at the photograph. What do you remember about this person?

Here are some of her quotations.

"We realize the importance of our voices only when we are silenced."

"Let us pick up our books and our pens. They are our most powerful weapons. One child, one teacher, one book and one pen can change the world."

"The Taliban could take our pens and books, but they couldn't stop our minds from thinking."

Discuss them. Which did you find the most inspiring?
Why do you think the Taliban are so against girls getting an education?

028 Textwork

Read *I Am Malala* on pages 20–22. Then fill in the missing information or choose the correct answer (a, b or c). The sentences are in no special order.

1 Before she climbed on to the bus Malala covered her face with her scarf. *a) True b) False*
2 Malala's last thought as she was shot was of *a) her own sisters b) school work c) the man killing chickens.*
3 While they were waiting for some teachers to arrive, Usman Bhai Jan ___________.
4 Gul Makai was Malala's ___________.
5 Malala was shot in the head *a) on her way to school b) on her way home from school c) in a car.*
6 The ice-cream boy's bicycle had ___________ painted on it.
7 Malala's mother was ___________ years old when she left school.
8 Malala didn't go out and buy some food herself because *a) she wasn't allowed to b) she was very tired c) she was chatting with her friends.*
9 At what time of the year does this take place? ___________
10 The poster near the army checkpoint showed men who were *a) soldiers b) crazy c) terrorists.*
11 The Malala Fund enables Malala to ___________.
12 Atal *a) hung off the tailboard of the bus b) didn't catch the bus home c) refused to speak to Usman Bhai Jan.*

Practise the vocabulary in Wordmatch/Spelling

029 Vocabulary: What does it mean?

You're now going to explain the meaning of some of the words used in the text *I Am Malala*. Complete the following sentences by giving English explanations of the words in bold. Make your explanations as exact as possible. Use a dictionary if necessary.

Example: A **non-profit** organization doesn't usually ________.
Answer: make a profit

1 She was holding a **pebble**. In other words, she was holding a ________.
2 He went home **in a huff**. In other words, he was feeling ________.
3 When you take a **shortcut**, you take a quicker ________ than the usual one.
4 A person who shows **courage** is a ________ person.
5 Malala **championed** universal access to education. This means she ________ it.
6 To **persuade** someone to do something is to ________.
7 The chicken's neck was **severed**. This means it was ________.
8 They refused him **permission** to leave early. In other words he ________ leave early.
9 When you're given an **award**, you're given ________.
10 Using a **loudspeaker** will help you ________.

030 Vocabulary: Choose the word

031 Interact

1 What in this text tells you that the story takes place in Pakistan? Give examples from the text.
2 Work in pairs and draw a mind map of the text about Malala. See Resource Section page 148.
3 In 2014 Malala was awarded the Nobel Peace Prize. What other recipients have you heard about?

032 Focus on verbs to do with looking

Complete the definitions below with a suitable verb. Choose from the following. Use a dictionary if necessary.

examine	glare	look up	peer
gaze	keep a lookout	make eyes at	squint
give a dirty look	keep an eye on	ogle	stare
glance	look for	peep	watch

1 To ________ is to look at a person doing something or at something happening.
2 To ________ is to look angrily at someone for a long time.

3 To __________ is to look at someone or something quickly, especially by raising your eyes and then lowering them again.

4 To __________ something is to try to find information in a book, computer, etc.

5 To __________ something or someone is to look after something or someone and make sure that they're safe.

6 To __________ at something is to look at it with difficulty because you can't see very well or there isn't enough light.

7 To __________ something is to look at it carefully because you want to find out more about it.

8 To __________ someone is to look at them in an offensive way, usually showing you're sexually attracted to them.

9 To __________ is to look steadily at someone or something for a long time, either because you're very interested or surprised, or because you're thinking of something else.

10 To __________ is to look at something with your eyes partly closed in order to see better.

11 To __________ is to keep watching carefully for something or someone, especially for danger.

12 To __________ is to look quickly and secretly at something, especially through a small opening, e.g. a keyhole.

13 To __________ something is to try to find it.

14 To __________ is to deliberately look at someone or something for a long time without moving your eyes.

15 To __________someone __________ is to look at them in a disapproving way.

16 To __________ someone is to make it clear to that person that you're sexually attracted to them by looking at them in a way that gets their attention.

WSM: MALALA YOUSAFZAI'S SPEECH AT THE UNITED NATIONS

LISTENING: INDIRA GANDHI ON EDUCATION

033 Starter

Look at the following list of women.

Benazir Bhutto	Kim Campbell
Helen Clark	Margaret Thatcher
Indira Gandhi	Portia Simpson-Miller
Julia Gillard	

1 How many have you heard of? They have one thing in common. What's that?

2 What do you know about these women?

034 **Listen and recall**

Born 19 November 1917 in Allahabad. The daughter of one Indian Prime Minister and the mother of another, Indira Gandhi was India's first female leader. The nationalization of India's banks, a programme for self-sufficiency and environmental policies contributed to her popularity. Initially nicknamed goongì gudiya ('dumb doll'), opinion was swiftly revised as she proved herself one of India's strongest leaders. Indira Gandhi strove to increase the participation of women in politics and society.
She was assassinated on 31 October 1984 in New Delhi.

Listen to the speech Indira Gandhi gave at Indraprastha College for Women and then decide which of the four alternatives (A, B, C or D) you think is correct. Before you start, read through the questions below.

1 What is the home according to an ancient Sankrit saying?
A ☐ A place that's friendly.
B ☐ The basis of society.
C ☐ A place of harmony.
D ☐ The place for a woman.

2 What happens if a country doesn't have harmony?
A ☐ It can't feel free.
B ☐ It loses its loving atmosphere.
C ☐ It can't grow in any direction.
D ☐ It becomes inadequate.

3 What does Indira Gandhi say about women's education?
A ☐ It's almost more important than male education.
B ☐ It's not neglected.
C ☐ It's not as important as male education.
D ☐ It's like the education in England.

4 What does she say about the present state of education in India?
A ☐ It needs a lot more investment.
B ☐ It needs to be thoroughly overhauled.
C ☐ It needs to adopt old customs.
D ☐ It needs to improve slowly.

5 Why do many well-educated Indians leave the country?
A ☐ They love travelling.
B ☐ They can't get jobs in India.
C ☐ They are forced to.
D ☐ They get more money and better working conditions.

6 What does she say about all that is old?
A ☐ It's neither all good nor all bad.
B ☐ It was a lot better than modern things.
C ☐ It's timeless.
D ☐ It's not as good as modern things.

7 Many people think that to being modern has to do with the way you dress or the way you speak or certain habits and customs. Which word does Indira Gandhi use to describe this way of thinking?

A ☐ superb
B ☐ superstitious
C ☐ superficial
D ☐ ultra modern

8 What does Indira Gandhi hope that education will enable young people to do?

A ☐ To fulfil their ambitions.
B ☐ To adjust to a changing world and to be able to contribute to it.
C ☐ To think a lot about life.
D ☐ To accept what comes from other parts of the world.

Practise the vocabulary in Wordmatch/Spelling

Assessment and strategies. Evaluate your listening skills! Use the Assessment in Resource Section page 149 and Listening strategies in the digital part.

035 **Vocabulary: Fill in the gaps**

Fill in the missing words in the sentences below. Choose from the following words, taken from the text. Then make up your own sentences for the four words that are left over.

affluent	contributed	inadequate	rational
ancient	current	neglected	recent
assassinate	demand	nickname	salary
content	extremely	participation	swiftly

1 One of the things I had to fill in on the form was the name of my __________ employer.
2 Governments need to act __________ to halt the dramatic spread of the Ebola virus.
3 India has a very __________ civilization.
4 There should be more __________ by ordinary workers in the company's decision-making.
5 The parking facilities were totally __________ for a busy shopping centre. There just weren't enough spaces.
6 Have you been following __________ political events in the Middle East?
7 The FBI have just foiled a plan to __________ the President.
8 He was given the __________ 'Ginger' because of his red hair.
9 Immigrants have __________ to British culture in many ways.
10 He lived in a very __________ neighbourhood, where every house was worth at least £1 million.
11 There's an increased __________ for organic produce these days.
12 The one regret in his life was that he had __________ his children in favour of his career.

036 **Pre-speaking**

Before you start working on a speech read and discuss On Speaking in Resource Section pages 157-159.

037 **Speaking/Writing**

Write a speech about the importance of education. You can take one or more of the following points into consideration when talking about the importance of education for everyone:

human rights - equality - class differences - intercultural understanding - future job career, etc.

Speak for 2–3 minutes to a small group and make use of Peer response - speaking in Resource Section page 159.

038 **Expand your vocabulary: Pairs of words that are easily confused**

Do you know the difference between 'rise' and 'raise' or 'remind' and 'remember'? And what about 'continual' and 'continuous'? English is full of so-called 'confusable' words.
Here are three pairs of words that are often confused. Fill in the correct word in each sentence. Make any necessary verb changes.

lend-borrow

1 I haven't got any money. Could you __________ me £10, please?
2 I often __________ books from the library.

rob-steal

3 Pickpockets usually find it easy to __________ from tourists - especially in large crowds.
4 Two masked men tried to __________ a bank this morning.

lie-lay

5 Does Swansea __________ to the east or the west of Cardiff?
6 She asked her daughter to __________ the table.

Now go to the Expand your vocabulary section of the book and do the exercise *Pairs of words that are easily confused* on pages 326–328.

FRIDAY 4TH APRIL (page 23)

039 Starter

Work in pairs or groups of three. Here are some famous diaries:

Diary of a Wimpy Kid *The Diary of Samuel Pepys*
Anne Frank: The Diary of a Young Girl *Bridget Jones's Diary*
The Secret Diary of Adrian Mole Aged 13 ¾

Have you read any of these? What other famous diaries can you think of?

040 Textwork

Show that you've understood the text *Friday 4th April* by completing the sentences below with information from the text. Sometimes one or two words are enough. The sentences are in no special order.

1 They don't have much money because their mother ________.
2 Alva got rid of her old posters and instead put up a poster of ________.
3 They only keep a small amount of cash at home so that they're not tempted to ________.
4 Is Alva older or younger than her sister? She's ________.
5 For Alva's Easter present this year, the sisters are going to ________.
6 The school the girls attend is a ________.
7 They decide to paint Alva's bedroom ________.
8 How old is Alva? She's nearly ________.
9 We learn from the text that the girls' parents are ________.
10 For emergencies, they keep a £5 note ________.
11 They don't have a spirit-level or other tools at home because ________.

Practise the vocabulary in Wordmatch/Spelling

041 Vocabulary: Definitions

Here are definitions of eight words from the text. Can you work out what they are? To help you, the first and last letter of each missing word is given.

1 The money you borrow from a bank in order to buy a house, which you then pay back over a period of years. m________e
2 A tool which tells you if a surface is level or not. s________t l________l

3 You use this to put your shopping in at a supermarket. t__________y
4 Spending or costing a lot of money, often more than you can afford. e__________t
5 If you're _____ with something, then you're very pleased. d__________d
6 The opposite of 'generous'. m__________n
7 To push someone gently, especially with your elbow, in order to get their attention. n__________e
8 A large picture or photograph which you often pin up on a wall. p__________r

042 **Interact**

1 How do you know that the family is not so well off? Give examples from the text.
2 How would you redecorate your present room? Which colours are trendy at the moment?

043 **Looking at words to do with the family and relationships**

Fill in the missing words in the definitions below. Choose from the following. Use a dictionary if necessary. Then write your own sentences for the four words left over.

adopted	fiancée	partner	split up
ancestors	get divorced	relatives	spouse
couple	extended family	sibling	stepfather
engaged	orphan	single	widower

1 Your __________ are members of your family, such as uncles, aunts, cousins, etc.
2 If a couple are __________, this means they've formally agreed to get married.
3 Your __________ is your husband or wife.
4 An __________ is a child whose parents are dead.
5 Your __________ are the people in your family who lived a long time ago.
6 If your mother remarries, you now have a __________.
7 A __________ parent is someone who has a child or children but doesn't live with a husband, wife or partner.
8 If a married couple __________, then their marriage legally comes to an end.
9 If a man's wife has died, then he's a __________.
10 Two people who are having a romantic relationship are often referred to as a __________.
11 If you're having a relationship and living together but you're not married, the word __________ is often used to describe your boyfriend or girlfriend.
12 An __________ is a family group that consists not only of parents and children but also of uncles, aunts, grandparents, etc.

WSM: SOME INTERESTING FACTS ABOUT IRELAND AND IRISH PEOPLE

FOR A LAUGH (page 26)

044 **Starter**

Work in pairs. Here are six riddles. See if you can work them out.

1 You answer me, although I never ask you questions. What am I?
2 Some months have 30 days, some months have 31 days; how many have 28?
3 The more it dries, the wetter it gets. What is it?
4 What has 4 fingers and a thumb, but is not alive?
5 What belongs to you but others use it more than you do?
6 What can you catch but not throw?

Now turn to page 209 for the answers.

045 **Textwork**

Work in pairs. Read through the text *For a Laugh* on pages 26–28. Take turns to ask and answer the following questions.

1 Was the woman really pregnant?
2 Why didn't the man immediately throw her out of his cab?
3 What does the woman offer to do instead of paying for her cab ride?
4 The taxi driver agreed under one condition. What was that?
5 The taxi driver liked the joke. Who else did he say would like it?
6 What had this exchange done to the woman?
7 What was the woman's problem?
8 What did the woman say to him when she got out of the cab?
9 How did the cab driver sum up the meeting with the woman?

046 **Interact**

1 How would you have reacted if you were the taxi driver when she told you that she had no money?
2 What do you think about the taxi driver's decision to give her a ride?
3 Why do you think the woman confides in the taxi driver?
4 This is a heart-warming story. Why is it so?

Practise the vocabulary in Wordmatch/Spelling

047 **Vocabulary: Choose the word**

048 **Let's talk! What if...?**

Work in two groups – A and B. Your teacher will give you more information.

NO PLANS AT ALL (page 29)

049 **Starter**

Here's a list of household chores. Put a cross (X) next to any you regularly do.

- ☐ clean the toilet/bathroom
- ☐ do the dusting
- ☐ do the gardening
- ☐ do the washing
- ☐ do the washing-up
- ☐ feed the dog/cat
- ☐ fill/empty the dishwasher
- ☐ hoover
- ☐ iron clothes
- ☐ make a meal
- ☐ make the bed
- ☐ mop the floor
- ☐ polish shoes
- ☐ polish the furniture
- ☐ recycle/take out rubbish
- ☐ tidy a room
- ☐ wash the car
- ☐ water the plants

Now find a partner. Compare your lists. Is there anything else you could add?

050 **Interact**

1 What impression do you get of the woman and her marriage from the text?
2 She says she doesn't have to do any household chores today. Why, do you think?
3 What do you think she means by this sentence? "She would rely on other people to feed her, wash her and buy her food. She didn't know who these people were but she believed that most people were longing to demonstrate their innate goodness."
4 What do we learn about her husband, Brian's job and what he thinks of Professor Brady?
5 What do you think will happen later on in the story?

Practise the vocabulary in Wordmatch/Spelling

051 Vocabulary: Right or wrong?

Work in pairs. Check that you've understood some of the words used in the text by stating whether they're used correctly in the following sentences. Mark each sentence R (Right) or W (Wrong). If wrong, explain why and write a new sentence to show how the word(s) should be used.

1. Some British people prefer blankets on their bed at night rather than a **duvet**. _____
2. One of my mother's favourite flowers is the **sycamore**. _____
3. She **pummeled** the weeds carefully. _____
4. Children have an **innate** ability to learn languages. _____
5. I always buy **annual** plants because they come back every year. _____
6. "I can't sleep in that bed. The sheets are **soiled**!" _____
7. "Could you pass me the **dial**, please? I want to change the TV channel." _____
8. The child was **lured** into a car but managed to escape. _____
9. They had a small **brook** at the bottom of their garden. _____
10. Jonathan went into the garden shed to tidy the **borders**. _____

052 Creating a situation from a dialogue

Work in pairs or groups of three. Look at the following dialogues. Your task is to choose one of them and expand it by adding 6–8 lines before and after the extract. Before you start, think of the following:

1. Who are the characters? (A and B)
2. Where are they and why are they there?
3. What is happening now. What might have happened just before and what is going to happen next?
4. Can you introduce a third person (C), either before or after the extract?

When you have finished writing your dialogue, act it out.

Dialogue 1

A Did you say you had a hobby?
B Yes.
A I think everyone should have a hobby, don't you?
B Yes, a hobby's very important.
A Fishing.
B Sorry?
A Fishing. That's my hobby – fishing.
B Oh, I see. Never been fishing.
A Never?
B No, never done that. I like fish though. Fish and chips. I like that.

Dialogue 2

A It's all right, I think he's gone.
B Are you sure?
A I think so.
B Do you think he'll come back?
A He might.
B I didn't like him very much.
A No, me neither.
B Shall we phone now or later, then?
A I'm not sure. What do you think?

053 Use of English: Sentence-changing 2

Here's another chance for you to try your hand at sentence-changing.
Complete the second sentence so that it has a similar meaning to the first sentence, using the words given. *Do not change the word given.* You must use between three and six words, including the word given.

1 "Will you lend me £20?" Mary asked.
BORROW
Mary asked if __________ £20.
2 How likely is he to win the race?
CHANCES
What are __________ the race?
3 It's a four-hour journey from Swansea to London.
TRAVEL
It __________ from Swansea to London.

Now go to the Use of English section of the book and do the exercise *Sentence-changing 2* on pages 350–351.

046 Starter: Sort out the riddles (from page 206)

Here are the answers :

1 a telephone / phone / mobile phone / smartphone
2 all of them
3 a towel / a tea towel
4 a glove
5 your name
6 a cold

054 **Sum up and comment**

1 What different challenges have people in this unit encountered?
2 How do you work with the different strategies for listening?

055 **Books to read and enjoy**

Evanovich, Janet: *Takedown Twenty*
Flynn, Gillian: *Gone Girl*
Fowler, Karen Joy: *We Are Completely Beside Ourselves*
Moyes, Jojo: *The One Plus One*
Oates, Joyce Carol: *Carthage*
Roth, Veronica: *Divergent*
Salomon, Eugene: *Confessions of a New York Taxi Driver*
Townsend, Sue: *The Woman Who Went to Bed For a Year*
Trollope, Joanna: *Balancing Act*
Yousafzai, Malala with Christina Lamb: *I Am Malala*

3 IN TRANSITION

FASTER THAN LIGHTNING

- ☐ Starter
- ☐ Textwork
- ☐ Interact
- ☐ Vocabulary: Choose the word
- ☐ Focus on verbs to do with walking
- ☐ Writing

WSM: THE OLYMPIC GAMES

NEXT STOP ALABAMA

- ☐ Starter
- ☐ Textwork
- ☐ Vocabulary: Choose the word
- ☐ Vocabulary: What does it mean?
- ☐ Interact

LISTENING: NEXT STOP ALABAMA CONT.

- ☐ Starter
- ☐ Listen and recall
- ☐ Vocabulary: Definitions
- ☐ Interact
- ☐ Expand your vocabulary: Homonyms and homophones
- ☐ Let's talk!

WSM: A PARENTS' AND TEENAGERS' ALPHABET BOOK

- ☐ Discuss

AT MUMBAI AIRPORT

- ☐ Starter
- ☐ Textwork
- ☐ Vocabulary: Words of similar meaning
- ☐ Interact
- ☐ Looking at words to do with travel
- ☐ Writing

HEMI'S GIFT

- ☐ Starter
- ☐ Textwork
- ☐ Vocabulary: Fill in the gaps
- ☐ Interact
- ☐ Use of English: One word only 1

WSM: MAORIS – THE ORIGINAL INHABITANTS OF NEW ZEALAND

- ☐ Sum up and comment
- ☐ Books to read and enjoy

FASTER THAN LIGHTNING (page 34)

056 **Starter**

Work in pairs or small groups.

1 Look at the following photograph. What do you know about this person?

2 Which other great 100 metres sprinters do you remember?
3 What about female sprinters?

057 **Textwork**

Read *Faster Than Lightning* on page 34. Then say whether the following sentences are true (T) or false (F). But if you can't definitely say if something is true or false from the information given, then mark the sentence don't know (DK) . The sentences are in no special order.

1 Usain Bolt considers his best season ever was in 2008. ______
2 If in the future he can't race at the top level, he'd like to become a field coach. ______
3 He's quite friendly with Cristiano Ronaldo. ______
4 Usain Bolt is very competitive. ______
5 He'll be 30 in April 2016. ______
6 Usain Bolt considers himself to be a legend for his generation. ______
7 Running 200 metres under 19 seconds would mean more to him than winning a gold medal. ______
8 He's hoping he'll be fit enough for the next Olympic Games in Moscow. ______
9 He doesn't mind being beaten by someone who's genuinely better than him. ______
10 He thinks he could play in the English Premier League. ______
11 He thinks it gets slightly easier to reach peak fitness the older you get. ______
12 He's confident he'll be able to run the 100 metres in 9.6 minutes by 2016. ______

058 Interact

1 What plans does Bolt have for his life outside track-and-field?
2 What do athletes do when their sporting careers are over? Give examples.
3 Do you play any sports? Are you a member of any sports team? If not, have you ever been? Do you prefer playing or watching sports?

Practise the vocabulary in Wordmatch/Spelling

059 Vocabulary: Choose the word

060 Focus on verbs to do with walking

Complete the definitions below with a suitable verb. Choose from the following. Use a dictionary if necessary.

creep	march	stomp	tiptoe
hike	roam	stretch your legs	trudge
hobble	shuffle	stroll	wade
limp	stagger	strut	wander

1 To ________ is to walk with stiff regular steps like a soldier.
2 To ________ is to walk in a slow, relaxed way, especially for pleasure.
3 To ________ is to walk through water with difficulty because of the pressure of the water on your legs.
4 To ________ is to walk slowly and with difficulty because of having an injured leg or foot.
5 To ________ is to walk or move unsteadily, almost falling over.
6 To ________ is to walk quietly and carefully in your toes, so that nobody hears you.
7 To ________ is to go for a long walk in the country, especially for pleasure.
8 To ________ is to go for a short walk after a long time sitting down.
9 To ________ is to walk or travel around an area without any definite aim or direction.
10 To ________ is to walk slowly or with heavy steps, because you're tired or carrying something heavy.
11 To ________ is to move slowly, quietly and carefully, because you don't want to be seen or heard.
12 To ________ is to walk with heavy steps or to put your foot down very hard, especially because you're angry.
13 To ________ is to walk with difficulty, especially because your legs or feet hurt.
14 To ________ is to walk proudly with your head up and chest out to show that you think you're important.
15 To ________ is to walk by pushing your feet slowly along the ground rather than lifting them.
16 To ________ is to walk slowly across or around an area without a clear purpose or direction.

061 **Writing**

Write a short newspaper article on a sporting event or a sports person you've seen either live or on TV. Use 150 – 200 words.
First use Checklist for writing in Resource Section page 156. Then exchange papers with your partner and use Peer response - writing in Resource Section page 156.

WSM: THE OLYMPIC GAMES

NEXT STOP ALABAMA (page 36)

062 **Starter**

Have you read any books by John Green? What are they about? What did you think of them?

063 **Textwork**

Read *Next Stop Alabama* on page 36. Then fill in the missing information or choose the correct answer (a, b or c). The sentences are in no special order.

1 Will and Marie stayed at the party for *a) less than an hour b) 90 minutes c) over 2 hours.*
2 Miles likes reading ___________ . *(a type of book)*
3 ___________ people came to Miles's farewell party.
4 The last words of François Rabelais were "___________."
5 Miles and his family live in *a) Alabama b) Florida c) Culver Creek.*
6 Miles was not very good at *a) singing b) dancing c) small talk.*
7 Miles's mother didn't really want him to ___________.
8 After everyone left, the family *a) watched TV b) ate some sandwiches c) went to bed.*
9 Miles was very popular at school and had lots of friends there. *a) True b) False*
10 Culver Creek is ___________.

Practise the vocabulary in Wordmatch/Spelling

064 **Vocabulary: Choose the word**

065 **Vocabulary: What does it mean?**

You're now going to explain the meaning of some of the words used in the text *Next Stop Alabama*. Complete the following sentences by giving English explanations of the words in **bold**. Make your explanations as exact as possible. Use a dictionary if necessary.

Example: An **artichoke** is a type of ________.
Answer: vegetable

1. To **persevere** is to ________ despite difficulties.
2. If you **excel** at something, e.g. sport, this means that you're ________.
3. Two children answered the teacher's question **simultaneously**. This means they answered ________.
4. A **geek** is a person's who's ________.
5. When you **underestimate** something, you guess that the amount, size or cost is ________.
6. "I need to **mull things over** before I decide whether to take the job or not." In other words, this person needs to ________ before making a decision.
7. His new book is **vastly** superior to his previous one. This means that it's ________.
8. A **couch** is something you can ________.
9. If you describe someone as **chunky**, you mean that they're ________.
10. To **head** for the coast means to ________ it.

066 **Interact**

1. What do you think "One Hundred and Thirty-six Days Before" refers to?
2. Describe the mood in the text. Give examples using quotes.
3. What impression do you get of Miles – the protagonist?
4. Miles says "That's why I'm going. So I don't have to wait until I die to start seeking a Great Perhaps." What do you think he means by this?

LISTENING: NEXT STOP ALABAMA CONT.

067 **Starter**

What do you remember of your first day at a new school? How were you feeling? What were your hopes, worries?

068 **Listen and recall**

Listen to the day Miles arrives at his new school and then answer the questions below by completing the sentences.

1 Why were his clothes sticking to him?
Because ________.
2 Where was his parents SUV parked?
It was parked outside ________.
3 Why did his dorm room surprise him?
Because it wasn't ________.
4 Why were the desks and dressers and bookshelves attached to the walls?
So that they couldn't ________.
5 What did he do while his mother opened his trunk?
He ________.
6 Which two things his mother offered to do did he say he could do himself?
He said he could ________ and ________.
7 When they hugged him, what did he feel he ought to do?
He felt he ought to ________.
8 His father warned him against doing three things. What?
He warned him against ________, ________ and ________.
9 What had his father done concerning hayfields when he was a pupil?
He had ________.
10 His parents saying "I love you!" made him feel uncomfortable. It was like what in his opinion?
It was like ________.

Practise the vocabulary in Wordmatch/Spelling

069 **Vocabulary: Definitions**

Here are definitions of eight words from the listening exercise. Can you work out what they are? To help you, the first and last letter of each missing word is given.

1 An area of land or water where mines have been hidden. m________d
2 A ______ headache would be a very bad or severe one. v________s
3 Something that's ______ has not been paid, done, returned, etc. by the required or expected time. o________e
4 If the weather is ______, you feel uncomfortable because the air is very wet and usually hot. h________d
5 To cover something with a layer of a substance, e.g. paint. c________t
6 To ______ is to complain in a sad, annoying, voice about something. w________e
7 If you describe something as ______, you mean that it's very comfortable, expensive, and of good quality. p________h
8 ______ beds are two beds fixed together, one above the other. b________k

070 **Interact**

1 How does Miles react to the room he gets? What had he expected?
2 How does Miles feel about saying goodbye to his parents?
3 Why can saying goodbye sometimes be difficult? Or isn't it?

071 **Expand your vocabulary: Homonyms and homophones**

Do you know the different meanings of the word 'leave'? What about 'lead' and 'faint'? And do you get mixed up between 'meet and 'meat' or 'check' and 'cheque'?

Read through the following pairs of sentences and try to decide which words (homonyms) are missing. The same word is used for both gaps but with two completely different meanings.

1 The captain stood on the __________ of the ship.
Now that they've built a __________ over the river, it only takes us ten minutes to drive into town.
2 We travelled to Amsterdam by __________.
This is Mr Davies, our new athletics __________.

Again, read through the following pairs of sentences and try to work out which two words (homophones) are missing. (They'll sound the same but will be spelt differently.)

3 To be perfectly __________ with you, I don't think your son has much chance of passing the exam.
Before the Euro, the currency in France was the __________.
4 The cut on my leg took a long time to __________.
She got badly spiked when one of the runners trod on her __________.

Now go to the Expand your vocabulary section of the book and do the exercise Homonyms and homophones on pages 329–330.

072 **Let's talk!**

What's your opinion?
Being able to hold discussions in English is a very important goal of language learning. You need to be able to express your opinions clearly and to agree or disagree with someone else's opinions.

There are many useful phrases in English which you can use when discussing things. These are to be found on pages 174–176 in the Resource Section. It's well worth learning many of these by heart.

Work in groups. Your teacher will give you more information.

WSM: A PARENTS' AND TEENAGERS' ALPHABET BOOK By David Crystal

073 **Discuss**

Can you think of any other adjectives you could use to describe a teenager or a parent? Can you make up your own alphabet poem to describe a parent or a teacher?

AT MUMBAI AIRPORT (page 39)

074 **Starter**

Write down 5–8 things you associate with airports and flying.

Compare your list with a partner.

075 **Textwork**

Work in pairs. Read through the text *At Mumbai Airport* on page 39. Take turns to ask and answer the following questions.

1. Why couldn't he relax at the airport?
2. Was he alone?
3. Which country was the delayed flight A1130 going to?
4. What does his uncle give him to eat on the journey?
5. For which Hindu festival does Ashish say he might come back to his aunt and uncle?
6. What was Ashish's familiar fear?
7. What smell did he notice as he boarded the plane?
8. How did he feel when the plane finally took off and was flying over Mumbai? Why did he feel like that?

Practise the vocabulary in Wordmatch/Spelling

076 **Vocabulary: Words of similar meaning**

Complete the pairs of words below with another word that is similar in meaning. Choose from the following words, all taken from the text.

abandoned	embrace	moulded	shove	specious
clutch	inquisitive	myriad	slender	urge

1 push, thrust, ________
2 formed, shaped, ________
3 craving, desire, ________
4 deserted, forsaken, ________
5 slim, slight, ________
6 cuddle, hug, ________
7 countless, innumerable, ________
8 curious, nosy, ________
9 false, phony, ________
10 grasp, grip, ________

077 **Interact**

1 Who is Ashish? What's your impression of him?
2 He phones Narayan from the airport. Who do you think he is? Why is he sad at leaving him?
3 Miles and Ashish are both saying goodbye to their families. Compare and discuss how the two young men experience the separation.

078 **Looking at words to do with travel**

Complete the definitions below with a suitable verb. Choose from the following.

Airbnb	destination	holidaymaker	peak season
backpacking	ecotourism	honeymoon	seaside resort
couch surfing	excursion	InterRail Global Pass	timeshare
crossing	globetrotter	itinerary	travel agency
departure lounge	guide	package holiday	youth hostel

1 A ________ is a holiday taken by a couple who've just got married.
2 A ________ is someone who often travels to a lot of different countries.
3 The ________ is the time of year when the greatest number of people are taking their holidays and when the prices are at their highest level.
4 The ________ is the area at an airport where passengers wait before getting onto their aircraft.
5 A ________ is a company that arranges travel and/or accommodation for people going on a holiday.

6 __________ is a community marketplace which connects people who have space to spare with those who are looking for a place to stay.
7 Your __________ is a plan or route of a journey, including the route and the places that you'll visit.
8 A __________ is a holiday home that you buy with other people so that you can each use it for a particular period of the year.
9 __________ is the activity of travelling for pleasure, usually without very much money, carrying your things in a large rucksack on your back.
10 A __________ is a person who's visiting a place on holiday.
11 Your __________ is the place where you're going to.
12 A __________ is a place where people - especially young people - who are travelling, can stay very cheaply for a short time.
13 An __________ is a short journey arranged so that a group of people can visit a place, especially while they're on holiday.
14 A __________ is a holiday organized by a company at a fixed price that includes the cost of travel, accommodation, etc.
15 __________ is the practice of sleeping overnight in the houses of friends or fellow members of a social network, especially as an alternative to staying in hotels, hostels, etc.
16 The __________ is a railway ticket available to European residents which is a fun and budget way to travel wherever you like across 30 countries in Europe.
17 __________ are holidays to places such as rain forests in which people can visit and learn about them in a way that won't damage the environment.
18 A __________ is someone whose job is to take tourists to a place and show them around.
19 A __________ is a place near the sea where a lot of people go for holidays.
20 A __________ is a journey by boat across the sea, a lake, or a river.

079 **Writing**

There are different ways of travelling. You can go on a package tours, you can use Airbnb or you can backpack, etc. What are the advantages or disadvantages of these different ways to travel?

For advice on discussion essay see Resource Section page 165. Also see page 176 for linking words. Don't forget to use the Checklist for writing on page 156.

HEMI'S GIFT (page 43)

080 **Starter**

Work in pairs. Here are 10 facts about a country.
Read through them and try to guess which country it is.

This country was the first major nation to give women the vote. It happened in 1893.

This country has the southernmost capital city in the world.

This country is very liberal and since 2003, same-sex marriages, brothels, prostitution and soliciting are all legal.

There are no snakes in this country.

Moa birds were once native to this country, but are now extinct. They were 12 feet tall and weighed about 230 kg.

The national sport of this country is rugby.

There are no nuclear power plants in this country.

A native flightless bird is also a slang term for a person from this country.

The first person to climb Mount Everest was from this country.

Organised commercial bungee jumping first began in this country.

Turn to page 222 to see if you were right.

081 **Textwork**

Without looking back at *Hemi's Gift* on page 43 choose the correct answer (a, b or c).

1. She caught the bus in *a) Wellington b) Auckland c) Whāngārei.*
2. Her *a) father b) mother c) sister* had died two days before.
3. The man with the guitar was *a) a Frenchman b) an Englishman c) a Māori.*
4. She hoped the man would sit next to her. *a) True b) False*
5. She takes *a) an iPhone b) an iPad c) an iPod* out of her bag.
6. She *a) has b) hasn't* read the last email her father sent her.
7. Her father had died of *a) cancer b) a heart attack c) a stroke.*
8. The bus stops at Kaiwaka for *a) a ten minute b) a half hour c) an hour's* break.
9. The girl is a smoker. *a) True b) False*
10. Hemi is *a) a musician b) an actor c) a writer.*
11. He buys her *a) a packet of cigarettes b) a drink c) some food.*
12. She's the first person in her family to *a) have a good job b) go to university c) marry a white man.*
13. Hemi's music helps her to *a) grieve for her father b) remember her childhood c) feel calm.*

Practise the vocabulary in Wordmatch/Spelling

082 Vocabulary: Fill in the gaps

Fill in the missing words in the sentences below. Choose from the following words, taken from the text. Then make up your own sentences for the four words that are left over.

flawless	permeated	shuddered	stroke
grieving	plucking	shuffled	swings
momentarily	relief	sloppy	tense
peered	rustled	solace	unfolded

1 The leaves ________ in the breeze.
2 The children were playing on the ________ in the park.
3 His grandchildren were a ________ to him in his old age.
4 As she ________ the letter and read it, I could tell the news wasn't good.
5 A strong smell of garlic ________ the whole house.
6 At home I tend to wear big ________ jumpers and jeans.
7 The supermodel had a ________ complexion. We were all so envious!
8 The old man ________ into the kitchen, leaning on his walking stick.
9 The coach ________ to a halt and the passengers got off.
10 My cousin is still ________ over the death of his mother.
11 Her grandfather died of a ________ at the age of eighty-nine.
12 When no one answered the door, she ________ through the window to see if anyone was there.

083 Interact

1 Describe the girl's feelings. What is on her mind? Why is she sad?
2 How does the girl's attitude to Hemi change during the bus ride?
3 How is Hemi? How is he described? Give examples from the text.
4 Why do you think is the story is called Hemi's gift?

086 Starter: Guess the country (from page 221)

The country is New Zealand

084 **Use of English: One word only 1**

In the previous two chapters you did an exercise on sentence-changing. Now it's time to try a different type of exercise, this time to try to fill gaps in various sentences with one suitable word only.
There's a gap in each of the sentences below. Each gap is to be filled with **ONE** word that makes sense in the context and that is grammatically correct.

1 You'd better take an umbrella with you in ________ it rains.
2 Even ________ he was very rich, he never travelled first class.
3 The open-air pop concert went ahead ________ the bad weather.
4 They left ________ saying goodbye.
5 You can't expect me to arrange a meeting ________ such short notice. I need at least a week.

Now go to the Use of English section of the book and do the exercise *One word only 1* on pages 352–353.

WSM: MAORIS – THE ORIGINAL INHABITANTS OF NEW ZEALAND

085 **Sum up and comment**

1 Which text did you find most interesting in this unit? Give reasons.
2 How can your writing improve by using peer response?
3 Write in your learning log, see Resource Section page 149, and comment on three questions of your own choice.

086 **Books to read and enjoy**

Achebe, Chinua: *Things Fall Apart*
Adams, Douglas: *The Hitchhiker's Guide to the Galaxy*
Bolt, Usain: *Faster Than Lightning*
Green, John: *Looking for Alaska*
Higgins Clark, Mary: *Daddy's Gone a Hunting*
Wilde, Oscar: *The Picture of Dorian Gray*

4 CLASSICS

HAMLET, PRINCE OF DENMARK

- [ ] Starter
- [ ] Textwork
- [ ] Vocabulary: Choose the word
- [ ] Vocabulary: Choose the meaning

LISTENING: HAMLET, PRINCE OF DENMARK CONT.

- [ ] Listen and recall
- [ ] Interact
- [ ] Speaking
- [ ] Looking at words to do with books and literature
- [ ] Expand your vocabulary: Words that go together (collocations)

WSM: A HISTORY OF THEATRE

PYGMALION

- [ ] Starter
- [ ] Textwork
- [ ] Vocabulary: Definitions
- [ ] Act it out
- [ ] Creating a situation from a dialogue

WSM: LOOKING AT COCKNEYS

SIXPENCE

- [ ] Starter
- [ ] Textwork
- [ ] Adjectives to describe a person's character
- [ ] Vocabulary: Fill in the gaps
- [ ] Interact
- [ ] Focus on 'make' and 'do'

CAT IN THE RAIN

- [ ] Starter
- [ ] Textwork
- [ ] Vocabulary: Choose the word
- [ ] Interact
- [ ] Project
- [ ] Use of English: One word only 2 & 3

- [ ] Sum up and comment
- [ ] Books to read and enjoy

HAMLET, PRINCE OF DENMARK

(page 50)

087 Starter

What is the play *Hamlet* about? Who is Hamlet? How would you sum up the plot in a few sentences?

088 Textwork

Read *Hamlet, Prince of Denmark* on page 50. Here is a summary of the extract, but the sentences are in the wrong order. Sort them out 1–10. Number 1 has been done for you.

_____ Hamlet decides to pretend to be mad.

_____ At the meeting with his mother, Hamlet suspects that Claudius is hiding behind a curtain. He stabs the person, only to find it is Polonius, Ophelia's father.

_____ Hamlet persuades the actors to put on the play *The Murder of Gonzago.* He makes changes to it.

__1__ Horatio tells Hamlet that his father has died from a snake bite.

_____ Hamlet tells his mother he'll meet her in her room and asks her to make sure she's alone and that no one knows about the meeting.

_____ Lady Ophelia begs Hamlet to attend a performance of the Royal Players. Hamlet agrees to attend.

_____ Claudius forces Hamlet to leave Denmark for England.

_____ A short while later, Hamlet's mother marries Claudius.

_____ At the end of the first scene of the play the actor playing Duke Gonzago pours poison into his nephew's ear. Claudius reacts angrily.

_____ Hamlet's father appears as a ghost and says he was murdered by Claudius and begs Hamlet to avenge his death.

Practise the vocabulary in Wordmatch/Spelling

089 Vocabulary: Choose the word

090 Vocabulary: Choose the meaning

The following words and expressions in **bold** are all found in the text. Mark the alternative (a, b, c or d) that best corresponds to the meaning of the words and expressions as they are used in the text.

1 Snowflakes **twirled** in the wind that moaned around the battlements.
a) fell lightly b) spun c) fell heavily d) were tossed around

2 ... bitten by a snake while he was sleeping in the **orchard.**
a) a place where fruit trees grow b) a small open space in a castle c) a private bedroom d) a field full of crops

3 Its voice was a groan of **despair** that sent shudders down my backbone.
a) great physical pain b) feeling desperate c) a feeling of disappointment d) a feeling of having lost all hope

4 ... because Horatio had **unwittingly** provided me with an answer.
a) unfortunately b) understandably c) unknowingly d) deliberately

5 The **strain** of pretending, ... was almost too great to bear.
a) effort b) problem c) tension d) situation

6 ... if I did not, my father's soul was doomed to **eternal** torment.
a) temporary b) very painful c) everlasting d) violent

7 Then one day, on a **bleak** afternoon, ... I drew my dagger and stared at it.
a) wet and windy b) cold and unpleasant c) frost-covered d) early winter's

8 It was Lady Ophelia, ... her eyes filled with love and **concern**.
a) great fear b) alarm c) sympathy D anxiety

9 ... and kiss her fingers in a way that filled me with **loathing.**
a) a feeling of disgust b) a feeling of hatred c) a feeling of hopelessness d) a feeling of envy

Assessment and strategies. Evaluate your reading! Use the Assessment in Resource Section pages 149-150 and reading strategies in the digital part.

LISTENING: HAMLET, PRINCE OF DENMARK CONT.

091 Listen and recall

Listen to the rest of the summary of the play *Hamlet*. As you listen, fill in the missing information or choose the correct answer (a, b or c). Before you start, read through the sentences below.

1 He couldn't see anything because the carriage he was riding in didn't have __________.

2 He boarded his ship and it set sail
a) after several hours b) almost immediately c) the following day.

3 Danish __________ captured the ship and murdered most of the crew.

4 Instead of killing Hamlet, they put him ashore in Elsinore. *a) True b) False*

5 He wrote to his mother telling her he would __________ that had been done.
6 Hamlet heads out for the castle and is met by Horatio who tells him that *a) Ophelia b) Claudius c) his mother* has died.
7 Laertes is Ophelia's *a) uncle b) brother c) lover* and he has sworn to kill Hamlet, but Claudius persuaded him to have a __________ in front of the whole court.
8 His mother and uncle are sitting on the royal thrones in the Great Hall. *a) Claudius b) Horatio c) His mother* looks proud.
9 During the fight, *a) Hamlet b) Laertes* gets the first hit.
10 During the fight Hamlet and Laertes change swords. *a) True b) False*
11 We learn that Claudius spread __________ on Laertes' sword blade and that Hamlet's mother dies because she drank from the cup intended for __________.
12 Hamlet kills __________ before dying himself. As he dies, he thinks he sees *a) Ophelia's b) Horatio's c) his father's* face.

Practise the vocabulary in Wordmatch/Spelling

---

092 Interact

When discussing literature make use of On Language in Resource Section page 172.

1 Describe Hamlet. What sort of personality does he have?
2 Describe the relationship between Hamlet and his mother. How do you think he feels about her new marriage?
3 Why do you think he waits such a long time before taking revenge?
4 Why are Shakespeare's plays still so popular all over the world, do you think?

093 Speaking

Work in pairs. Imagine BBC News or Sky News or CNN had been around at the time of Hamlet. A piece of breaking news has just come into the studio about what has happened in Denmark. Prepare a short news broadcast trying to give the main events of the story plus any background to it.

You can start:
Some breaking news is just coming in from Denmark ...

Now let one of you make the broadcast while your partner films it.
When you've finished, compare your result with another pair.

094 Looking at words to do with books and literature

A Work in pairs. Below are 30 words in alphabetical order which have something to do with books and literature. Put them under the correct heading (6 words under each). Use a dictionary, if necessary and make a special note of any new words you come across.

appendix	critic	index	rhyming couplet

atlas
author
autobiography
bibliography
biographer
blank verse
blurb
detective story
dictionary
encyclopedia
epigram
fairy tale
glossary
haiku
lyricist
manual
memoirs
novel
novelist
playwright
poem
short story
sonnet
table of contents
thriller
whodunit

TYPES OF FICTION

____
____
____
____
____

OTHER BOOKS (non-fiction)

____
____
____
____
____

WORDS TO DO WITH POETRY

____
____
____
____
____

TYPES OF WRITERS

____
____
____
____
____

PARTS OF A BOOK

____
____
____
____
____

B Fill in the missing words in the eight definitions below. They're all words found in A.

1 An __________ is a short poem, phrase or poem that expresses an idea in a clever or amusing way.
2 A __________ is a story about a murder in which you don't know who did the murder until the end.
3 The __________ is a short description of a book, written by the people who've produced it, that's intended to attract your attention and make you want to buy it.
4 An __________ is a list of names or topics that are referred to in a book, usually arranged at the end of a book in alphabetical order.
5 An __________ is the story of a person's life, written by that person.
6 An __________ is a separate part at the end of a book which gives extra information.
7 A __________ is a person who expresses opinions about the good and bad qualities of books, music, etc.
8 __________ are an account written by someone – especially someone famous – about their life and experiences.

095 Expand your vocabulary: Words that go together (collocations)

Do you know why we say 'knife and fork' rather than 'fork and knife'? Or why you have a 'vivid' imagination rather than a 'bright' imagination? Or why you 'commit' a crime rather than 'do' a crime? Certain words go together. They're called collocations and you really have to learn them by heart as they don't follow any rules. Here's your chance to test your knowledge of collocations using adjectives + nouns (a juicy orange) and verbs + nouns (to pass a law).

Fill in the gaps in the sentences below by taking an adjective from A and a noun from B. Use each word once only.

A			B		
heavy	roaring	splitting	fire	headache	traffic

1 'I think I'll go to bed. I've got a __________ __________.'
2 We took longer than expected to get to the city centre because of the __________ __________.
3 There's nothing nicer on a winter's evening than to come home to a __________ __________.

Again fill in the gaps in the sentences below, this time by taking an verb from A and a noun from B. Use each word once only. Make any necessary verb changes.

A			B		
catch	draw	set	curtains	example	fire

4 'It's getting dark. Can you __________ the __________ please?'
5 For reasons that are not yet known, the factory __________ __________ in the middle of the night.
6 A teacher should __________ a good __________ to his or her pupils.

Now go to the Expand your vocabulary section of the book and do the exercise *Words that go together (collocations)* on pages 331–333.

WSM: A HISTORY OF THEATRE

PYGMALION (page 56)

096 Starter

Work in pairs or groups of three. Discuss the following.

1 What do you know about the various accents in the United Kingdom?
2 Do you know what's typical of the Cockney accent?

097 Textwork

1 How is the flower girl described?
2 What kind of work does the note taker do?
3 What does he hope to achieve with the flower girl?

Practise the vocabulary in Wordmatch/Spelling

098 Vocabulary: Definitions

Here are definitions of eight words from the text. Can you work out what they are? To help you, the first and last letter of each missing word is given.

1 Another word for to 'need'.	r_________e
2 An _____ person is very good at expressing ideas or feelings clearly in words.	a_________e
3 You use this word to describe things that you hate very much.	d_________e
4 Another word for 'immediately'.	i_________y
5 The wife of a Duke.	d_________s
6 Another word for 'very weak'.	f_________e
7 To _____ doing something is to stop doing it.	c_________e
8 If you're feeling _____ you feel you might vomit soon.	b_________s

099 Act it out

Work in groups of four. Try acting out the scene from *Pygmalion*. Three people are actors while the fourth is the director. Your teacher will give you copies of the script.

100 Creating a situation from a dialogue

Work in pairs or groups of three. Look at the following dialogues. Your task is to choose one of them and expand it by adding 6–8 lines before and after the extract. Before you start, think of the following:

1 Who are the characters? (A and B)
2 Where are they and why are they there?
3 What is happening now? What might have happened just before and what is going to happen next?
4 Can you introduce a third person (C), either before or after the extract?

When you've finished writing your dialogue, act it out.

Dialogue 1

A It was in Egypt, wasn't it?
B No, I'm sorry. I've never been to Egypt.
A Are you sure?
B Of course I'm sure!
A Well, it must have been Spain.
B I haven't been to Spain, either.
A No? So where have you been, then?
B Why do you want to know?
A Just curious... maybe we met there.

Dialogue 2

A And then she walked out!
B No! Really?
A Yes, just walked out.
B What – just like that?
A Yes. Didn't even say goodbye to anyone.
B Well, I never!
A Yes, it was quite a shock.
B Mind you, I blame her mother.
A Her mother?
B Yes. Her mother's got a lot to answer for, if you ask me.

WSM: LOOKING AT COCKNEYS

Strictly speaking, to call yourself a Cockney you should have been born 'within the sound of Bow Bells' – that is, within the sound of the bells of St. Mary-le-Bow, which stands nearly in the centre of the City of London. However, nowadays, it's used to describe anyone who speaks with a Cockney or working-class London accent.

Cockneys have their own special language called 'rhyming slang', where the original words are replaced by words that rhyme with them. They usually rhyme with the last word.

For example:

apples and pears (stairs), plates of meat (feet), bread and cheese (sneeze), custard and jelly (telly, television), and China plate (mate = friend).

So what do you think these are?

1 mince pies ________
2 bees and honey ________
3 daisy roots ________
4 Uncle Ned ________
5 Rosy Lee ________

Another thing worth noting is that Cockneys don't usually pronounce the letter 'h'. So the word *hot* becomes *'ot*, *have* becomes *'ave*, *happy* becomes *'appy*, and so on. So how would a Cockney say this sentence?
How many handsome house-guests are having halibut instead of hamburgers in Hampstead?

Turn to page 237 to see if you got it right.

SIXPENCE (page 59)

101 Starter

1 How do you think children 100 years ago were raised differently from today?
2 Who was the head of the family at that time? What did that mean?

102 Textwork

Work in pairs. Read through the text *Sixpence* on page 59. Take turns to ask and answer the following questions.

1 What were Dicky's sisters' reaction when he dropped the plate?
2 Why didn't Dicky's mother chase after him?
3 What does Mrs Spears suggest should happen to Dicky?
4 Mrs Spears's children are often beaten. Who does the beating?
5 Mrs Bendall asks her husband to whip Dicky. How does he react?
6 How many slaps did he give Dicky? How did Dicky react?
7 How did the father feel after the whipping?
8 Dicky's father returns to his room and gives him something. What?

Practise the vocabulary in Wordmatch/Spelling

103 Adjectives to describe a person's character

104 Vocabulary: Fill in the gaps

Fill in the missing words in the sentences below. Choose from the following words, taken from the text. Then make up your own sentences for the four words that are left over.

according to	impress	on purpose	sprained
dodging	lawn	punish	startled
for granted	leapt	seize	thimble
hissing	obedient	sensitive	upside down

1 The dog __________ over the gate into the field.
2 We should try to help prisoners, not just __________ them.
3 The steam escaped from the kettle with a loud, __________ noise.
4 Adiba __________ her ankle playing tennis at the weekend.
5 Ben is very __________ – he just can't take criticism.
6 "Your son's been absent from school six times this term __________ our records," said the head teacher to his parents.
7 To get the ketchup out, turn the jar __________ and then shake it.
8 He ran across the road, carefully __________ the traffic.
9 "It wasn't an accident at all. You did it __________," she said accusingly.
10 It's embarrassing the extremes Harry will go to in order to __________ his boss.
11 A sudden flash of lightning made my sister jump back like a __________ rabbit.
12 She seemed to take it __________ that I would go with her to New York.

105 Interact

1 Dicky is described as being 'good as gold, as a rule'. What would your idea be of a child like this?
2 Mrs Spears says, "To be weak with children when they are little. It's such a sad mistake, and one so easy to make. It's so unfair to the child." Do you agree or disagree? Give reasons.
3 Dicky's father says at the end, "But could even that – could even a whole sixpence (worth about £5 in today's money) blot out what had been?" What do you think he means by that?
4 What's the moral of this story?

106 **Focus on 'make' and 'do'**

A Place the following words and phrases under the correct headings (12 words/phrases under each).

an excuse, a mistake, research, an appointment, the washing-up, friends, a good job, your hair, a noise, a speech, homework, your duty, a complaint, business, an effort, harm, your best, a journey, an exam, fun of someone, a fuss, an exercise, a lot of money, someone a favour

MAKE	DO

B Pair work

Work in pairs – A and B. Your teacher will give you more information.

CAT IN THE RAIN (page 66)

107 **Starter**

1 What do you know about Ernest Hemingway?
2 Hemingway used the "Iceberg Theory" when writing. Do you know or can you guess what that is?

108 **Textwork**

Read *Cat in the Rain* on page 66. Then say whether the following sentences are true (T) or false (F). But if you can't definitely say if something is true or false from the information given, then mark the sentence don't know (DK). The sentences are in no special order.

1 The husband offers to go and get the kitten. ______
2 The kitten is in a doorway sheltering from the rain. ______
3 The husband, George, is an accountant. ______
4 They were the only two Americans at their hotel. ______
5 George is on the bed reading a spy novel. ______
6 The cat is a present from the maid. ______
7 When the American lady goes downstairs, she finds the cat has gone. ______
8 George likes the idea of his wife letting her hair grow. ______
9 The maid brings the American woman a black and white cat. ______
10 George tells his wife to get something to read. ______
11 They'd been at the hotel for over a week. ______
12 The hotel-keeper was quite young. ______

Practise the vocabulary in Wordmatch/Spelling

109 Vocabulary: Choose the word

110 Interact

1 How would you describe the woman? What is she mainly interested in? What do you think of her behaviour?
2 Do you think the couple have a good relationship? Give examples of situations in the text.
3 The short story *Cat in the Rain* is partly about the desire for material things in contrast to another way of vacationing. Give examples of this from the text. Look at how the woman, George and the Italian tourists spend their holiday. Compare their activities.
4 How would you explain why the woman behaves the way she does?

111 Project

For a project on classic and contemporary authors go to pages 238–240 for suggestions on what to do.

112 Use of English: One word only 2 & 3

In the previous chapter you did an exercise on filling gaps in separate sentences with one word only. Now it is time to try the same exercise, this time using complete texts.

In this text there are a number of gaps. Each gap is to be filled with **ONE** word that makes sense in the context and that is grammatically correct.

You learn English and other foreign (1)______ in order to be able to communicate (2)______ people who don't speak your (3)______ language. Many people feel they (4)______ to be as good as or sound (5)______ native speakers. This is not necessary (6)__________ you're (7)__________ to be an interpreter or possibly an English teacher. Others feel (8)__________ if they make mistakes. This is silly as (9) __________ mistakes is an integral part of learning anything. Can you imagine learning to drive (10)__________ ever doing anything wrong?

Now go to the Use of English section of the book and do the exercises *One word only 2* and *One word only 3* on pages 354–355.

113 **Sum up and comment**

1 What different themes can you find in the texts?
2 How much better are you at "reading between the lines", that is, really understanding the message of the text?

114 **Books to read and enjoy**

Austen, Jane: *Emma, Pride and Prejudice*
Brontë, Charlotte: *Jane Eyre*
Brontë, Emily: *Wuthering Heights*
Dickens, Charles: *Oliver Twist, David Copperfield*
Fitzgerald, Scott: *The Great Gatsby*
Golding, William: *Lord of the Flies*
Hemingway, Ernest: *The Old Man and the Sea, A Farewell to Arms*
Huxley, Aldous: *Brave New World*
Mansfield, Katherine: *Short Stories*
Orwell, George: *1984*
Steinbeck, John: *Of Mice and Men, The Grapes of Wrath*
Twain, Mark: *Huckleberry Finn*

WSM: LOOKING AT COCKNEYS

1 mince pies – eyes
2 bees and honey – money
3 daisy roots –boots
4 Uncle Ned – bed
5 Rosy Lee – tea

AUTHORS OF THE ENGLISH-SPEAKING WORLD (page 72

On these pages you will find various suggestions on how to work with classical and contemporary writers. When working with literature make use of the following pages in Resource Section:

1 Analyzing and discussing a novel p. 170
2 Writing a review
3 The language of literary criticism p. 172
4 On Speaking p. 157
5 Writing a project p. 168
6 Checklist for writing p. 156
7 Peer response – writing p. 156
8 Peer response – speaking p. 159

See also:
A Brief History of English Literature p. 74–75.

A Read a novel and write a review

Classical and contemporary writers in your textbook p. 72–78 will give you some names of writers from the English-speaking world and some titles that you might want to try reading. There are also suggestions for further reading under the heading **Books to read and enjoy** at the end of each unit.

B Find an interesting group project, and present it orally to the class

Suggestions for literary projects to work with:

1 Presenting a classical writer

Pick one of the writers on p. 72–73 and prepare a 3–5 minute presentation. You can work as follows:

1 Present briefly the period in which the writer can be placed.
2 Present the writer: background information, year of birth, year of death, place of birth, some interesting trivia.
3 Major works: define genre, name a few of the works and briefly summarize the content of one or two of them.
4 If presenting Shakespeare you might want to act out a scene or comment on some famous quotes.
5 If presenting Emily Dickinson or Walt Whitman you might want to read a poem or parts of a poem.
6 If possible: find a clip from a filmed version of one of the works to show in connection with your presentation.

2 Working with contemporary writers

When working with contemporary writers it is a good idea to present them in a wider context. Firstly use the writers on p. 76–78 and present them country wise: Canada, the US, Ireland, India, New Zealand, England and Africa.

1 Present the writer: background information, year of birth, place of birth, some interesting trivia
2 Major works: define the genre, name a few of the works and briefly summarize the content of one or two of them.
3 If possible: find a clip from a filmed version of one of the novels to show in connection with your presentation.

C Other suggestions for literary projects – to be presented orally

When presenting these groups of writers and titles use the same outline as above. One additional point is suggested for each project.

Please note that these are suggestions – use any books of your choice!

1 Dystopian novels

George Orwell's *1984*, Aldous Huxley's *Brave New World*, William Golding's *Lord of The Flies* and Suzanne Collins' *The Hunger Games* all deal with dystopian societies.

- What societies are these writers depicting in their works?

2 Chick lit

Carrie Bradshaw's *The Carrie Diaries*, Marian Keyes' *Watermelon,* Helen Fielding's *Bridget Jones' Dairy*, and Sophie Kinsella's *Can You Keep a Secret* are all categorized as chick lit.

- Who is the main character in each book? What is typical of her/him?

3 Lad lit

Nick Hornby's *About a Boy*, Tony Parsons' *Man and Boy,* Mike Gayle's *My Legendary Girlfriend* and David

Nicholl's *Starter for Ten* fall under the category of lad lit.
- Who is the main character in each book? What is typical of her/him?

4 Filmed versions of novels

Many novels have been made into films or TV series e.g. *Game of Thrones, Hunger Games, Divergent, Fever Pitch, Lord of the Rings, The Fault in our Stars, The Great Gatsby* and *Pride and Prejudice*
- Find some film clips on YouTube and present these and give your opinion on whether this is a good film version or not. Compare the film clip with the episode in the book.

5 Fantasy novels

Present a writer of fantasy novels such as J.R.R. Tolkien's *Lord of the Rings*, George R.R. Martin's *Game of Thrones* and Kristin Cashore's *Graceling.*
- When and where does the action take place? Who is the "good guy" and who is the "bad guy"? What is the struggle about?

6 Childhood

Richard Ford's *Canada*, Jeanette Winterson's *Why Be Happy When You Could Be Normal?* Donna Tartt's *The Goldfinch* and Charles Dickens' *Great Expectations.*
- What kind of childhood is described?

D Suggestions for written projects

A literary project can also be presented in writing. You can choose to work with one or two novels or a novel and a film in order to analyze some aspect of the works. You can focus on: the characters, the environment, the theme, the historical period etc.

Some suggestions are:

1 The description of the society in a dystopian novel.
2 The protagonists in one or two chick lit novels/lad lit novels.
3 Compare the novel and the filmed version.
4 How good and evil are presented in a fantasy novel.
5 How childhood can be described in a novel.

5 SHOP TILL YOU DROP

A GOOD PRICE!

- [ ] Starter: How to haggle
- [ ] Textwork
- [ ] Vocabulary: Choose the word
- [ ] Vocabulary: What does it mean?
- [ ] Interact
- [ ] Looking at words to do with money

WSM: THE PARROT SKETCH FROM MONTY PYTHON

LISTENING: MEET NUNU NTSHINGILA-NJEKE FROM SOUTH AFRICA

- [ ] Starter
- [ ] Listen and recall
- [ ] Interact
- [ ] Expand your vocabulary: Synonyms
- [ ] Project

CREATIVE DESTRUCTION

- [ ] Starter
- [ ] Textwork
- [ ] Vocabulary: Choose the word
- [ ] Interact
- [ ] Writing

WSM: IT'S POLAROIDS WORLD – WE JUST LIVE IN IT

SHOPPING, SEDUCTION & MR SELFRIDGE

- [ ] Starter
- [ ] Textwork
- [ ] Vocabulary: Unscramble the letters
- [ ] Interact
- [ ] Project
- [ ] Follow up
- [ ] Use of English: Word-building 1
- [ ] Speaking/Writing

LISTENING: NEWS ITEMS

- [ ] Listen and recall
- [ ] Critical reading and reviewing

- [ ] Sum up and comment
- [ ] Books to read and enjoy

A GOOD PRICE! (page 80)

115 Starter: How to haggle

Read the following short text about haggling. A number of words have been left out. Below you will find four alternatives for each gap. Choose the **best** alternative and write your choice, A, B, C or D in the appropriate box below.

In many countries around the world such as Thailand, Indonesia, China, Jamaica, Turkey, Egypt and Sri Lanka, haggling or bartering is almost __**1**__. If you don't haggle, then it's highly likely that you'll get __**2**__, because vendors expect a bit of haggling which is why their opening price is always higher than what they expect to receive. And if you're willing to pay the asking price, then you probably __**3**__ to pay too much. If, however, you're interested in shopping like a seasoned traveller rather than a gullible tourist, here are a few rules of __**4**__ on how to haggle.

1 Set your top price and stick to it, Once you go above that, it's a slippery __**5**__ to paying the full price.

2 Know your product. It's hard to set a realistic price goal if you don't know the item's true value. If you know what you want, do a little research before you get there, or check around in various shops for similar items. Carpets in Turkey, for example, are worth researching before you ever walk into a rug-seller's shop. Prices vary wildly __**6**__ what you look like.

3 Double up. You may be able to get that discount if you buy more than one item from the same shop. Buy more and sellers should be willing to come down, if only to __**7**__ more of their stock .

4 Be willing to walk away. Chances are you can live without that camel-skin belt or whatever you were interested in. If the seller isn't __**8**__ on the price, just turn and head for the door. They may even shout that perfect final offer before you're gone for good. And never worry about having taken too much of the vendor's time. They're experienced business people who know they won't close every deal.

5 Finally, don't take it too seriously. Have a sense of humour and know when to accept an offer. Remember that usually the amounts you are arguing over are actually a __**9**__ to a traveller from the West, but will definitely mean a lot more to the vendor.

Haggling can be exhausting – especially if you've been at it all day. But don't give in. It's satisfying to get what you think is a great __**10**__, even if the price on your 50%-off piece was actually marked up 200%!

1 **A**) normal **B**) expected **C**) compulsory **D**) usual
2 **A**) abused **B**) bowled over **C**) ripped off **D**) done up
3 **A**) demand **B**) deserve **C**) hope **D**) justify
4 **A**) advice **B**) finger **C**) law **D**) thumb
5 **A**) slope **B**) deal **C**) result **D**) drop
6 **A**) banking on **B**) in the event of **C**) depending on **D**) according to
7 **A**) do away with **B**) dispose **C**) remove **D**) get rid of
8 **A**) budging **B**) nudging **C**) going away from **D**) changing
9 **A**) fortune **B**) pittance **C**) small change **D**) peanuts
10 **A**) contract **B**) compromise **C**) discount **D**) deal

116 **Textwork**

Read *A Good Price!* on pages 80–83. Then complete the statements below, basing your answers on information in the text. Answer briefly and, as far as possible, in your own words. Read each statement very carefully so that your completion fits in with it.

1 Ma's main aim every Saturday morning at Chatuchak is to get the vendors ...

2 When she puts on a pair of Armani glasses, her son tells her that ...

3 When the vendor tells her the glasses will cost twelve hundred, Ma ...

4 We can gather from the text that the husband of the Chinese couple ...

5 The vendor calls Ma back and insists that the Armani glasses ...

6 It appears that the vendor's boyfriend ...

7 The vendor lowers her price to a thousand. Ma replies by ...

8 The girl refuses Ma's offer saying that ...

9 Ma offers seven hundred and fifty and tells the girl that she needs the glasses because ...

10 Ma's entreaties to the girl result in ...

Practise the vocabulary in Wordmatch/Spelling

117 **Vocabulary: Choose the word**

118 Vocabulary: What does it mean?

You're now going to explain the meaning of some of the words used in the text *A Good Price!* Complete the following sentences by giving English explanations of the words in **bold**. Make your explanations as exact as possible. Use a dictionary if necessary.

Example: A **raspy** voice sounds ________.
Answer: very rough

1 To **slash** the price of something is to ________..
2 A **shrill** sound is________.
3 **Stubborn** people don't find it easy to change ________.
4 That Rolex watch is a **fake**. Anyone can see it's ________.
5 Vendors often **submitted** to Ma's entreaties. This means that they often ________ to her.
6 When you get a **discount**, the amount you pay is________.
7 A **vendor** is someone who ________.
8 English is compulsory for all students, but Art and Music are **optional**. So you ________ those subjects.
9 She **feigned** being ill. In other words, she was only ________.
10 A huge **throng** had gathered around the speaker. This means that the speaker was surrounded by ________.
11 When you're **mute**, you don't ________.
12 They made accusations which couldn't be **substantiated**. This means they couldn't ________.

119 Interact

1 What do you think about the woman's haggling methods to get a better price?
2 Have you ever tried to haggle for something while on holiday? Where was it? Did you succeed?
3 Which do you prefer – fixed prices for goods or having to haggle? Why?

120 Looking at words to do with money

A Each of the missing words in the sentences below is to do with money. Fill each gap with one of the following:

affluent	economical	purchase
bargain	fee	recession
boom	gross income	refund
budget	inheritance	rise (BrE), raise (AmE)
deposit	instalments/payments	savings
discount	loan	tip
donation	net income	worthless
economy	priceless	

1 A ________ is when the economy is doing badly. The opposite is a ________.
2 I got this dress in a sale. It only cost £10. It was a real ________.
3 As they had enjoyed the meal and service so much, they left the waiter quite a large ________.
4 He had paid too much by mistake, so the Gas company gave him a ________.
5 He asked me if I would like to make a small ________ to Oxfam.
6 It is very easy to take out a ________. The difficult part is in paying it back.
7 There was a large advertisement in the shop which said, 'When you make your first ________ using your store card, you will be given a 10% ________'.
8 Your ________ is the money you earn before tax, etc. has been deducted. Your ________ is the money you actually get in your hand.
9 Most companies make a ________ every year, where they try to predict their income and expenses.
10 She'll be a very rich woman indeed when her father dies and she comes into her ________.
11 When he lost his job he had to dip into his ________ to make ends meet.
12 The lawyer's ________ came to £650.
13 Most of the paintings in the Louvre in Paris are ________. It's impossible to say how much they're worth.
14 I think I deserve to be paid more, so I'm going to ask my boss for a ________ today. She can only say 'No'.
15 In Britain, the Chancellor of the Exchequer is responsible for the country's ________.
16 A more formal word for 'rich' is ________.
17 I had to pay a 10% ________ when I bought the TV, followed by ten monthly ________ of £50.
18 It's not a genuine Picasso. So I'm afraid the painting's ________.
19 People are changing to small cars because they are far more ________ than big ones.

B Now work in pairs or small groups and discuss the following.

1 Give some examples of things that could be described as **priceless**.
2 Have you bought anything in the last six months that you consider to be a **bargain**? If so, tell the others about it.
3 In the UK there are lots of **discount** shops, for example, Poundland. Are there such shops in Sweden? Have you ever bought anything from them?
4 Tell the others about three **purchases** you have made in the past 2-3 months. Did you buy anything that you really didn't need?

WSM: THE PARROT SKETCH FROM MONTY PYTHON

How many different ways of saying 'It's dead' can you find?
If you like, you can try acting it out.

LISTENING – MEET NUNU NTSHINGILA-NJEKE FROM SOUTH AFRICA

121 Starter

Steve Jobs, the former Chief Executive Officer of Apple, Bill Gates the former CEO of Microsoft and Mark Zuckerberg the present CEO of Facebook are all household names. They are also all men.

But what about women? There are a lot more female CEOs, nowadays but perhaps they're not as well-known as many of their male counterparts.

Here are five women that are or have been a CEO for a company. But for which company?

________ 1	Indra Nooyi	a)	Hewlett-Packard (formerly eBay)
________ 2	Virginia Rometty	b)	PepsiCo
________ 3	Meg Whitman	c)	Kraft Foods
________ 4	Marissa Mayer	d)	IBM
________ 5	Irene Rosenfeld	e)	Yahoo

122 Listen and recall

Listen to the interview with Nunu Ntshingila-Njeke and then answer the questions below by completing the sentences.

1 Was Nunu's career in advertising planned from an early age?
No, she got into it ________.
2 Her first job in advertising was working with the Unilever brand, Omo. Why was she chosen to read the testimonials for the product?
Because she could ________.
3 Were there a lot of women in advertising when Nunu started?
No, it was ________.
4 Have things changed now?
Not a lot, but in the last 25 years it has ________.
5 What does Nunu say about consumers?
She says that they're both ________.
6 How will having more women affect creative work?
The portrayal of women in advertising ________.
7 Why do women often leave a company?
In order to ________.
8 When Nunu started in advertising, who wasn't the industry really friendly towards?
It wasn't friendly towards ________ or ________.

9 What did Nunu study at university that has helped her a lot?
She studied ______.

10 What other characteristic do you need in order to succeed in advertising?
You need ______.

11 Which advertising campaign is Nunu particularly proud of?
The campaigns she did for ______.

12 Does Nunu read or watch TV in her spare time?
No, she prefers to ______.

13 What, in her opinion, is especially important for black women?
Having a woman as a ______.

Practise the vocabulary in Wordmatch/Spelling

123 Interact

1. Nunu speaks of women mentorship. How can a mentor help you in your career?
2. Do you have any experience of mentorship?
3. According to Forbes magazine, women still make up less than 3% of the CEOs of companies. Why do you think there are still so few women at the head of companies?

124 Expand your vocabulary: Synonyms

A 'synonym' is a word that is similar in meaning to another word. English is full of synonyms or near synonyms and it's worth knowing some of the most common ones.

Complete the sentences below with an adjective that is similar in meaning to the word in **bold type**. Choose from the following words. Not all of them will be used.

arrogant	risky	strict	very angry
lazy	rough	unfriendly	very sociable
puzzling	short	uninteresting	weak

1. An **irate** person is ______.
2. A **choppy** sea is ______.
3. A **hostile** reception is ______.
4. A **baffling** problem is ______.
5. A **flimsy** structure is ______.
6. A **curt** message is ______.
7. A **hazardous** journey is ______.

Now go to the Expand your vocabulary section of the book and do the exercise *Words of similar meanings (synonyms)* on pages 334–335.

125 **Project**

Use the Internet to find out more about a successful company. Describe their line of business, how it all started, how it's run today, where they're active, etc.

For advice on writing a project see Resource Section pages 168–169.

CREATIVE DESTRUCTION (page 84)

126 **Starter**

Put a cross (X) next to any of the following hi-tech gadgets that you or someone in your family have ever owned or still own?

- ☐ a 3D printer
- ☐ a blue-ray player
- ☐ a Sony Walkman
- ☐ a Bluetooth earpiece
- ☐ a camcorder
- ☐ a cassette recorder
- ☐ a CD player
- ☐ a digital camera
- ☐ a DVD player
- ☐ a Game Boy
- ☐ a laptop
- ☐ a Nintendo Wii
- ☐ a smartphone
- ☐ a Sony playstation
- ☐ a tablet (e.g. iPad)
- ☐ a video player
- ☐ an HD TV
- ☐ an Mp3 player (e.g. iPod)
- ☐ an X-box
- ☐ a Polaroid camera
- ☐ stereo headphones
- ☐ an e-book reader (e.g. Kindle)

Which of the ones you crossed have you stopped using?
Are there any other gadgets you could add to the list?
What's the 'must-have' gadget for you at the moment?

127 **Textwork**

Without looking back at the text *Creative Destruction* on page 84, match the opening words of sentences 1–8 with the correct endings.

1 The phrase 'creative destruction'
2 New emerging companies create new jobs and
3 When digital cameras came along
4 Creative destruction
5 Traditional economics focuses on
6 Ruined companies and disappearing industries
7 Creative destruction focuses on
8 Capitalism can only thrive if

A are both inevitable and necessary.
B there is innovation.
C was coined by Joseph Schumpeter.
D price competition.
E Polaroid's market disappeared.
F new products or technologies.
G is driven by entrepreneurs.
H allow economies to grow.

Practise the vocabulary in Wordmatch/Spelling

128 Vocabulary: Choose the word

129 Interact

1 Why do you think it's important for some people to have the latest hi-tech gadgets? What about you?
2 What hi-tech products will be out-dated next? What will come instead?

130 Writing

Write a letter to the editor complaining about the use of mobile phones everywhere and asking for a no-mobile sign in some public areas.

For advice on how to write a letter to the editor see the digital Resource Section. Also remember to use linking words in your letter. See Resource Section pages 176–179.

WSM: IT'S POLAROID'S WORLD - WE JUST LIVE IN IT

SHOPPING, SEDUCTION & MR SELFRIDGE (page 85)

131 Starter

There are many famous department stores in London. What do you know about the following stores: Harrods, Marks & Spencer, Primark and Selfridges?

132 Textwork

Read through the text *Shopping, Seduction & Mr Selfridge* on pages 85–87 and decide which of the four alternatives (A, B, C or D) you think is correct.

1 What was the main thing that department stores offered?
- A ☐ high fashion
- B ☐ great cathedrals
- C ☐ seduction
- D ☐ good architecture

2 What do we learn about Harry Gordon Selfridge?
- A ☐ He wasn't very modest.
- B ☐ He was fairly tall.
- C ☐ He had visions.
- D ☐ He had music hall entertainment at his store.

3 What was the main result of positioning the perfume and cosmetics department immediately inside the main entrance?
- A ☐ The sales floor smelled nice.
- B ☐ Women shoppers were happier.
- C ☐ His store became the third biggest tourist attraction in London.
- D ☐ He made more money.

4 Which of these is **not** true about Mr Selfridge?
- A ☐ He was a celebrity.
- B ☐ He didn't spend very much on advertising.
- C ☐ He created window dressing as an art form.
- D ☐ He personally inspected his store every morning.

5 How did Britain's industrial revolution help Selfridge's?
- A ☐ Most of the population had big houses to equip.
- B ☐ There was a huge demand for servants.
- C ☐ People were proud to show off their homes.
- D ☐ People had lots of money to spend.

6 How did department stores change women's lives?
  - A ☐ They were now able to go out and buy things for themselves.
  - B ☐ They didn't need to spend all their time in church.
  - C ☐ They could walk to them rather than go by carriage.
  - D ☐ Shopping began to jeopardize their reputations.

7 What did Selfridge introduce at his Marshall Field's Store in Chicago?
  - A ☐ A doctor's waiting-room with a nurse.
  - B ☐ Fixed prices only.
  - C ☐ The art of just looking at goods without having to buy them.
  - D ☐ A small library.

Practise the vocabulary in Wordmatch/Spelling

133 Vocabulary: Unscramble the letters

Unscramble the letters to find a word that fits into the sentence. All the words are taken from the text. To help you, the first letter of the word is given.

1	satingob	"I hope you don't think I'm b__________, but I can actually speak six languages."
2	cyanfin	Genetic engineering is still in its i__________.
3	ticengin	The offer was just too e__________ to refuse.
4	baitaliens	There seems to be an i__________ demand for more powerful smartphones and tablets.
5	puritantoe	Apple is a company that has a r__________ for innovation and good design.
6	hearstog	In the UK there's a s__________ of teachers in the big cities, especially in London.
7	ragsped	Harry Selfridge really g__________ the idea of consumption as a sensual entertainment.
8	laidspy	There's been a beautiful floral d__________ outside the Town Hall all week.
9	garlabuy	Ayrton Senna was a__________ the greatest racing driver of all time.
10	swobgrin	"Can I help you, madam?" asked the shop assistant. "No, thank you. I'm just b__________."
11	tinompoor	Marks & Spencer are doing a special p__________ of New Zealand wines this week.
12	liratree	Tesco is the largest food r__________ in the UK.
13	rivalyanib	Our bus to work is i__________ late in the morning.
14	manscopes	The festival is to e__________ everything from music, theatre and ballet to literature, cinema and the visual arts.

134 Interact

1 How did Mr Selfridge change the department store to make shopping more fun?

2 Do men and women have different shopping habits? Give examples.

3 Are you a price conscious shopper? Do you compare prices at different stores when you shop?
4 When you buy something, what things are most important to you? Price? Quality? Fashion trends? Status or image? Anything else?
5 How do you shop? On the Internet, in regular stores? Have you come across a pop up store?

135 Project

What makes a good print ad? Here's one example that brings the message of global warming home to people.

Work in pairs. Type into your favourite search engine the following words: good print ads

You should be shown lots of websites with good print ads. Look through some of them and try to choose two that you think are really good and that you're also able to explain why they're so good. Download them, if possible. Now find another pair and compare your choices.

See Resource Section *On Advertising* for help when analysing your ads.

136 Follow up

1 Are there any memorable TV adverts you can remember? What made them so memorable?
2 What different methods of advertising are there? (newspapers, television, etc.)? Which do you think is the most effective?
3 What do you think of celebrity endorsements? Do they work? Can you remember which celebrities advertise which products?

137 Use of English: Word-building 1

In the two previous chapters you did exercises on filling gaps with one word only. Now it is time to look at word-building.

Complete the following sentences by changing the words in **bold type** into a word (noun, adjective, adverb or verb) that fit suitably in each gap.

1 I'm sorry , I'll be ____________ to attend the meeting tomorrow. **ABLE**
2 There was a loud ____________ when the bomb went off. **EXPLODE**
3 "Do sit down and make yourself ____________." **COMFORT**
4 Gagana was the only ____________ for the job. **APPLY**
5 My ____________ is to leave by the first available plane. **INTEND**

Now go to the Use of English section of the book and do the exercise *Word-building 1* on page 356.

138 Speaking/Writing

Write a short argumentative speech and speak for 2-3 minutes to a small group.
Choose one of the following topics or make up your own dealing with shopping in one way or another.

Have a shopping detox for a year - Buy only recycled clothes - Buy this fantastic item - Buy only fairtrade products

For advice on argumentative writing see Resource Section page 166. Also make use of linking words on pages 176-179.

LISTENING: NEWS ITEMS

139 Listen and recall

You're going to hear 7 news items. They'll be read ONCE only. After each news item there'll be a pause for you to answer the questions by choosing one of the letters A, B, C or D. After writing your answer, you may also like to look at the question which follows.

1 Why did the pensioner decide to grow cannabis?
A To help people with health problems.
B To help a friend and share half the profits with him.
C Because he was unemployed.
D Because his pension wasn't big enough.

2 What does this news item tell us about the wheelchairs?
A They've been modified to enable disabled visitors to enjoy a future event in Dubai.
B The wheels are not very easy to remove.
C They will be used in 80 percent of the beach parks in Dubai.
D They can be reserved and used for a small fee.

3 What is this news item about?
A Police violence.
B Banning violent football supporters.
C Violent clashes between rival football supporters.
D Local football team rivalry.

4 Choose the most suitable headline for this report.
A 91-year-old woman battles cancer
B 91-year-old women sets two new records
C 91-year-old women raises money to fight cancer
D 91-year-old cancer victim promises to run again

5 What do we learn about the food that's served at the La Cocinita de San Juan restaurant in Mexico?

A The customers often send dishes back.

B The tacos include scorpions which waiters catch in the hills.

C The tacos they serve contain unusual ingredients.

D It includes insect soup.

6 What do we learn about the cloning of cats?

A They can be cloned either before or after a cat dies.

B It takes about three months to clone a cat.

C You pay $50,000 when you receive the clone.

D At present, the company clones about 50 kittens a year.

7 What would be the most suitable headline for this report?

A Snakes don't like eating hamsters

B A snake and a hamster are great friends

C A snake shares some mice with a hamster

D A relationship doomed to end in disaster

Practise the vocabulary in Wordmatch/Spelling

---

140 Critical reading and reviewing

Pick an article from either *The Sun* or the *Daily Mirror* and analyse it critically by using the questions in Resource Section page 151.

141 Sum up and comment

1 What different aspects of consumerism have you come across in this unit?

2 How did your argumentative text turn out? What do you need to improve until next time?

3 Write in your learning log, see Resource Section page 149, and comment on three questions of your own choice.

142 Books to read and enjoy

Kinsella, Sophie: *Confessions of a Shopaholic*
Lapcharoensap, Rattawut: *Sightseeing*
Martin, Steve: *Shopgirl: A Novel*
Weisberger, Lauren: *The Devil Wears Prada, Revenge Wears Prada*
Woodhead, Lindy: *Shopping, Seduction & Mr Selfridge*

6 THE ARTS

NIPPLE JESUS

- ☐ Starter
- ☐ Textwork
- ☐ Vocabulary: Definitions
- ☐ Interact
- ☐ Let's talk!

WSM: TWO SHOCKING EXAMPLES OF PERFORMANCE ART

PAINTING IS NOTHING NEW

- ☐ Starter: One word only
- ☐ Textwork
- ☐ Vocabulary: Choose the word
- ☐ Interact
- ☐ Activity
- ☐ Project
- ☐ Expand your vocabulary: Two words make one (compound words]

TWO LOVE POEMS

- ☐ Starter
- ☐ Textwork
- ☐ Interact
- ☐ Writing a Limerick

LISTENING: THE CARRIE DIARIES

- ☐ Starter
- ☐ Listen and recall
- ☐ Vocabulary: Which word?
- ☐ Interact
- ☐ Use of English: Word-building 2 & 3

FAREWELL, CAMDEN TOWN

- ☐ Starter
- ☐ Textwork
- ☐ Vocabulary: Right or wrong?
- ☐ Interact
- ☐ Writing

WSM: MITCH'S EULOGY FOR AMY

REHAB

- ☐ Textwork
- ☐ Interact
- ☐ Project

WSM: ELVIS PRESLEY – STORY OF A SUPERSTAR

LISTENING: MEET JUDI DENCH

- ☐ Starter
- ☐ Listen and recall
- ☐ Vocabulary: Choose the word
- ☐ Vocabulary: Fill in the gaps
- ☐ Interact
- ☐ Project
- ☐ Looking at words to do with the theatre
- ☐ Act it out

- ☐ Sum up and comment
- ☐ Books to read and enjoy

NIPPLE JESUS (page 90)

143 Starter

Look at the following poster

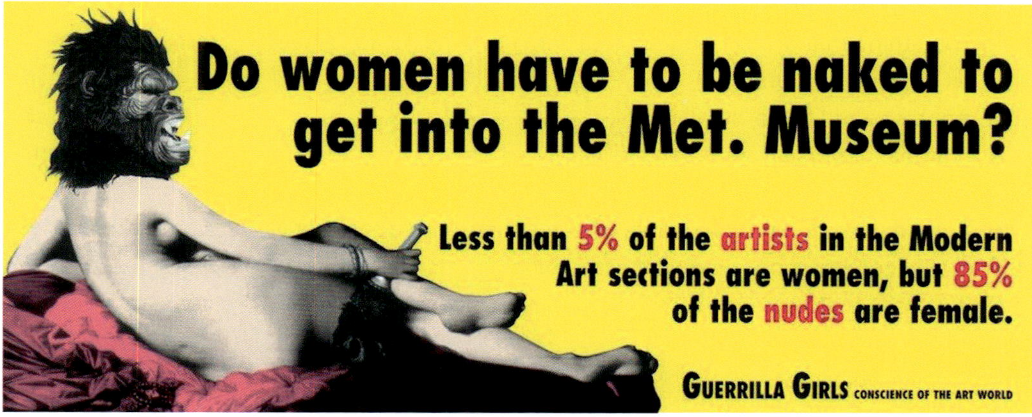

(Guerilla Girls, *Do Women Have to be Naked to get into the Met. Museum?* (1990), New York)

Which adjectives would you use to describe it? Shocking, amusing, etc.
What do you think about the picture introducing this unit (page 89)?

144 Textwork

Read *Nipple Jesus* on pages 90–93. Then fill in the missing information or choose the correct answer (a, b or c). The sentences are in no special order.

1 Only people over the age of __________ were allowed to see the picture.
2 At first Dave couldn't understand why anyone would be offended by the picture. *a) True b) False*
3 The artist has cut all the pictures out of __________ magazines.
4 At first glance, the painting of Jesus seemed *a) quite normal b) very unusual c) startling.*
5 Dave finally notices that the picture is made up of tiny squares, each of which is a picture of a __________.
6 Dave had got a new job as a*) a sentry b) a guard c) an art critic.*
7 The painting made Dave feel Jesus really was suffering a lot of __________.
8 In Dave's opinion, religious people are *a) posh b) very unpleasant c) a bit mad.*
9 The young couple looked at *a) each other b) Dave c) the picture* and laughed.
10 The exhibit behind the curtain was described as *a) offended b) out of order c) controversial.*
11 The *a) posh woman b) man* seemed to like the picture.
12 Dave was shocked that the artist was a woman. *a) True b) False*

Practise the vocabulary in Wordmatch/Spelling

145 Vocabulary: Definitions

Here are definitions of eight words from the text. Can you work out what they are? To help you, the first and last letter of each missing word is given.

1	Something that's ______ causes a lot of angry public discussion and disagreement	c__________l
2	Something that a king or queen wears on his or her head, usually on official occasions.	c__________n
3	Another word for to 'steal'.	p__________h
4	A stupid or unpleasant person. (*slang*)	t__________r
5	A slightly offensive word for a young woman.	b__________d
6	A word used to describe people who belong to a high social class.	p__________h
7	A soldier whose job is to guard something.	s__________y
8	If you say that someone is out of ______, you mean that their behaviour is unacceptable.	o__________r

146 Interact

1. How does the man's attitude to the painting and the artist change throughout the story? Give examples from the text.
2. Can you understand why this picture was given an R-certificate? Would you have found this picture offensive? Why? Why not?
3. Do you think it's the duty of an artist to shock people?
4. Why does art have an important role in society?

147 Let's talk!

Name three things ...

Work in two teams – A and B (2–3 people per team). You're going to be asked to name three things as quickly as possible. For example:

Can you name three things that would be useful on a desert island?
For each answer that's considered appropriate you score 1 point.
Your teacher will give you more information.

WSM: TWO SHOCKING EXAMPLES OF PERFORMANCE ART

PAINTING IS NOTHING NEW (page 94)

148 **Starter: One word only**

Read the following text about the famous graffiti artist Banksy and write ONE word in each gap. The word you write must make sense in the text and be grammatically correct.

The Story Behind Banksy

On his way to becoming an international icon, the subversive and secretive street artist turned the art world upside-down.

When *Time* magazine (1)__________ the British artist Banksy - graffiti master, painter, activist, filmmaker and all-purpose *provocateur* - for its (2)__________ of the world's 100 most influential people in 2010, he found himself in the company of Barack Obama, Steve Jobs and Lady Gaga. He supplied a picture of himself with a paper bag (recyclable, naturally) (3)__________ his head. Most of his fans don't really want to know who he is (and have loudly protested at newspaper journalists' (4)__________ to unmask him). But they do want to follow his upward trajectory from the outlaw "bombing" (i.e. spraying) - walls in Bristol, England, during the 1990s to the artist (5)__________ work commands hundreds of thousands of dollars in the auction houses of Britain and America. Today, he has bombed cities from Vienna to San Francisco, Barcelona to Paris and Detroit. And he has (6)__________ from graffiti on gritty urban walls to paint on canvas, conceptual sculpture and even film, with his documentary *Exit Through the Gift Shop* even (7)__________ nominated for an Academy Award.

'Pest Control', the tongue-in-cheek-titled organization (8)__________ up by the artist to authenticate the real Banksy artwork, also protects him from prying outsiders. Hiding behind a paper bag, or, more commonly, e-mail, Banksy relentlessly controls his own narrative. His last face-to-face interview took (9)__________ in 2003.

While he may shelter behind a concealed identity, he advocates a direct connection (10)__________ an artist and his constituency. "There's a whole new audience out there, and it's never been easier to sell [one's art]," Banksy has maintained. "You don't have to go to college, drag 'round a portfolio, mail off transparencies to snooty galleries or sleep with someone powerful, all you need now is a few ideas and a broadband (11)__________. This is the first time the essentially bourgeois world of art has (12)__________ to the people. We need to make it count."

(Extract from *The Story Behind Banksy* by Will Ellsworth-Jones, Smithsonian Magazine February 2013)

What do you know about Banksy?

149 Textwork

Work in pairs. Read through the text *Painting Is Nothing New* on pages 94–95. Take turns to ask and answer the following questions.

1 What is meant by the phrase "Painting is nothing new"?
2 Why are man-made images important for people?
3 Give three examples of things which paintings have adorned?
4 Do paintings have the same value, meaning and purpose for every culture?
5 What has happened to people's experience of life in the last 100 years?
6 How has this affected the artist?
7 Why did Haring say that the image maker is more important now than at any other time in the history of man?

Practise the vocabulary in Wordmatch/Spelling

150 Vocabulary: Choose the word

151 Interact

1 Do you think computers will one day also have imagination comparable to human imagination? Why?/Why not?
2 How important is imagination and creativity in everyone's life? In society?
3 What does it take to be a successful artist? Which of the following do you think is most important?
a) natural talent b) hard work c) marketing skills d) luck e) help from other people
f) choosing shocking or controversial subjects g) something else (what?)
4 Do you like visiting art museums? Have you ever been to any famous ones?
5 Do you think of cartoons, comics and graffiti as art? Why? Why not?
6 Do you think performance art should be considered art? Give reasons.

152 Activity

1 According to a well-known saying, " The camera never lies". Do you agree or disagree with this?
2 Give some arguments for or against the claim that photography is an art.
3 How can we learn about the way a culture sees the world by studying its art?

153 Project

You're going to talk about your favourite painting/picture. If you need some suggestions here are some artists you can look at.

William Turner, David Hockney, Francis Bacon, Annie Leibovitz, Cindy Sherman, Andy Warhol, Yoko Ono, Roy Lichtenstein, Edward Hopper.

Your teacher will give you more information. Speak to a small group and make use of *Peer-response speaking* in Resource Section page 159.

154 Expand your vocabulary: Two words make one (compound words)

In English, many words are made up of two words joined together, e.g. cupboard (cup + board), earring (ear + ring), etc. or two separate words with a new meaning, e.g. washing machine, post office, car park, etc. In this unit you're going to practise forming some common compound nouns and adjectives.
Take a word from A and a word from B to form a new word. Write each word next to the correct definition below. Some words will be a single word, e.g. postman, while others will be two words, e.g. shop assistant.

A		**B**	
alarm	time	clock	mare
frog	youth	hostel	table
night		man	

1 ________ A very bad dream.
2 ________ A cheaper place to stay compared to a hotel.
3 ________ You need this if you want to be on time for work.
4 ________ This person could help you to search a lake in search of a murder weapon or a dead body.
5 ________ If you have one of these you shouldn't miss your bus.

Now go to the Expand your vocabulary section of the book and do the exercise *Two words make one (compound words)* on pages 336–338.

TWO LOVE POEMS (page 96)

155 Starter

How would you explain to a ten-year-old what a poem is?

Practise the vocabulary in Wordmatch/Spelling

156 Textwork

1 What is the difference in the description of love in the two poems?
2 What similarities are there between the poems?

157 **Interact**

1 Which of the *Two Love Poems* on page 96 did you prefer? Why?
2 What other topics apart from love are found in poems?
3 In music lyrics the theme is often about love. Find some examples.

158 **Writing a Limerick**

A limerick is a humorous poem which contains 5 lines altogether.
Lines 1, 2 and 5 must rhyme with each other, so must lines 3 and 4. Here's an example:

1 Smith Minor, whose first name was Paul
2 Just narrowly missed a bad fall.
3 He broke several teeth
4 And the jawbone beneath,
5 Seven ribs, and a leg, but that's all!
(Rhymes: *Paul-fall-all ... teeth-beneath*)

A Work in pairs. Fill in the missing words in the limerick below. Choose from the following. Remember: Lines 1, 2 and 5 must rhyme with each other, so must lines 3 and 4.

a	bus	made	again	fuss
on	all	Jane	on	lady
she	terribly	threw	was	young

A nervous ________ ________ called ________,
________ ________ sick ________ ________ train.
People ________ such a ________,
________ got ________ a ________,
And ________ up ________ over ________.

B Now try your hand at writing your own limerick. You can choose one of these openings (or use one of your own).

1 There was a fat waiter from Spain ...
2 A teacher, whose first name was Pete ...
3 While brushing her hair by the fire ...
4 While travelling from Bangkok by train ...
5 There was a deaf lady from Reading ...
6 I once had a bulldog called Rover ...
7 A chef by the name of Jill Brown ...
8 There was a young lady from Chile ...
9 A young man as bald as a bat ...
10 A very strange fellow called Clark ...

Before you start, think up as many rhyming words as you can for the word at the end of the first line. This will help you to get some ideas. Here's an example for the first one.

Spain: rain, drain, pain, again, plain, plane, gain, main, cane, Dane, feign, grain, Jane, Kane, lain, insane, stain, attain, vain, vein, wane, regain, inane

LISTENING: THE CARRIE DIARIES

159 Starter

What do you know about *The Carrie Diaries*?

160 Listen and recall

Listen to an extract from *The Carrie Diaries.* As you listen, fill in the missing information or choose the correct answer. Before you start, read through the sentences below.

1 The woman with white hair is drinking __________.
2 We understand from George that Carrie is *a) a dancer b) a singer c) a writer.*
3 According to the woman, the work of writers *a) from the upper-classes b) from the middle classes c) who have suffered greatly* are of no real value.
4 Carrie has met the woman once before at a bookshop in Castlebury. *a) True b) False*
5 Carrie had asked the woman to sign a book for __________.
6 Carrie's mother is dead. *a) True b) False*
7 Bunny remembers that Carrie was wearing __________ ribbons.
8 Carrie thinks the sherry she's drinking tastes like __________.
9 From the text we gather that Carrie is a) *a movie star b) pretty c) amusing.*
10 According to George's aunt if you want to be a great writer then you shouldn't have any __________.
11 Something Carrie says makes Bunny *a) cry b) laugh c) become sarcastic.*
12 Bunny gives Carrie a signed copy of her latest book. *a) True b) False*
13 On the way home, George buys Carrie a __________.
14 According to the author of *The Writer's LIfe*, you shouldn't write about who you know. Instead you should write about what you know about __________.

Practise the vocabulary in Wordmatch/Spelling

161 Vocabulary: Which word?

Here are some words found in the listening exercise *The Carrie Dairies.*

audible	choked	in astonishment	journal
beam	fearful	indicate	meretricious
by rote	guffaw	interject	simulacrum

Which of the above...

1 is another word for 'frightened'? __________
2 is something that's made to look like something else? __________
3 is something loud enough to be heard? __________
4 fits into this sentence: *She _____ on a piece of bread.* __________
5 is another word for 'to show'? to __________

6 is something that seems attractive but has no real value? __________
7 is to laugh noisily? to __________
8 is another word for 'to exclaim'? to __________
9 fits into this sentence: *He learnt the poem _____.* __________
10 is another word for a 'diary'? a __________
11 fits into this sentence: *He looked at me _____ when I told him he'd won £1 million on the National Lottery.* __________
12 is to smile with obvious pleasure? to __________

162 **Interact**

1 What kind of person is Bunny, do you think?
2 What do you think about the advice on writing Bunny gives to Carrie?
3 Have you ever seen *The Carrie Dairies*? What do you think of it?
4 What series, if any, are you following now?

163 **Use of English: Word-building 2 & 3**

In the previous chapter you did an exercise on word-building. Here's another chance to practise.

Complete the following sentences by changing the words in **bold type** into one word (noun, adjective, adverb or verb) that fits suitably in each gap.

1 I'm sorry to __________ with you, but I think you're wrong. **AGREE**
2 We heard their __________ as they ran along the corridor. **FOOT**
3 It's __________ in some countries for the bride's father to pay for the wedding. **CUSTOM**
4 "Pay __________ to what I'm saying!" **ATTEND**
5 This year's exam was __________ easy. It's usually a lot harder. **COMPARE**

Now go to the Use of English section of the book and do the exercises *Word-building 2 & Word-building 3* on pages 357–358.

FAREWELL, CAMDEN TOWN (page 97)

164 **Starter**

How much do you know about Amy Winehouse? Did you like her music? Why? Why not? Do you remember where you were when you heard about her death?

165 **Textwork**

Read *Farewell, Camden Town* on pages 97–99. Then complete the statements below, basing your answers on information in the text. Answer briefly and, as far as possible, in your own words. Read each statement very carefully so that your completion fits in with it.

1 At the news of Amy's death, her father was obviously ...

2 According to Andrew, Amy had been ...

3 When Andrew checked on Amy for the second time in the morning, he realized that ...

4 It wasn't really true that during the year and a half before her death, ...

5 Amy's clothes were neatly arranged in her wardrobe in the time before her death, which meant that ...

6 Her father was unaware that a week before her death, Amy ...

7 Amy couldn't have died from a drug overdose because ...

8 The following day they had to go to the mortuary to ...

9 The slight red blotchiness to her skin could be proof that she ...

10 The police weren't sure if Amy's death ...

11 The square where Amy lived ...

12 Amy's Foundation was intended to help ...

13 The post-mortem examination ...

14 Amy's funeral took place ...

15 Amy's body ...

Practise the vocabulary in Wordmatch/Spelling

166 Vocabulary: Right or wrong?

Work in pairs. Check that you've understood some of the words used in the text by stating whether they're used correctly in the following sentences. Mark each sentence R (Right) or W (Wrong). If wrong, explain why and write a new sentence to show how the word(s) should be used.

1 He gave a moving **eulogy** when he received an Oscar for Best Actor. __________
2 The death was very suspicious and the police suspected **foul play**. __________
3 "I've been in a complete **daze** since hearing the news of the President's death in a plane crash. I just can't believe it." __________
4 A **coroner** is someone you go to when you have to arrange a funeral. __________
5 You can't think straight when you're mind's in a **turmoil**. __________
6 The course is designed to **equate** students for a career in nursing. __________
7 He wasn't very drunk, but he was certainly a bit **tipsy**. __________
8 There was a large wooden **partition** around the garden. __________
9 The meeting was **adjourned** until Tuesday. __________
10 Manchester City's performances at home have been very **inconclusive** this season. Last season they won most of their home games. __________

167 Interact

1 Amy Winehouse was only 27 when she died. Can you remember any other pop stars who died young?
2 Why do you think so many pop stars and film stars become drug addicts or alcoholics?

168 Writing

Write a discussion essay about drug abuse. Describe the medical and social consequences of taking drugs.

For advice on discussion essays see Resource Section page 165. Remember to use linking words on pages 176–179 and make use of the Checklist for writing on page 156.

WSM: MITCH'S EULOGY FOR AMY

"Amy was the greatest daughter, family member and friend you could ever have. I will talk a lot about her fantastic recovery. Recently Amy found love with Reg. He helped her with her problems and Amy was looking forward to their future together.

She was the happiest she has been for years. We all remember that great night at the 100 Club on Oxford Street, her voice was good, her wit and timing were perfect. She told me that she had "thoroughly, thoroughly enjoyed herself".

The last time she called me she had found a box of old family photos and called me to go over to look. We spoke three times a day at least, she was very excited.

Three years ago, Amy conquered her drug dependency, the doctors said it was impossible but she really did it. She was trying hard to deal with her drinking and had just completed three weeks of abstinence. She said, "Dad I've had enough of drinking, I can't stand the look on your and the family's faces anymore".

She was not depressed. She saw Janis and Reg on Friday and was in good spirits. That night, she was in her room, playing drums and singing. As it was late, her security guard said to keep it quiet and she did. He heard her walking around for a while and when he went to check on her in the morning he thought she was asleep. He went back a few hours later, that was when he realised she was not breathing and called for help.

But knowing she wasn't depressed, knowing she passed away happy, it makes us all feel better.

I was in New York with my cousin Michael when I heard and straight away I said I wanted an Amy Winehouse Foundation, something to help the things she loved – children, horses, but also to help those struggling with substance abuse. In this country, if you cannot afford a private rehabilitation clinic, there is a two-year waiting list for help. With the help of Keith Vaz MP, we are trying to change that.

Goodnight my angel, sleep tight. Mummy and Daddy love you ever so much."

REHAB (page 100)

169 Textwork

1 What reasons does Amy give for not going to rehab?
2 Who are Ray and Mr. Hathaway?

170 Interact

This song is obviously written about Amy Winehouse's own experiences. Do you like the song? What about her other songs?

Practise the vocabulary in Wordmatch/Spelling

171 Project

Choose one of your favourite songs and analyse the lyrics. Present the singer, the lyrics and the interpretation to a group of classmates. For help with vocabulary on figurative language see page 174.

WSM: ELVIS PRESLEY – STORY OF A SUPERSTAR

LISTENING: MEET JUDI DENCH

172 **Starter**

Unlike people in some other jobs, actors can go on working well after they might have retired. Here are 10 actors 1–10, all over the age of 70 who are still working. See if you can match them up with the correct films a-j.

1 ________	Al Pacino b. 1940	a) *Gran Torino*
2 ________	Anthony Hopkins b. 1937	b) *The Dark Knight*
3 ________	Clint Eastwood b.1930	c) *Star Wars*
4 ________	Donald Sutherland b. 1935	d) *Skyfall*
5 ________	Harrison Ford b. 1942	e) *The Godfather*
6 ________	Ian McKellen b. 1939	f) *Harry Potter*
7 ________	Judi Dench b. 1934	g) *The Hunger Games*
8 ________	Maggie Smith b. 1934	h) *The Shawshank Redemption*
9 ________	Michael Caine b. 1933	i) *Silence of the Lambs*
10 ________	Morgan Freeman b. 1937	j) *Lord of the Rings*

Have you seen any of the above films? Which of the actors do you like best? Why?

173 **Listen and recall**

Listen to the British actress Judi Dench talking about her life in the theatre. As you listen, say whether the sentences are true (T) or false (F). Before you start, read through the sentences below.

1 Judi Dench doesn't seem to want to encourage people to be actors. ________
2 Judi Dench does the usual routine things at home, including ironing. ________
3 She always gets to the theatre early before a performance. ________
4 Judi Dench enjoys doing word-runs. ________
5 Before every performance she has a cup of honey. ________
6 A steamer is something you use to help your voice. ________
7 Judi Dench likes to hear the audience over the tannoy while she's waiting in her dressing room. ________
8 She doesn't agree with her husband that you should 'live each day as if it's the last'. ________
9 She hopes to retire once she's sixty-five. ________
10 She would hate to do a one-woman show. ________
11 She thinks she needs to be more choosy about the plays she does. ________
12 She'd love to do a play in New York as she's never worked there. ________

Practise the vocabulary in Wordmatch/Spelling

174 Vocabulary: Choose the word

175 Vocabulary: Fill in the gaps

Fill in the missing words in the sentences below. Choose from the following words, taken from the listening extract *Meet Judi Dench*. Then make up your own sentences for the four words that are left over.

appealing	dressing-gown	royal jelly	tannoy
chanted	on the dot	spout	tedious
conscious	phial	steam	treasure
decline	repertoire	tad	vocal

1 The announcement came over the ________: "The train now standing on platform 6 is the 17.45 to Brighton."
2 George was suddenly very ________ of the fact that he was the only one at the party wearing a tie.
3 "Breakfast is served at 8 o'clock ________," said the owner of the guest house we were staying at.
4 Steam was coming out of the ________ of the kettle.
5 My girlfriend and I split up last week, but I shall always ________ the memory of our time together.
6 "Come on Arsenal! Come on Arsenal!" ________ the home supporters.
7 The Royal Shakespeare Company also has many modern plays in their ________.
8 The fish was OK, but the chips were a ________ greasy.
9 My sister is looking forward to retiring. The idea of not having to get up early every morning is very ________ to her.
10 I never go to the gym as I find all forms of exercise so ________.
11 Industry in our country has been in ________ since the 1980s.
12 The singer's ________ style was strongly influenced by country and blues music.

176 Interact

1 What do you think about Judi Dench's attitude to her job?
2 What films, if any, have you seen, starring Judi Dench?
3 Would you consider working after retirement age? Give reasons.

177 Project

Present your favourite film. Retell the plot briefly and show some clips. Comment on setting, acting, costumes, visual effects etc. Explain why the film has certain qualities that you appreciate. Speak for 3–4 minutes to a small group.

178 Looking at words to do with the theatre

Fill in the missing words in the definitions below. Choose from the following.
Use a dictionary if necessary. Then write your own sentences for the four words left over.

actor	cast	foyer	review
applause	critics	interval	stalls
audience	curtain	matinée	understudy
auditorium	curtain calls	playwrights	usher
box office	dress rehearsal	rehearse	wings

1 The __________ really loved the new musical, as they showed by their loud __________ at the end.
2 The __________ was terrible. Several of the actors forgot their lines, one or two dancers fell over and there was a problem with the lighting. Let's hope the play's a lot better when it opens on Saturday.
3 Not many of the __________ liked the new Andrew Lloyd-Webber musical. In fact, most of them gave it a terrible __________.
4 Nowadays we refer to an __________ as someone who performs on the stage, on television or in films, irrespective of whether they're a man or a woman.
5 Two of the most famous British __________are Tom Stoppard and Harold Pinter.
6 If you can't get to see the play in the evening, then you can always go to a __________ or afternoon performance.
7 She told us that she was once an __________ to Maggie Smith, but no one believed her.
8 We wanted to sit in the circle, but there weren't any tickets left. So we had to sit in the __________ instead.
9 After the final performance of *War Horse*, the director threw a party for the whole __________.
10 We waited for our friends in the __________ before going into the __________.
11 The audience became very quiet as the lights dimmed and the __________ went up.
12 Before actors go on stage, they often wait in the __________, that is, the area on either side of the stage which is hidden from the audience.
13 We picked up the tickets we had ordered on the Internet at the theatre __________.

179 Act it out

Here's your chance to see what you're like as actors. You're going to act out some sketches. Your teacher will give you copies of a sketch to work with.

180 Sum up and comment

1 What kind of art is your favourite? Give reasons.
2 How is your writing progressing? What strategies can you use to be even better?

181 **Books to read and enjoy**

Atwood, Margaret: *Cat's Eye*
Bushnell, Candace: *The Carrie Diaries*
Chevalier, Tracy: *Girl with a Pearl Earring*
Chopin, Kate: *The Awakening*
Cody Epstein, Jennifer: *The Painter from Shanghai*
Doyle, Roddy: *The Commitments*
Hornby, Nick: *Fever Pitch*
Maugham, Somerset: *Of Human Bondage*
Rand, Ayn: *The Fountainhead*
Tremain, Rose: *Music and Silence*
Vonnegut, Kurt: *Bluebird*
West, Rebecca: *The Fountain Overflows*
Winehouse, Mitch: *Amy, My Daughter*

7

7 GLIMPSES OF ENGLAND

TORN ON THE PLATFORM

- [ ] Starter
- [ ] Textwork
- [ ] Interact
- [ ] Focus on types of people 1

WSM: INTERESTING FACTS ABOUT LONDON

WSM: INTERESTING FACTS ABOUT THE UK

A LION WITH A PRICE TAG

- [ ] Starter
- [ ] Textwork
- [ ] Vocabulary: Words of similar meaning
- [ ] Interact

LISTENING: A LION WITH A PRICE TAG CONT.

- [ ] Listen and recall
- [ ] Vocabulary: What's the word?
- [ ] Interact
- [ ] Vocabulary: Sick of the Parrot
- [ ] Expand your vocabulary: Phrasal verbs 1

THE ROAD TO WIGAN PIER

- [ ] Starter
- [ ] Textwork
- [ ] Vocabulary: Definitions
- [ ] Interact
- [ ] Use of English: Find the mistakes 1
- [ ] Retell the stories 1

NO BOUNDARIES

- [ ] Starter
- [ ] Textwork
- [ ] Vocabulary: Fill in the gaps
- [ ] Interact
- [ ] Speaking/Writing
- [ ] Retell the stories 2

THE PEOPLE YOU NEVER HEAR FROM

- ☐ Starter
- ☐ Textwork
- ☐ Vocabulary: Choose the meaning
- ☐ Interact
- ☐ Debate

WSM: WHY BRITAIN'S FALLEN OUT OF LOVE WITH THE WELFARE STATE

- ☐ Sum up and comment
- ☐ Books to read and enjoy

TORN ON THE PLATFORM (page 104)

182 Starter

Check the video 'Torn on the Platform' on YouTube.

183 Textwork

1 Why is he 'torn' on the platform?
2 How long is his trip to be?
3 What time is the train leaving?
4 Which city is he in? Does he leave or does he stay?
5 What examples of rhymes can you find in the song?

184 Interact

1 Have you ever heard this song or seen the video on YouTube? If so, did you like it? Why? Why not?
2 Have you ever had strong feelings about a particular city? If so, describe your feelings.
3 In the song, the singer is undecided as to whether to go or to stay. Have you ever had an experience where you had to make a decision, one way or the other, about something? Describe it and say what you did in the end and if it was the right decision or not.

Practise the vocabulary in Wordmatch/Spelling

185 Focus on types of people 1

Complete the definitions below with a suitable person. Choose from the following. Use a dictionary if necessary.

acquaintance	bystander	gatecrasher	miser
ancestor	casualty	guinea pig	orphan
benefactor	figurehead	hostage	scapegoat
bully	fugitive	lodger	scrounger

1 A __________ is someone who's been captured by a person or organisation and may be killed unless certain demands are met.
2 A __________ is someone who's been hurt in an accident or in a battle.
3 An __________ is someone you know, but not well enough to be called a friend.
4 An __________ is a child whose parents are dead.
5 A __________ is someone who's always hitting or picking on people who are smaller or weaker than himself or herself.
6 A __________ is someone who's running away or hiding, often from the law.
7 An __________ is a member of your family who lived a long time ago.
8 A __________ is someone who loves money and really hates spending it.

9 A ____________ is someone who turns up at a party without being invited to it.
10 A ____________ is someone who rents a room with a family.
11 A ____________ is person who gets money or something they want by asking other people for it rather than by paying for it themself.
12 A ____________ is a person who's standing near or watching something that's happening but isn't taking part in it.
13 A ____________ is a person who's used as a subject in medical or other experiments.
14 A ____________ is a person who's in a high position in a country or an organization but who has no real power or authority.
15 A ____________ is someone who gets the blame for something, even though he or she may not really be responsible for it.
16 A ____________ is someone who gives money or other help to a person or an organization such as a school or charity.

WSM: INTERESTING FACTS ABOUT LONDON

WSM: INTERESTING FACTS ABOUT THE UK

A LION WITH A PRICE TAG (page 106)

186 Starter

Would you consider having a lion as a pet? Give reasons for your answer.

187 Textwork

Read *A Lion with a Price Tag* on pages 106–107. Then say whether the following sentences are true (T) or false (F). But if you can't definitely say if something is true or false from the information given, then mark the sentence don't know (DK). The sentences are in no special order.

1 The female lion cub seemed to be wilder than her brother. ____________
2 They had often fantasized about or dreamed of owning an exotic pet. ____________
3 Harrods were interviewing prospective buyers to make sure they were responsible people who would look after the lions properly. ____________
4 The lion cubs were on sale just before Christmas. ____________
5 They'd first become interested in lions after reading the book *Born Free* by Joy Adamson. ____________

6 They were given the first option to buy Christian. ____________
7 Harrods wanted £250 for the male cub. ____________
8 They were from Australia and had only been in Europe for 6 months. ____________
9 The staff had named the male lion cub Christian. ____________
10 Roy Hazle worked at London zoo. ____________
11 Their interview at Harrods was at 9.30 in the morning. ____________

Practise the vocabulary in Wordmatch/Spelling

188 Vocabulary: Words of similar meaning

Complete the pairs of words below with another word that is similar in meaning. Choose from the following words, all taken from the text.

assimilate	incessantly	investigate	thoroughly
demand	intrigued	irresponsible	undaunted
enchanted	intuitively	restrain	urge

1 examine, inspect, ____________
2 insist on, require, ____________
3 meticulously, systematically, ____________
4 longing, impulse, ____________
5 continually, non-stop, ____________
6 fascinated, interested, ____________
7 digest, take in, ____________
8 curb, suppress, ____________
9 negligent, reckless, ____________
10 not discouraged, undeterred, ____________
11 instinctively, naturally, ____________
12 bewitched, captivated, ____________

189 Interact

1 When do you think the story takes place? In what decade?
2 Do you think it's possible to purchase a lion as a pet today?
3 Give examples of extreme things you can buy today.

LISTENING: A LION WITH A PRICE TAG CONT.

190 Listen and recall

Listen to the continuation of the story *A Lion with a Price Tag.* As you listen, fill in the missing information or choose the correct answer (a, b or c). Before you start, read through the sentences.

1 They took Christian from Harrods to *a) Knightsbridge b) Chelsea c) Mayfair.*
2 They had to stop the car frequently because Christian was feeling ___________.
3 Christian calmed down when they gave him a huge teddy bear to play with.
a) True b) False
4 Sophistocat is the name of *a) a street b) a restaurant c) a shop.*
5 Name one group of people that London in the 1990s had become a Mecca for.
___________.
6 London at this time was called ' ___________ London'.
7 Mary Quant was a popular *a) fashion designer b) singer c) painter.*
8 Name one other exotic pet mentioned in the text.
___________.
9 It took Christian quite a long time to adjust to his new home. *a) True b) False*
10 Christian was now ___________ months old.
11 Which part of his body dominated his appearance?
a) his paws b) his head and ears c) his eyes
12 Which two things did Christian quickly learn?
His ___________.

Practise the vocabulary in Wordmatch/Spelling

191 Vocabulary: What's the word?

What are the missing words in the following sentences? To help you, some letters of the word are already given. All the words are from the listening exercise.

1 He s _ _ _ mb _ _ d up the cliff and raced towards the car. ___________
2 Jake is a _ _ s _ d _ _ t of Chicago. ___________
3 We go to the cinema quite f _ _ q _ _ n _ _ y. ___________
4 So far the escaped prisoner has _ v _ d _ d capture. ___________
5 Not enough is often done for the v _ _ t _ m of a crime. ___________
6 Much to her e _ b _ rr _ ss _ _ _ t she realized that everybody had been listening to her singing. ___________
7 It didn't take long for the lion cub to adjust to his _ u _ r _ _ nd _ _ g _. ___________
8 Something that's _ ph _ m _ _ _ l lasts or is used for only a short period of time.
____
9 My keys were here a minute ago but now they've v _ _ _ s _ _ d. ___________
10 Do you think boys are more b _ _ st _ r _ _ s than girls? ___________
11 We c _ dd _ _ _ up together under the blanket. ___________
12 "Careful you don't tread in that p _ _ d _ e," she said as we were walking along the path after heavy rain. ___________

192 **Interact**

1 How long do you think it's possible to keep a lion in a house?
2 Why do you think people want to keep exotic animals?
3 What do you think happened next? Check *Christian the Lion/ A Lion Called Christian* on YouTube.
4 What, if anything, do you know about 'Swinging London'? Have you heard of any of the groups or fashion designers mentioned?

193 **Vocabulary: Sick of the Parrot**

Read the following short text about a parrot. A number of words have been left out. Below you will find four alternatives for each gap. Choose the **best** alternative A, B, C or D.

At first parishioners thought it was a blessing when the pigeons living in God's house were joined by an exotic companion. The __**1**__ of the African Grey parrot's glorious plumage adorning the tower of their 13th century church raised the congregation's spirits on even the cloudiest of days. But the creature's foul manners are __**2**__ the feathers of anyone who is brave enough to venture into the churchyard of St Mary's at Mirfield in Yorkshire. For the bird's behaviour and language are just as colourful as its bright red tail.

The vicar, The Reverend Peter Craig-Wilde, is being swamped with __**3**__ from passers-by who have become regular __**4**__ for wolf-whistling and abuse from the bird. The parrot, which is thought to have escaped from its owner, arrived four months ago.

The shocked vicar first became aware of it when an unfamiliar voice from above started telling him in no __**5**__ terms where to go. The bird has been taught to swear by its previous owner and repeatedly uses - very loudly - the only expression it knows: "**** off!"

Mr Craig-Wilde said. "It's very friendly and that's causing the problems. It doesn't just sing, it wolf-whistles at people as they walk past, especially me. Most people find this very funny but we are a working church and when it flies about at funerals it can cause problems. He added: "We have tried to __**6**__ the bird down from the bell tower, but it seems to have settled in." Mr Craig-Wilde said the parrot also wolf-whistles __**7**__ church services and weddings.

Tim Wood, who runs the nearby Old Colonial pub, __**8**__ the parrot while walking his three dogs past the church. "I couldn't believe it when I first heard the parrot," he said. "I thought I must have __**9**__ someone because of the language that was being used. It was only when I looked up and saw the parrot with its long red tail that I realised who was telling me to "**** off."

Mr Craig-Wilde said the bird's __**10**__ has created a lot of interest in his church. "People keep coming just to see the parrot," he said. "There's not a lot that anyone can do until he decides he's had enough. But it looks like he's enjoying his freedom a bit too much at the moment."

1	A ☐ incident	B ☐ report	C ☐ view	D ☐ sight
2	A ☐ shaking	B ☐ ruffling	C ☐ cutting	D ☐ messing
3	A ☐ complaints	B ☐ grumbling	C ☐ objections	D ☐ annoyance
4	A ☐ goals	B ☐ intentions	C ☐ objects	D ☐ targets
5	A ☐ exact	B ☐ unclear	C ☐ uncertain	D ☐ definite
6	A ☐ twist	B ☐ coax	C ☐ trap	D ☐ urge
7	A ☐ through	B ☐ under	C ☐ into	D ☐ around
8	A ☐ caught up with	B ☐ glanced	C ☐ spotted	D ☐ viewed
9	A ☐ surprised	B ☐ distressed	C ☐ shaken up	D ☐ upset
10	A ☐ company	B ☐ presence	C ☐ absence	D ☐ behaving

194 **Expand your vocabulary: Phrasal verbs 1**

A verb followed by a particle or preposition (e.g. come across, bring up, call off, etc.) is called a phrasal verb. To be really fluent in English – especially spoken English – it's essential that you know the most common ones.

Fill in the missing phrasal verbs in the sentences below. Choose from the following and make any verb changes that may be necessary. To help you, there's a Swedish translation in brackets after each sentence.

call on	give up	hand in
give away	go on	look after

1 We were so tired that we just couldn't __________ working any longer. *(fortsätta)*
2 If you're visiting Liverpool next week, why don't you __________ my sister. I know she'd be delighted to see you again. *(hälsa på)*
3 'Could you __________ my bag while I make a phone call?' *(se efter, passa)*
4 John __________ smoking in 1995 and hasn't smoked since. *(sluta)*
5 The teacher asked the students to __________ their homework on Friday. *(lämna in)*
6 Last week *PC World* __________ a free printer with each computer system bought. *(ge bort)*

Now go to the Expand your vocabulary section of the book and do the exercise *Phrasal verbs 1* on pages 339–340.

THE ROAD TO WIGAN PIER (page 108)

195 Starter

What sort of things do you associate with mining? What films set in a mining area have you seen?

196 Textwork

Without looking back at the text *The Road to Wigan Pier* on pages 108–110, match up the sentence openings 1–12 with the correct endings a–l.

______ 1 Most miners have experienced	a)	to be brought to the surface.
______ 2 Miner's use a Davy lamp to	b)	the death of a workmate.
______ 3 A spark from a pick striking a stone	c)	as fast as an express train.
______ 4 Most mine accident are caused by	d)	test the air for gas.
______ 5 Gas explosions are	e)	a roof isn't safe.
______ 6 Better machinery has made mining	f)	it can sometimes crash into the pit bottom.
______ 7 A blue flame from the Davy lamp	g)	more dangerous.
______ 8 Injured miners can take hours	h)	gas explosions.
______ 9 Because the cage is operated by someone on the surface	i)	they give some warning before they collapse.
______ 10 The cage often moves	j)	signals a high level of gas.
______ 11 Wooden props are used because	k)	can set off a gas explosion.
______ 12 Experienced miners know instinctively when	l)	the chief danger of mining.

Practise the vocabulary in Wordmatch/Spelling

197 Vocabulary: Definitions

Here are definitions of ten words from the text. Can you work out what they are? To help you, the first and last letter of each missing word is given.

1 A narrow crack in a rock or wall. c__________e
2 A strong beam, made of iron or steel, that supports a floor, roof, or bridge. g__________r
3 To discover or notice something, especially something that's not easy to see, hear, etc. d__________t
4 To some extent; not completely. p__________y
5 To burn slowly without a flame. s__________r

6 A sudden event such as a flood, storm, or accident which causes great damage or suffering. d__________r

7 The top layer of an area of water or land. s__________e

8 The piece of string in the centre of a candle which you light so that the candle burns. w__________k

9 An ability to do something well, especially because you've learned and practised it. s__________l

10 When you _____ your teeth or fists, you press or squeeze them together tightly, usually because you feel angry or determined. c__________h

198 Interact

1 Why do you think people take on dangerous jobs?

2 Orwell describes life in the 1930s in Great Britain. Where do accidents happen today?

3 What do you think causes accidents in mines or other workplaces nowadays?

199 Use of English: Find the mistakes 1

In the previous chapters you did exercises on word-building. It's time for another type of exercise now – trying to find various mistakes in sentences, usually an extra word that doesn't belong there.

Read the following text and look carefully at each line. Some of the lines are correct and some have a word that should **not** be there. If a line is correct put a tick (✔) next to it. If a line has a word that should not be there, write down that word. The first two lines have been done for you.

The song 'Yesterday'

1 Paul McCartney's song 'Yesterday', which it was ______it______

2 voted the most popular song of the century by a BBC ______✔______

3 poll, had music written before the lyrics. Paul was used the ____________

4 working words 'Scrambled eggs' before coming up with ____________

5 'Yesterday' while he composing this song. ____________

Now go to the Use of English section of the book and do the exercise *Find the mistakes 1* on pages 359–360.

200 Retell the stories 1

Work in pairs – A and B. Your teacher will give you more information.

NO BOUNDARIES (page 111)

201 **Starter**

What do you know about Stephen Hawking? What autobiographies have you read?

202 **Textwork**

Show that you have understood the text *No Boundaries* on pages 111–113 by completing the statements below with information from the text. Sometimes one or two words are enough.

1 Three hundred years before he was born, another great scientist, Galileo ______ .
2 Due to ______ with the Germans during World War II, neither Oxford nor Cambridge ______.
3 When he found out he had contracted ALS, his first thought was, "Why ______ to me?"
4 He thought then that his life was over, but now he ______ with his life.
5 He believes that the only reason he's never won the Nobel Prize is that his theory is very difficult to ______.
6 One advantage of having his disability is that he didn't have to ______.
7 Stephen Hawking is probably the ______ in the world.
8 He was the ______ at the 2012 Paralympic Games in London.
9 Hawking has concentrated on things that his handicap hasn't ______ him from doing rather than ______ things he can't do.
10 He was once detained in Russia for ______.
11 He's visited every continent in the world apart from ______.
12 His later work has shown how quantum theory can predict what happens at the ______ and ______ of time.

Practise the vocabulary in Wordmatch/Spelling

203 **Vocabulary: Fill in the gaps**

Fill in the missing words in the sentences below. Choose from the following words, taken from the text. Then make up your own sentences for the four words that are left over.

agreement	despite	emission	return
asset	detained	estimate	significance
continent	devote	potential	tedious
contracted	disguise	prediction	verify

1 Scientists ________ that smoking reduces life expectancy by around 12 years on average.
2 He says he was captured by aliens and taken to their spaceship. Unfortunately he's unable to ________ his story.
3 An ________ has finally been reached between management and employees.
4 The police have ________ five suspects for questioning in an alleged plot to blow up Buckingham Palace.
5 The discovery of this new drug has great ________ for people suffering from cancer.
6 Famous people, when they go out shopping, often try to ________ themselves to avoid being mobbed by fans.
7 Not many people agree with the government's ________ that the economy will improve this year.
8 In the UK this year, there's been an increase in the number of people who've ________ AIDS.
9 Helen's still out of work ________ applying for hundreds of jobs.
10 The Green Party have called for a substantial reduction in the ________ of greenhouse gases.
11 Being able to speak Mandarin is a big ________ when trying to do business in China.
12 George didn't feel he was achieving his true ________ in his present job.

204 **Interact**

1 What is your impression of Hawking from reading parts of his autobiography?
2 "I believe that disabled people should concentrate on things that their handicap doesn't prevent them from doing and not regret those they can't do." What do you think of this statement?

205 **Speaking/Writing**

It's a great achievement for any person to perform extraordinary acts - but it's even more so when this is done despite some kind of disability. Here are 10 people - some dead, some still alive - who've made a major mark on society through their actions or through succeeding against all odds.

Use the Internet to prepare a short presentation of one of the following people. When you've finished, give your presentation to a partner or to the whole class.

Christy Brown (1932 -1981)
Frida Kahlo (1907-1954)
Hellen Keller (1880 -1968)
Jean-Dominique Bauby (1952 -1997)
John Nash (1928-2015)
Ludwig van Beethoven (1770 -1827)
Marla Runyan (1969-)
Stephen Hawking (1942-)
Sudha Chandran (1964-)
Vincent Van Gogh (1853 -1890)

206 **Retell the stories 2**

Work in pairs - A and B. Your teacher will give you more information.

THE PEOPLE YOU NEVER HEAR FROM (page 114)

207 **Starter**

How does the state help people financially in Sweden? What sort of benefits can you get, for example, if you're unemployed, homeless, have a large family, are disabled, are ill, wish to go to university?

208 **Textwork**

Work in pairs. Read through the text *The People You Never Hear From* on pages 114–117. Take turns to ask and answer the following questions.

1 How many people are dependent on benefits and why don't many people know that?
2 What does she mean by 'post-grad kidults in urban flat-share'?
3 What sort of response did the writer normally get when she wrote about benefits?
4 What do we learn about her friend, Richey?
5 What sort of people were sympathetic to Richey's situation?
6 What did many people who were unsympathetic to Richey's situation suggest the writer should do?
7 Why doesn't the writer agree with this criticism?
8 Why do you think she calls this solution 'MoranAid'?
9 Which adjectives does she use to describe disabled, mentally ill and poor people?
10 What was the UK like before the Welfare State came into being?
11 What do we learn about the writer's own upbringing?
12 How does she feel about the Welfare State?
13 What does the Welfare State enable people from poor backgrounds like hers to do?

Practise the vocabulary in Wordmatch/Spelling

209 Vocabulary: Choose the meaning

The following words and expressions in **bold** are all found in the text. Mark the alternative (a, b, c or d) that best corresponds to the meaning of the words and expressions as they are used in the text.

1 A third of the people in this country are **dependent on** benefits.
a) entitled to b) need (benefits) to survive c) addicted to d) eligible for

2 Judging by the lives of our popular fictional characters, you'd **presume** that...
a) believe it to be true b) guess c) rely on d) be doubtful

3 ... writing about benefits **prompts** a very mixed, and often confused, response.
a) stimulates b) gives a hand to c) influences d) provokes

4 For the unsympathetic, one idea seemed **paramount**...
a) really unusual b) really good c) more important than anything else d) urgent

5 ...instead of taking to my column and **whining** about it.
a) complaining b) writing angrily c) being very upset d) disagreeing (with)

6 ... a lot of disabled / mentally ill / poor people are **grumpy**...
a) depressed b) bad-tempered c) not very attractive d) prejudiced

7 ...rather than the Big Society, which is wholly optional and **ad hoc**...
a) informal b) confusing c) disorganized d) not planned

8 ... instead of seeking out local, **winsome** widows and pressing bread into their grateful hands...
a) grieving b) rather ugly c) pleasant and attractive d) well-deserving

9 ... the State stepped in, and acted like the well-paid columnist our social circle so **sorely** lacked...
a) hardly b) greatly c) painfully d) definitely

10 ... and opened a library where we all read so much, we all **subsequently** went to university
a) consequently b) finally c) eventually d) afterwards

210 Interact

1 What does she tell us in her introduction?
2 What do some people criticize her for?
3 What arguments does Moran have for her defence of the Welfare State?
4 What do you think of Moran's text as an argumentative piece of writing?

211 Debate

Arrange a debate about the welfare system. One group is in favour of higher taxes and wants to spend more money on social benefits while the other group advocates heavy cuts by reducing taxes drastically. Instead you should get private insurances and pay for what you use.

Focus on the following matters:

paid sick leave - parental benefits - unemployment benefit - medical care - education and schools- students loans

For advice on how to work see *On Debating* in Resource Section in the digital part.

Also make use of Useful phrases for discussion on pages 174-176.

WSM: WHY BRITAIN'S FALLEN OUT OF LOVE WITH THE WELFARE STATE

212 Sum up and comment

1. What have you learnt about England that you didn't know before?
2. How has your spoken English improved since the beginning of this course? How can you get even better?
3. Write in your learning log, see Resource Section page 149, and comment on three questions of your own choice.

213 Books to read and enjoy

Bourke, Anthony & Rendall, John: *A Lion Called Christian*
Hornby, Nick: *A Long Way Down*
Joyce, Rachael: *The Unlikely Pilgrimage of Harold Fry*
McEwan, Ian: *Sweet Tooth, Atonement*
Moran, Caitlin: *Moranthology, How to Be a Woman*
Smith, Zadie: *White Teeth*

8 YES OR NO!

THE MOTHER'S PRAYER FOR ITS DAUGHTER

- [ ] Starter
- [ ] Textwork
- [ ] Interact
- [ ] Vocabulary: Unscramble the letters

CHICKY

- [ ] Starter
- [ ] Textwork
- [ ] Vocabulary: Right or wrong?
- [ ] Interact
- [ ] Expand your vocabulary: Phrasal verbs 2

LISTENING: ONLINE ALL THE TIME

- [ ] Starter
- [ ] Listen and recall
- [ ] Vocabulary: Matching pairs
- [ ] Interact
- [ ] Speaking/Writing
- [ ] Use of English: Find the mistakes 2
- [ ] Let's talk

WSM: ARE WE TURNING INTO A NATION OF WEB ADDICTS?

EVERYTHING YOU NEED TO KNOW ABOUT GENERATION Z

- [ ] Starter
- [ ] Textwork
- [ ] Vocabulary: Fill in the gaps
- [ ] Interact
- [ ] Critical reading and reviewing
- [ ] Writing
- [ ] Focus on types of people 2
- [ ] Creating a situation from a dialogue

LISTENING: NEWS ITEMS

- [ ] Starter: One word only
- [ ] Listen and recall
- [ ] Looking at words to do with newspapers
- [ ] Interact
- [ ] A News Broadcast

WSM: NEWSPAPER MISPRINTS

- [ ] Sum up and comment
- [ ] Books to read and enjoy

THE MOTHER'S PRAYER FOR ITS DAUGHTER (page 120)

214 Starter

What do parents usually wish for regarding their teenage children?

215 Textwork

1 Give five examples what the mother wants to protect the daughter from?
2 Find one example of what she wishes for her daughter?
3 When do you think the daughter understands her mother's good intentions?

216 Interact

1 What do you think the mother means by 'May she be Beautiful but not Damaged'?
2 What does the mother mean by saying "lead her away from Acting but not all the way to Finance"?
3 What in the mother's prayer can you sympathize with? Give reasons.

Practise the vocabulary in Wordmatch/Spelling

217 Vocabulary: Unscramble the letters

Unscramble the letters to find a word that fits into the sentence. All the words are found in the *The Mother's Prayer for Its Daughter.* To help you, the first letter of the word is given.

1	deadmag	The fire badly d__________ the town hall.
2	weirdifmy	If you like babies, then maybe a career in m__________ is for you.
3	yewins	The boxer had a strong, s__________ body.
4	batsdeb	The shopkeeper was s__________ several times in the chest.
5	aidsnet	The juice from the berries s__________ her fingers red.
6	locales terror	Whenever I take a r__________-__________ ride, I keep my eyes closed the whole time. I'm so scared! (*2 words*)
7	yefir	My daughter has a really f__________ temper.
8	evictvine	He gave a speech full of i__________ against the government.
9	acnehush	They were squatting on their h__________ playing dice.
10	secef	The disease is spread by the contamination of food and water by f__________.
11	dayken	She y__________ open the cupboard and everything fell out.
12	seper	British children did less well in Maths than their p__________ in Korea.

CHICKY (page 123 ⧉)

218 Starter

What do you associate with Ireland? Do you know of any Irish writers?

219 Textwork

Read *Chicky* on pages 123–127. Then complete the statements below, basing your answers on information in the text. Answer briefly and, as far as possible, in your own words. Read each statement very carefully so that your completion fits in with it.

1 Each of the children on the Ryan's farm in Stoneybridge ...

2 Chicky was the nickname ...

3 Stoneybridge lies ...

4 Chicky needed to find a job because ...

5 Her life changed when ...

6 Chicky couldn't sell Walter an Aran sweater because ...

7 Chicky was surprised that Walter thought Stoneybridge ....

8 Walter suggested to Chicky that they ...

9 After six weeks together, Chicky ...

10 Her brothers and sisters seemed to be ...

11 According to her father, Chicky had ...

12 Her mother didn't believe ...

13 Her mother refused to give Chicky ....

14 Chicky and Walter left Shannon airport ...

Practise the vocabulary in Wordmatch/Spelling

220 Vocabulary: Right or wrong?

Work in pairs. Check that you've understood some of the words used in the text by stating whether they're used correctly in the following sentences. Mark each sentence R (Right) or W (Wrong). If not, explain why and write a new sentence to show how the word(s) should be used.

1. To young children, someone over the age of 60 probably looks really **ancient**. ________
2. Catholic priests take a **vote** of celibacy. In other words, they may not have sex or get married. ________
3. The factory **provides** nearly 2,000 cars a week. ________
4. There was a very high **fence** around the garden. ________
5. The ring was really **endearing**. It cost over £5,000! ________
6. I really must go on a diet again. I'm suffering from **infatuation**. ________
7. Taking a warm bath can help to **soothe** tense, tired muscles. ________
8. An Aran sweater is a type of knitted **garment**. ________
9. My sister was **adamant** to stop smoking. ________
10. He drove through the town at 80 kilometres per hour and was found guilty of **reckless** driving. ________
11. I usually wake up at 7.30, have a shower and then I **dress up** before having breakfast and going to work at the local library. ________
12. You can't usually buy things directly from a factory, because it's not a **retail outlet** like a department store. ________

221 Interact

1. What's the difference between Walter Starr's background and Chicky's?
2. How does Walter Starr charm Chicky? What is Chicky impressed by?
3. Why is Chicky such a disgrace to the family?
4. What do you think will happen to their relationship?
5. How would you feel if your parents disliked your present boyfriend/girlfriend? Would it influence you in any way?

222 Expand your vocabulary: Phrasal verbs 2

In the previous unit you looked at phrasal verbs. Here's your chance to learn some more. Fill in the missing phrasal verbs in the sentences below. Choose from the following and make any verb changes that may be necessary. To help you, there's a Swedish translation in brackets after each sentence.

look back on	look up to	wear off
look into	take in	wear out

1 She sounded so convincing when she told us that she was a famous Russian ballerina that we were all completely __________. It was only later that we found out that she was really a check-out girl at Tesco's. *(lura)*
2 I often __________ my childhood and remember how happy I was then. *(se tillbaka på)*
3 The effect of the drug should __________ in a few hours. *(gå över)*
4 The manager asked his assistant to __________ the complaints they had received. *(undersöka)*
5 I walked so much during my holidays that I __________ two pairs of trainers. *(slita ut)*
6 There are very few political leaders worth __________ these days. *(se upp till)*

Now go to the Expand your vocabulary section of the book and do the exercise *Phrasal verbs 2* on page 341–342.

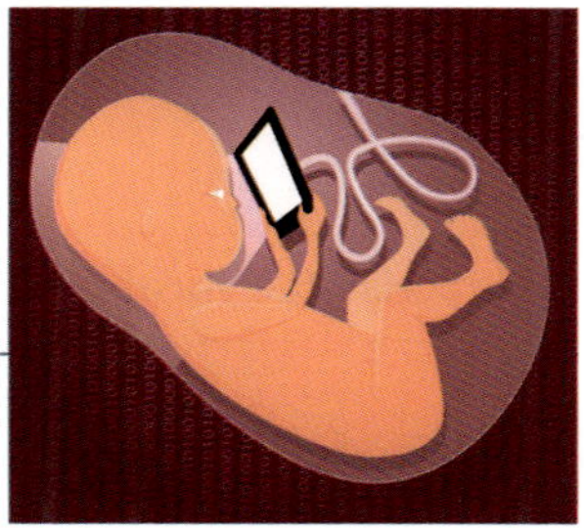

LISTENING: ONLINE ALL THE TIME

223 Starter

Answer Yes or No to the following questions.

Do you...

1 spend an increasing amount of time on the Internet? __________
2 wish you could spend more time on the Internet? __________
3 feel restless when not on the Internet for a while? __________
4 tend to neglect family and friends? __________
5 find the Internet interferes with your job or studies? __________
6 lie about how much time you spend on the Internet? __________
7 feel really good when surfing the Web? __________
8 check your email or social media accounts very often? __________
9 tend to withdraw from other activities? __________
10 prefer chatting on the Internet to meeting people? __________

Answering YES to three of these questions suggests Internet abuse. Five or more indicates addiction, Do you agree?

224 Listen and recall

Listen to the text *Online All the Time.* As you listen, fill in the missing information or choose the correct answer. Before you start, read through the sentences below.

1 The 24-year-old woman lived in __________.
2 She presented herself to a psychiatric clinic because she *a) didn't have any friends b) spent too much time on Facebook c) had lost her job.*
3 Many people nowadays wonder how people managed to live without access to the __________.
4 Nowadays, the Internet is *a) mainly for geeks b) hated by most people c) used by all sorts of people.*

5 Which of the following do people worry about regarding the Internet?

a) The time we spend using it.

b) Our inability to sleep.

c) Spending too much time in the real world.

6 The real 'killer application' that caused the Internet to expand was ___________.

7 Most people check their email more often than they think. *a) True b) False*

8 Nearly 60% of people admitted checking their email in the *a) bedroom b) toilet c) bathroom.*

9 Some emails are more interesting and ___________ than others.

10 We're still very obsessive about checking our email despite the fact that most of it is ___________.

11 Unwanted emails such as advertising material is called ___________.

12 If we can't check our email frequently, this can often lead to *a) tension b) frustration c) anger.*

Practise the vocabulary in Wordmatch/Spelling

---

225 Vocabulary: Matching pairs

On the left are twelve words found in the extract you listened to. Check that you understand them by finding a word, phrase or sentence on the right that can be 'paired off' in some way.

___________	1	ambivalence	a) The way of life or set of beliefs accepted by most people.
___________	2	compulsion	b) Causing problems and preventing something from continuing in its usual way.
___________	3	device	c) Unwanted email.
___________	4	disruptive	d) "I both love and hate the Internet!"
___________	5	fate	e) e.g. about people's Internet habits.
___________	6	habitual	f) Another word for 'earlier'.
___________	7	mainstream	g) "It was bound to happen!"
___________	8	previously	h) A strong and unreasonable desire to do something.
___________	9	servile	i) "My life' s got worse!"
___________	10	spam	j) "I can't stop doing it. It's become _______."
___________	11	survey	k) Very eager to obey someone because you want to please them.
___________	12	take a nosedive	l) e.g. a smartphone, a tablet, etc.

226 Interact

1 Can Facebook be addictive? Give reasons.

2 What problems does the Internet create? What problems does it solve?

3 Why do you think Facebook and Twitter have so many subscribers?

4 Do you find emailing or texting habit-forming? Why/ Why not?

227 Speaking/Writing

Argue for or against one of the following topics:

Facebook - Playing games online - One Internet free day a week

Speak for 3 minutes to a small group/the class. Make use of linking words in Resource Section pages 176–179 and advice on argumentative essays on page 166.

228 Use of English: Find the mistakes 2

In the previous chapter you did exercises on finding various mistakes in sentences. Here's your chance to try again.

Read the following text and look carefully at each line. Some of the lines are correct and some have a word that should **not** be there. If a line is correct put a tick (√) next to it. If a line has a word that should not be there, write down that word. The first two lines have been done for you.

Basketball

1	In December 1891, a physical-education instructor at the	✔
2	YMCA Training School in the Springfield, Massachusetts,	the
3	invented a new game. He asked the school janitor for	______
4	to find two boxes and nail them at opposite ends of the	______
5	gymnasium balcony. The janitor couldn't not find any	______
6	boxes so he substituted for two peach baskets. If the	______
7	janitor had been able to find some boxes, the game	______
8	would probably have become known as 'box-ball'.	______
9	Instead it was named as 'basketball'.	______

Now go to the Use of English section of the book and do the exercise *Find the mistakes 2* on page 361.

229 Let's talk!

Ask the right question

Work in two groups - A and B (2 or 3 people per group). Your teacher will give you more information.

WSM: ARE WE TURNING INTO A NATION OF WEB ADDICTS?

EVERYTHING YOU NEED TO KNOW ABOUT GENERATION Z

(page 128)

230 Starter

What's typical of your generation compared to your parents'? For example, compare your attitudes to work, money and friends.

231 Textwork

Read *Everything You Need to Know about Generation Z* on pages 128–129. Then fill in the missing information or choose the correct answer (a, b or c). The sentences are in no special order.

1 They get all their latest trends from *a) YouTube b) online magazines c) social media.*
2 Older people often find it hard to understand what they're talking about because __________.
3 More than 80% of them are hooked on *a) drugs b) social networks c) dating websites.*
4 FOMO is an acronym for '__________'.
5 Some academics have nicknamed them "the mutants" because __________.
6 Generation Z people put themselves on YouTube in the hope of *a) becoming famous b) making new friends c) teaching people things.*
7 Apart from 'always being in a rush', the following three adjectives are used to describe the life of Generation Z people. __________, __________ and __________.
8 They dance to Korean K-Pop. *a) True b) False*
9 Most Generation Z people are stressed out by the future, especially the __________ and the __________.
10 Generation Z people like reading books. *a) True b) False*
11 A large number of them *a) would like to create their own company b) believe success comes from qualifications c) aim to have an interesting hobby.*
12 Their habit of skim-reading rather than reading properly can often lead to __________.
13 25% of American Generation Z teenagers are doing __________.
14 The average Generation Z person spends over __________ hours a day in front of a screen.
15 Generation Z people find it harder to talk to people in person than online. *a) True b) False*
16 They object to paying for a film or a song because they __________.

Practise the vocabulary in Wordmatch/Spelling

232 Vocabulary: Fill in the gaps

Fill in the missing words in the sentences below. Choose from the following words, taken from the text. Then make up your own sentences for the four words that are left over.

achieve	blockbuster	in a rush	outlook
acronym	ethical	in the know	pals
attention	hierarchy	incomprehensible	stubborn
bleak	in a nutshell	obsolete	ultimate

1 Gas lamps became ___________ when electric lighting was invented.
2 Nuclear weapons are the ___________ deterrent.
3 "To put it ___________," said the managing director, "the company is bankrupt."
4 'AIDS' is an ___________ for 'acquired immune deficiency syndrome'.
5 The new James Bond film has become another ___________.
6 Unlike me, my sister has a fairly positive ___________ on life.
7 It may be possible in the future to clone human beings, but is it ___________?
8 Young people always seem to be ___________ nowadays. They really need to learn how to slow down.
9 The government has failed to ___________ their target of less than 3% inflation.
10 The speaker had such a strong Scottish accent that his speech was ___________ to most of the audience.
11 The ___________ span of most young people nowadays is about 8 seconds.
12 He rose quickly through the political ___________ to become party leader.

233 Interact

1 Sum up what's typical of generation Z. How does generation Z look at the future?
2 What do you think about their attitude to life?
3 Do you think the text gives a correct description of generation Z? Give reasons.
4 Can you identify with generation Z? Why/Why not?

234 Critical reading and reviewing

Analyze the text *Everything You Need to Know about Generation Z* critically by using the questions in Resource Section page 151.

235 Writing

Write a summary of the text *Everything You Need to Know about Generation Z* and comment on the content. Use 300 - 400 words. Remember to use linking words in Resource Section pages 176–179.

236 **Focus on types of people 2**

Complete the definitions below with a suitable person. Choose from the following.

adversary	daredevil	invalid	stowaway
busker	deserter	next-of-kin	successor
busybody	heir	predecessor	teetotaller
castaway	interpreter	refugee	underdog

1 A ________ is someone who's been driven from his or her country because of war or for political reasons.
2 A ________ is a musician who plays in the street, at underground stations, etc.
3 A ________ is a person who leaves the army, navy, etc. without permission.
4 A ________ is someone who never drinks alcohol.
5 An ________ is someone who translates the words a person speaks into another language, often at the same time as the person is speaking.
6 A ________ is someone who's left on a lonely shore or island after their ship has sunk.
7 Your ________ is your closest relative. If you're married, it would be your husband or wife.
8 A ________ is someone who hides in a ship, aircraft or some other form of transport, in order to travel in secret and without paying.
9 An ________ is a person who has the legal right to receive someone's property, money or title when that person dies.
10 An ________ is a person who's usually expected to lose in a competition with someone else.
11 An ________ is someone who's disabled or very ill and needs to be cared for by someone else.
12 An ________ is a country or person you're fighting or competing against.
13 Your ________ is the person who had your present job before you.
14 A ________ is someone who's too interested in other people's private activities.
15 A ________ is a person who enjoys doing dangerous things, in a way that other people may think is stupid.
16 Your ________ is the person who takes over your job from you when you finish.

237 **Creating a situation from a dialogue**

Work in pairs or groups of three. Look at the following dialogues. Your task is to choose one of them and expand it by adding 6–8 lines before and after the extract. Before you start, think of the following:

1 Who are the characters? (A and B)
2 Where are they and why are they there?
3 What is happening now? What might have happened just before and what is going to happen next?
4 Can you introduce a third person (C), either before or after the extract?

When you've finished writing your dialogue, act it out.

1

A Don't take any notice of him.
B That's easier said than done.
A He's not as bad as you think.
B There was no need for him to say that!
A He didn't mean it.
B Yes, he did!
A No, he didn't. You just don't know him, that's all.
B And you do, I suppose?

2

A This is out of date!
B Out of date?
A Yes, out of date. See – it's only valid till the tenth.
B The tenth? It's the tenth today, isn't it?
A No, today's the eleventh.
B Are you sure?
A Quite sure! It says on my phone too. See!

LISTENING: NEWS ITEMS

238 **Starter: One word only**

Read the following text about a young boy who has become a chess grandmaster and write ONE word in each gap. The word you write must make sense in the text and be grammatically correct.

Boy Becomes Youngest-Ever US Chess Grandmaster

Sam Sevian likes watching hockey and basketball and hates (1)__________ chores, but most American teen boys don't have the title of chess grandmaster (2)__________ their belt. This was an honour Sam (3)__________ last week at a St. Louis tournament, making him the youngest US grandmaster ever. Sam, who trains with chess guru Garry Kasparov, won all four games he played, elevating him over the 2,500-point mark (4)__________ for the title.

"He really outplayed his (5)__________ in three games," said his father, "but the fourth, it was really back and forth."

The California teen is (6)__________ to winning: When he was just 8, he (7)__________ the youngest person ever in the US to become an official "chess expert," and in 2009, he became the country's youngest "national master." He's been playing (8)__________ he was 5, and he and his dad are the only ones in the family who play.

His father sometimes (9)__________ if his son's passion will pay off.

"I actually told Sam, 'Maybe we (10)__________ do something else', but that doesn't go (11)__________ well with Sam." The teen's next goal: to get to 2,600 points so he can compete in more-elite tournaments and someday become world (12)__________.

239 **Listen and recall**

You're going to hear 7 news items. They'll be read ONCE only. After each news item there'll be a pause for you to answer the questions by choosing one of the letters A, B, C or D. After writing your answer, you may also like to look at the question which follows.

1 What do we learn about the taxi driver?

A He was an honest person.
A He was hoping for a reward.
B He liked sweets.
C He knew the name of the poker player.

2 What does this news item tell us about Italian drivers?

A They usually have more than one car.
B They all have Twitter accounts.
C They often park illegally.
D They're put in prison if they park in the wrong places.

3 What do we learn from this news item?

A The solo voyage around the world will take 6 months.
B Michael Perham used his voyage to raise money for charity.
C He has tried this once before.
D He wasn't a bit nervous about the trip.

4 What are we told in this news item?

A Roundabouts are confusing.
B The man was driving in the slow lane of a motorway.
C Pensioners drive slowly.
D The man had got lost on his way home.

5 What would be the most suitable headline for this report?

A Farmer attacked by a Siberian tiger.
B President Putin's pet tiger found in China.
C 18 goats killed by wild animal.
D Chinese Farmer told to buy more goats.

6 What is this news item about?

A The joy of walking in a forest.
B Mushroom picking.
C Romance in the countryside.
D Illegal drugs.

7 What do we learn from this news item?

A The funeral took place in Sydney.
B The carjacker had a health problem.
C The deceased was Tobias Richardson's brother-in-law.
D The coffin was in the stolen hearse.

Practise the vocabulary in Wordmatch/Spelling

---

240 Looking at words to do with newspapers

Write the missing words in the sentences below. Choose from the following.

advertisement	correspondent	obituary
caption	editor	popular
circulation	editorial	quality
colour supplement	feature	review
column	gossip column	tabloid
comic strip	headline	weather forecast

1 There was a large __________ on the front page which said 'EARTHQUAKE SHAKES TOKYO'.
2 The person in charge of the newspaper is called the __________.
3 Since the newspaper changed owners, it's__________ has increased by nearly 10,000 copies a month.
4 Before we go for picnic this afternoon, we'd better check the __________. There's no point in going if it's going to rain.
5 In Britain, the national newspapers can be divided into __________ papers, such as *The Times*, and *The Telegraph*, which report the news seriously and thoroughly and the __________ papers, such as *The Sun* and the *Daily Mirror* which often go in for sensational news and use lots of pictures.
6 Editors usually think very carefully about what __________ to write under a photograph.

7 A __________ is the set of drawings telling a story, often humorous. There are usually words showing the speech of the characters in the story.
8 You read the __________ to find out about the private lives and scandals of famous people.
9 Many Saturday and Sunday newspapers include a free magazine to read called a __________.
10 An __________ is a piece of writing about the character and achievements of someone who's just died.
11 For many years before returning to Britain he worked as a foreign __________ in Paris and in Turkey.
12 There was a very interesting __________ today, giving the newspaper's opinion of the government's new plans for the health service.
13 I prefer reading __________ newspapers as they are smaller and easier to handle. Reading newspapers like *The Telegraph* makes my arms ache after a while.
14 The new television series got a very bad __________ in today's newspaper. It was described as 'the worst series the BBC has ever made'.
15 All this week the newspaper's running a special __________ on love and marriage.
16 A large proportion of newspapers income comes from __________, especially full-page ones.
17 There wasn't enough room on the front page for the complete article, so it was continued on page 2, __________ 4.

241 **Interact**

1 Which kind of news is the best for you – newspapers, television, radio, the Internet? Why?
2 Do you trust the information you get from the news?
3 Due to the Internet, do you think printed newspapers will disappear in the future?
4 Do you think the news media influences people too much? How has it changed over the years?

242 **A News Broadcast**

Work in groups. Your task is to prepare a news broadcast, where two of you will present the news you've decided on, plus a weatherman/weather girl. Your teacher will give you more information.

WSM: NEWSPAPER MISPRINTS

243 **Sum up and comment**

1 Which was the most interesting text in this unit? Give reasons.
2 What strategies have been most useful to you until now? Which skill do you still need to improve?

244 **Books to read and enjoy**

Egan, Jennifer: *Look at Me*
Eggers, Dave: *The Circle*
Fey, Tina: *Bossypants*
Lin, Tao: *Taipei*
Kasischke, Laura: *The Raising*
Shteyngart, Gary: *Super Sad True Love Story*
Simone, Alina: *Note to Self*

9 OUTLOOK ON THE US

QUIET STRENGTH

- [ ] Starter: One word only
- [ ] Textwork
- [ ] Vocabulary: Definitions
- [ ] Interact

WSM: MARTIN LUTHER KING'S SPEECH: 'I HAVE A DREAM'

THE NEGRO MOTHER

- [ ] Starter: USA Quiz
- [ ] Textwork
- [ ] Interact
- [ ] Expand your vocabulary: Idioms

WSM: ON SLAVERY IN AMERICA

WE ARE THE FUTURE

- [ ] Starter
- [ ] Textwork
- [ ] Interact
- [ ] Writing
- [ ] Focus on types of people 3

LISTENING: KAVES – THE GRAFFITI AND TATTOO MASTER

- [ ] Starter
- [ ] Listen and recall
- [ ] Vocabulary: Definitions
- [ ] Interact
- [ ] Debate
- [ ] Use of English: Find the mistakes 3

THE AGE OF EXCITEMENT

- [ ] Starter
- [ ] Textwork
- [ ] Vocabulary: Words of similar meaning
- [ ] Interact
- [ ] Politics – political – politician – policy?
- [ ] Project
- [ ] Let's talk!

WSM: LOOKING AT GOVERNMENT IN THE USA

THE BIRTH OF HELA

- ☐ Starter
- ☐ Textwork
- ☐ Vocabulary: What does it mean?
- ☐ Interact
- ☐ Activity
- ☐ Project

LISTENING: WHAT'S THE TOPIC?

- ☐ Listen and recall
- ☐ A-Z Quiz

- ☐ Sum up and comment
- ☐ Books to read and enjoy

QUIET STRENGTH (page 132)

245 Starter: One word only

Read the following text about the U.S. Civil Rights Movement and write ONE word in each gap. The word you write must make sense in the text and be grammatically correct.

The U.S. Civil Rights Movement

During the early 20th (1)__________ in Southern states, racial segregation was the norm, and blacks had (2)__________ opportunities. But the 1950s brought forces to bear that (3)__________ launch a powerful civil rights campaign.
Black soldiers who had (4)__________ in the war beside whites came home (5)__________ to work beside them. The black media flourished, spreading news of injustice. Black lawyers chipped (6)__________ at legal justifications for segregation. And black students, (7)__________ times disobeying their parents, planned demonstrations.
Ministers saw a religious context to the civil rights struggle. (8)__________ them, the Reverend Martin Luther King Jr., a gifted orator who had been (9)__________ by India's Mahatma Gandhi in his belief in nonviolent protest, rose quickly to (10)__________ the movement.
It was a movement of children and adults, preachers and lawyers, sharecroppers and presidents. They all (11)__________ a sense of urgency, a sense that, no matter what, they could not (12)__________ back.

What do you know about this movement?
What do you know about Martin Luther King Jr.?

246 Textwork

Without looking back at the text *Quiet Strength* on page 132–133, see if you can sort out the following summary as the sentences are in the wrong order. Number them 1–10. To help you, the first one has already been done.

_____ She doesn't care and tells him he can send for the police if he wishes.
_____ The Reverend Martin Luther King Jr. addresses the crowd and tells them "There comes a time that people get tired of being trampled over by the iron feet of oppression."
__1__ A black woman gets onto a bus in Montgomery and sits in the first row of the Colored section.
_____ A police officer arrives and arrests her.

_____ This action changes the course of American history.
_____ The bus fills up and the bus driver asks her to give up her seat to a white passenger.
_____ The woman who started it all - Rosa Parks - died in 2005 at the age of ninety-two.
_____ On the afternoon of her trial 5,000 people gather in a church to support the woman's act of courage.
_____ The association launches a citywide bus boycott that lasts for 381 days.
_____ The woman refuses and the driver threatens to have her arrested.

Practise the vocabulary in Wordmatch/Spelling

247 Vocabulary: Definitions

Here are definitions of ten words from the text. Can you work out what they are? To help you, the first and last letter of each missing word is given.

1 To start to burn; to make something start to burn. i_____e
2 Brave and confident; not afraid to say what you feel or to take risks. b_____d
3 To walk slowly or with heavy steps, because you're tired or carrying something heavy. t_____e
4 Something that you think is true although you have no definite proof. a_____n
5 Reasonable, practical, and showing good judgment. s_____e
6 Courage shown by someone who's suffering great pain or facing great difficulties. f_____e
7 A room that's _____ is dark and dirty. d_____y
8 An article about someone's life and achievements, that's printed in a newspaper soon after they've died. o_____y
9 To shock or surprise someone so that they do something to solve a problem, improve a situation, etc. g_____e
10 _____ is when someone treats a group of people unfairly or cruelly and prevents them from having the same rights as other people have. o_____n

248 Interact

1 What does the heading 'Quiet Strength' refer to?
2 Why don't we usually give credit to being shy and quiet?

WSM: MARTIN LUTHER KING'S SPEECH: 'I HAVE A DREAM'

In **Want some more** in Unit 2 you read the memorable and moving speech Malala Yousafzai made at the United Nations in 2013. Fifty years before that the Rev. Martin Luther King Jr. made a speech which is among the most acclaimed in U.S. history. His soaring close "to let freedom ring" still resonates today and inspires those who are moved by his dream. Here's that extract from it.

THE NEGRO MOTHER (page 135)

249 Starter: USA Quiz

How much do you know about the United States? Here's your chance to find out. Your teacher will give you more information.

250 Textwork

1 Sum up the poem in your own words.
2 She says, 'Now, through my children, I'm reaching the goal'. What goal is she referring to?

Practise the vocabulary in Wordmatch/Spelling

251 Interact

1 What is the message of the poem?
2 What did you think of this poem? How did you find it?

252 Expand your vocabulary: Idioms

In the previous unit you looked at phrasal verbs. In this, the final chapter, you are going to look at idioms. Like phrasal verbs, to be really fluent in English you need a good passive knowledge of these.

Each of the sentences below contains an idiom. Unfortunately they're incomplete. Choose the missing word or words from the ones given (a, b or c).

1 Do you like my chicken-bone earrings? They're **all the** ________ in London at the moment.
a) fashion b) way c) rage

2 You're **flogging a** ________ trying to persuade James to come with us.
a) stray cat b) dead horse c) drowned rat

3 I wouldn't like to live in John's flat. **There's no room to** ________!
a) swing a cat b) bounce a budgie c) throw a rabbit

4 Of course they're in love. It's **as plain as the** ________.
a) birds and the bees b) sun in the sky c) nose on your face

5 I **had my** ________ **in my mouth** watching the man crossing the Niagara Falls on a tightrope.
a) shoe b) heart c) hand

Now go to the Expand your vocabulary section of the book and do the exercises Idioms 1–2 on pages 343–346.

WSM: ON SLAVERY IN AMERICA

Read the following short text about slavery. A number of words have been left out. Below you will find four alternatives for each gap. Choose the *best* alternative and write your choice, A, B, C or D in the appropriate box below.

In America, slavery began in the 17th century. Slaves usually __**1**__ of women and men between the ages of 18 and 35, __**2**__ children were enslaved as well. These men, women, and children were then __**3**__ into portholes where many fell into depression or tried resisting and were therefore killed. The __**4**__ living were then sold and forced to work at long hours and had no rights to vacations, wages, marriages, or property.

Some slave owners would threaten to beat their slaves if they resisted or __**5**__ to do the labor they were ordered. If a slave was beaten, they couldn't fight back or try to go to court for it, they were required to simply __**6**__ it. Also, many families were forced to __**7**__ and were then sold to different slave owners. Although women and children usually were allowed to stay together.

Many slaves would find strength to endure the hardship of it all __**8**__ religion, but some also began to be rebellious to their slave owners. They would work slower, __**9**__ to not know how to do certain things, "accidentally" break equipment in order to slow the work process down, and a lot of slaves attempted to run away and find a free state in which they could become free.

Some of the slaves that attempted to run away, would escape through a series of trails known as the underground railroad. It had many people who were __**10**__ to hide slaves in their homes and they would conduct them to the next station or safe house until they could reach the free North. Many of the slaves did not __**11**__ the hardships of the trails and some of them were caught and returned to their owners. But this did not stop slaves from attempting to gain the freedom they well __**12**__.

	A	B	C	D
1	A involved	B consisted	C contained	D made up
2	A despite	B however	C because	D although
3	A moved	B forced	C demanded	D made
4	A rest	B outstanding	C only	D remaining
5	A refused	B denied	C evaded	D turned down
6	A put up	B sustain	C endure	D receive
7	A break away	B split up	C divide	D share
8	A by	B under	C through	D among
9	A claim	B deny	C request	D retaliate
10	A reluctant	B enthusiastic	C voluntary	D willing
11	A survive	B undergo	C pull over	D last
12	A earned	B gained	C deserved	D required

1	2	3	4	5	6	7	8	9	10	11	12

WE ARE THE FUTURE (page 137)

253 **Starter**

Here are some predictions for the next 25 years. Mark with a cross (X) any that you think are likely to come true.

1 ☐ China will be the major power in the world.
2 ☐ The world will be faced with a new financial crisis.
3 ☐ A vaccine will be developed to rid the world of AIDS.
4 ☐ The use of fossil fuels will be reduced from 80% to 50%.
5 ☐ Computers will be more intelligent than humans.
6 ☐ Internet use will reach 5 billion.
7 ☐ Smoking in public places will be banned in every state in the US.
8 ☐ Astronauts will land on Mars.
9 ☐ Global average temperatures will rise by 1°C.
10 ☐ Automated (i.e. self-driving) cars will become very popular.
11 ☐ Brain implants will be able to restore lost memory.
12 ☐ In Africa, gorillas, elephants and rhinos in the wild will become extinct.
13 ☐ Rising sea levels will wreak havoc on the Maldives.
14 ☐ The UK population will reach 75 million.
15 ☐ Extinct species will be resurrected through cloning.

Now work in small groups and compare your answers. Suggest 2–3 predictions of your own for the next 25 years.

____

____

____

254 **Textwork**

Without looking back at the text *We Are the Future* on pages 137–138, match the opening words of sentences 1–8 with the correct endings.

1 The Intel Science Talent Search contest
2 According to the text, it's important to

3 The guests at the dinner were all
4 The winner had developed a software navigation system which would
5 There were 40 guests at the
6 Magic happens when these high-aspiring people
7 For the competition, the student had to
8 The winner of the contest

A enable spacecraft to travel through the solar system more efficiently.
B was from Mexico.
C honors top students in math and science.
D gala dinner in Washington D.C.
E find solutions to scientific problems.
F continue attracting high-aspiring immigrants.
G are mixed together with a democratic system and free markets.
H American high school students.

Write your answers here, then turn to pages 137–138 to check them.

1	2	3	4	5	6	7	8

Practise the vocabulary in Wordmatch/Spelling

255 **Interact**

1 Why do you think so many people emigrate to the USA?
2 In what ways does the USA benefit from immigration?

256 **Writing**

You're going to apply for a job abroad and need to send off a letter of application together with your CV. Advice on how to write is in Resource Section pages 163–164. Use Checklist for writing on page 156.

257 **Focus on types of people 3**

Complete the definitions below with a suitable person. Choose from the following.

battle-axe	offspring	road hog	swot
blackleg	participant	skinflint	tomboy
junkie	picket	spouse	victim
killjoy	rival	survivor	whizz kid

1 A __________ is a person's husband or wife.
2 A __________ is someone who takes part in a contest, course, etc.
3 A __________ is a young girl who enjoys activities and games that are traditionally considered to be for boys.
4 A __________ is someone who carries on working when the rest of the workers are on strike.
5 A __________ is a person, group, or organization that you compete with in sport, business, a fight, etc.
6 A __________ is a person who's been attacked, injured or killed as the result of a crime, a disease, an accident, etc.
7 A __________ is a person who intentionally spoils the pleasure of other people.
8 A __________ is a very selfish and careless driver.
9 A __________ is someone who's still alive after being involved in a plane crash, car accident, etc.
10 A __________ is someone who's unable to stop taking drugs.
11 A __________ is someone, usually a child, who spends too much time studying. Often used to show disapproval.
12 A __________ is someone on strike who stands at the entrance to a factory trying to persuade other workers not to carry on working.
13 A __________ is a person with modern ideas who works with great energy and who achieves great success in his job, profession while still young.
14 An __________ is someone's child.
15 A __________ is someone who dislikes spending money or giving it away.
16 A __________ is an aggressive and unpleasant older woman who tries to control other people.

LISTENING: KAVES – THE GRAFFITI AND TATTOO MASTER

258 **Starter**

What do you think of the following tattoos?

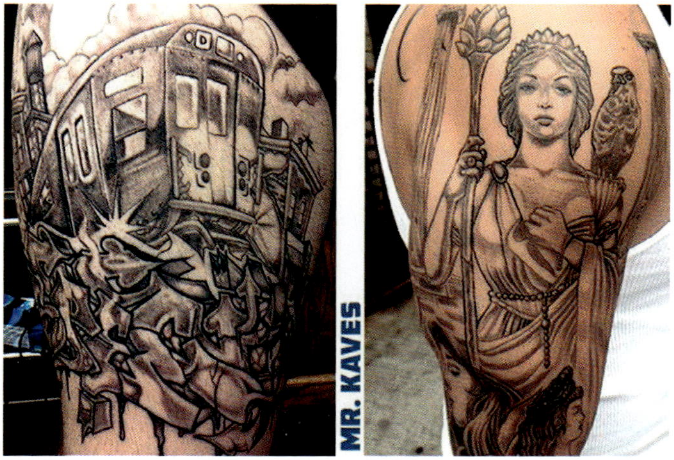

These are done by Michael McLeer, who goes under the name Kaves. Have you ever heard of him?

259 Listen and recall

Listen to the text about Kaves and then answer the questions below by completing the sentences. Before you start, read through the questions.

1 What type of band is Lordz of Brooklyn?
It's ______________________________.
2 What's Brooklyn Made Tattoo?
It's the name ______________________________.
3 How old was he when he started writing graffiti?
He was ______________________________.
4 What did kids in his school talk about?
They talked about ______________________________.
5 Who was RR?
He was an older writer who ______________________________.
6 Why did his father take him and his brother to the Bronx or Harlem at weekends?
So that they could ______________________________.
7 What was the dot in his father's hand?
It was ______________________________.
8 What did Danny Boy give him?
He gave him a ______________________________.
9 Who was Baba?
He was someone who ______________________________.
10 Why is skin the hardest canvas to work on?
Because it's ______________________________.
11 How does Kaves describe tattooing?
He describes it as ______________________________.

Practise the vocabulary in Wordmatch/Spelling

260 Vocabulary: Definitions

Here are definitions of eight words from the text. Can you work out what they are? To help you, the first and last letter of each missing word is given.

1 A feeling of sadness mixed with pleasure and affection when you think of happy times in the past. n__________a
2 A _____ situation or period of time is one in which there are a lot of sudden changes. t__________t
3 To explain something in a more detailed way. e__________e
4 Not seen or found very often, or not happening very often. r__________e
5 A strong heavy rough material used by artists for painting on. c__________s

6 All the people who regularly use a shop, restaurant, etc. c_________e
7 To officially introduce someone into a group, gang or organization. i_________t
8 _____ memories, dreams, descriptions etc. are so clear that they seem real. v_________d

261 Interact

1 Do you consider graffiti and tattooing as art? Why? Why not?
2 How long do you think the tattoo trend will last?
3 When can a very visual tattoo stop you from getting a certain kind of job?
4 In the UK at the moment there's a trend for young men to grow Victorian-style beards. What trends, if any, are there in Sweden?

262 Debate

Work in two groups - A and B. Group A are for tattoos and body-piercings while Group B are against them. Your teacher will give you more information.

263 Use of English: Find the mistakes 3

In the previous two chapters you did exercises on finding various mistakes in sentences. Here is your last chance to try this sort of exercise. But this time it's going to be slightly different. Read the text below and look carefully at each line. Some of the lines are correct, and some have a word missing. If a line is correct put a tick (✔) after it. If a line has a missing word, use a stroke (/) to show where a word has been left out and on the right suggest what the missing word might be. There are two examples at the beginning.

500 parrots to go

1 A bird lover has / ordered to find a new home for __been__
2 his collection of 500 exotic parrots. Peter Hammond's __✔__
3 exhausted neighbours said squawking from the exotic ________
4 menagerie in his house made their lives unbearable ________
5 for five years. Mr Hammond, 76, has been to move ________
6 the birds from his home. Mrs Griffiths, his neighbour ________
7 said, "The parrots emit what can only described ________
8 as alarming primeval squawks at random intervals." ________
9 Mr Hammond has been six months to appeal. ________

Now go to the Use of English section of the book and do the exercise *Find the mistakes 3* on page 362.

THE AGE OF EXCITEMENT (page 139)

264 **Starter**

Work in small groups. Look at the following two adverts from the 50s. What do they say about that decade?

265 **Textwork**

Read *The Age of Excitement* on pages 139–141. Then fill in the missing information or choose the correct answer (a, b or c). The sentences are in no special order.

1 A haircut in the 50s which resulted in every hair standing to attention and sheared off in a perfect horizontal plane was known as *a) a horizontal-top b) a flat-top c) a shaved-top.*

2 The fact that rocket mail wasn't feasible didn't really matter. The important thing was knowing that ___________.

3 Mrs Chase set *a) 4 b) 5 c) 6* small fires as she wandered through the White House.

4 The *Des Moines Register* reported that mail would be delivered by *a) submarine b) a Regulus I rocket c) guided missile.*

5 When Mrs Chase was eventually found, she *a) was arrested b) wrote a book about her adventure c) was given a cup of tea and allowed to go home.*

6 Find three examples from the text of things done in the 50s which are now controlled or advised by the government.

____

____

____

7 If anyone was loose in the White house nowadays, name one thing that might happen.

8 Name one problem associated with missile mail.

9 In 1956, a woman on a tour of the White House *a) went missing b) slipped c) couldn't find her tour group.*

Practise the vocabulary in Wordmatch/Spelling

266 Vocabulary: Words of similar meaning

Complete the pairs of words below with another word that is similar in meaning. Choose from the following words, all taken from the text.

benign	dishevelled	lavish	preposterous
combust	endearing	lucid	prevailing
custody	instantaneous	penetrate	soothe

1 in a flash, immediate, __________
2 scruffy, unkempt, __________
3 absurd, ludicrous, __________
4 benevolent, non-threatening, __________
5 calm, comfort, __________
6 articulate, eloquent, __________
7 enter, pass through, __________
8 care, safekeeping, __________
9 appealing, lovable, __________
10 extravagant, lush, __________
11 current, existing, __________
12 catch fire, ignite, __________

267 Interact

1 What picture do you get of society in the 1950s from the text?
2 Compare the 1950s with the present time described in the text.
3 What kind of writing style does Bryson have? What do you think of it?

268 Politics – political – politician – policy?

Do you know the difference? Fill in the correct words in the sentences below. Use each word twice.

1 My husband's in the government. He's a __________.
2 The __________ situation in the country is very serious at the moment.
3 Fewer and fewer people nowadays seem to be interested in __________.

4 The Conservative party's __________ on taxation is simple - keep taxes as low as possible.
5 Which __________ party do you usually vote for?
6 The Government's __________ on unemployment isn't working. They're going to have to change it.
7 Tony Blair's interest in __________ began at an early age.
8 "I wouldn't trust a __________ as far as I could throw him or her. They're all rotten, if you ask me."

269 **Project**

Present an American politician, e.g. Abraham Lincoln, Eleanor Roosevelt, Dwight Eisenhower, John F. Kennedy, Richard Nixon, Hillary Clinton, Nancy Pelosi, Barack Obama.

When were they active? What did they achieve? Present your findings in a paper.

For advice on writing a project see Resource Section page 168. Also make use of

Checklist for writing on page 156.

270 **Let's talk!**

Work in groups of 3-4. How logical are you? Here's your chance to find out. Your teacher will give you more information.

WSM: LOOKING AT GOVERNMENT IN THE USA

THE BIRTH OF HELA (page 142)

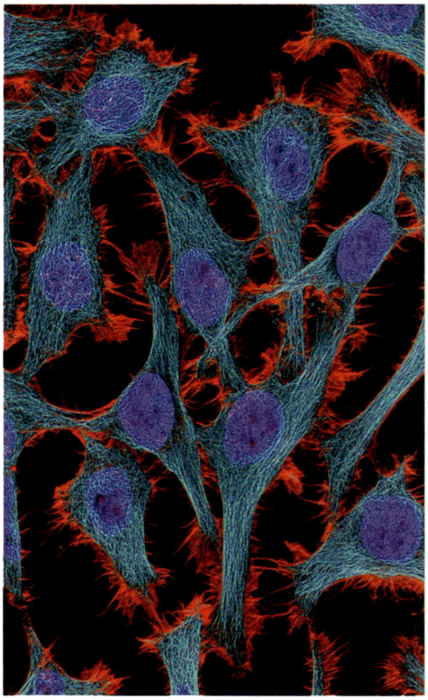

271 **Starter**

What do you know about HeLa? Why is research on stem cells so important?

272 **Textwork**

Read through the text *The Birth of HeLa* on pages 142-146 and decide which of the four alternatives (A, B, C or D) you think is correct.

1 Henrietta's biopsy report showed that her cancer was malignant. This means that ...

☐ A it wasn't very serious.
☐ B it was likely to cause her death.
☐ C it was curable.
☐ D the result was negative.

2 Which of these is true?

☐ A Henrietta lied to her husband.
☐ B The doctor had given her some medicine to take.
☐ C She was feeling really scared.
☐ D She had to go back to the hospital in a week's time.

3 What happened to Henrietta on her first day in hospital?

☐ A She was given an early dinner.
☐ B She was shown into a ward with lots of white women.
☐ C They checked her heart.
☐ D She underwent lots of tests.

4 How were invasive tumors treated in those days?

☐ A With very strong drugs.
☐ B With an operation.
☐ C With radium.
☐ D With gas and electricity.

5 Which of these is not true about radium?

☐ A It was discovered in the early 19th century.
☐ B Patients who'd taken it for trivial problems began dying.
☐ C It kills cancer cells.
☐ D At high doses it can burn the skin off a person's body.

6 What was the probable cause of Howard Kelly's death?

☐ A Exposure to radium during an operation.
☐ B Being overworked.
☐ C Carrying too many Brack plaques in his pockets.
☐ D Being regularly exposed to radium.

7 What happened in the operating theatre?

☐ A Henrietta's stomach was filled with radium.
☐ B The doctor took two tissue samples from her cervix.
☐ C The radium was packed into rolls of gauze.
☐ D TeLinde sat on a stool between her legs.

8 What do we learn about Henrietta's cell samples?

☐ A They died after only a few days.
☐ B They doubled their number every thirty-six hours.
☐ C Dr George Gey believed they'd grown the first immortal human cells.
☐ D They looked like crabgrass.

Practise the vocabulary in Wordmatch/Spelling

273 Vocabulary: What does it mean?

You're now going to explain the meaning of some of the words used in the text *The Birth of HeLa*. Complete the following sentences by giving English explanations of the words in **bold**. Make your explanations as exact as possible. Use a dictionary if necessary.

Example: A **malignant** tumour is likely to get worse and may lead ________.
Answer: to death

1 A **biopsy** can tell you more about________.
2 If you're writing is **illegible** then it's ________.
3 A **procedure** is another word for an ________.
4 A team leader was appointed to **oversee** the project. In other words to make sure that ________.
5 The study was **conducted** by Howard Jones. In other words he was the person who ________.
6 To **empty your bladder** means to ________.
7 The **eerie** sound of an owl hooting at night. This means that the sound was ________.
8 A **ward** is ________.
9 **Invasive** surgery means that a surgeon ________.
10 An **anaesthetic** is a substance that stops you from ________.
11 The girl was crying and obviously in **distress**. In other words she was ________.
12 The optician put drops in her eyes to **dilate** her pupils, that is, to make them ________.

274 Interact

1 What do you think of the medical treatment Henrietta Lacks received?
2 Why were the cells from Henrietta Lacks so different? Why have her cells become so important to research all over the world?
3 Would you consider donating your organs after your death? Why? Why not?

275 Activity

1 What connotations does the word 'science' have for you? Are they positive, negative or mixed?
2 Do you think there is a hierarchy of sciences? If so, try to order the various sciences according to any criteria of your choice. If not, explain why.
3 How are scientists viewed in popular culture, such as novels and movies? Are they generally seen as heroes or villains?

276 **Project**

Present a medical discovery such as X-rays, DNA or a Nobel Prize Winner.

For advice on writing a project see Resource Section page 168. Also make use of Checklist for writing on page 156.

LISTENING: WHAT'S THE TOPIC?

277 **Listen and recall**

You're going to hear 10 speakers, each one talking about a different topic. After each item, there'll be a short pause for you to choose from the list below which topic you think is being mainly talked about. Then write the letter of the topic you choose in the appropriate box. The items will be read ONCE only. You can only use each letter ONCE.

A Art
B Changing Attitudes
C Climate
D Crime
E Dress Code
F Economy
G Fashion
H Health advice
I Information Technology
K Internet privacy
L Language Usage
M Leisure Activity
N Pets
O Relationships
P Senior Citizens
R Shopping
S Sports
T Study on Behaviour
V Surprising Conclusion
X Travel

Write your answers here:

1	2	3	4	5	6	7	8	9	10

Practise the vocabulary in Wordmatch/Spelling

278 **A-Z Quiz**

Work in groups of 3–4. Your teacher will give you more instructions.

279 **Sum up and comment**

1 What do you remember best from your English studies this year?
2 Write in your learning log, see Resource Section page 149, and comment on three questions of your own choice.
3 Time for your last assessment. Did you achieve your goals? Why?/ Why not?

Adichie, Chimamanda: *Americanah*
Auster, Paul: *New York Trilogy*
Belfort, Jordan: *The Wolf of Wall Street*
Bryson, Bill: *The Life and Times of The Thunderbolt Kid*
Lee, Harper: *To Kill a Mockingbird*
Kerouac, Jack: *On the Road*
Passos, Don John: *USA*
Salinger, J.D: *Catcher in the Rye*
Selasi, Taiye: *Ghana Must Go*
Skloot, Rebecca: *The Immortal Life of Henrietta Lacks*
Stockett, Kathryn: *The Help*
Williams, John: *Stoner*

EXPAND YOUR VOCABULARY

1 BRITISH AND AMERICAN ENGLISH

A Find the words

What are the British and American words for the Swedish words below? Choose from the following:

apartment	check	flat	purse
apartment house	closet	French fries	queue
autumn	chips	gasoline	shop
baby carriage	cookies	handbag	stand in line
bill	curtains	label	store
biscuits	diaper	lift	sweets
block of flats	drapes	nappy	tag
can	elevator	parking lot	tap
candy	fall	petrol	tin
car park	faucet	pram	wardrobe

	Swedish	British	American
1	affär, butik	____________	____________
2	barnvagn	____________	____________
3	bensin	____________	____________
4	blöja	____________	____________
5	burk	____________	____________
6	etikett	____________	____________
7	garderob	____________	____________
8	gardiner	____________	____________
9	godis	____________	____________
10	handväska	____________	____________
11	hiss	____________	____________
12	höghus	____________	____________
13	höst	____________	____________
14	kex	____________	____________
15	kran	____________	____________
16	köa	____________	____________
17	lägenhet	____________	____________
18	nota	____________	____________
19	parkeringshus	____________	____________
20	pommes frites	____________	____________

B Complete the sentences

Now complete the sentences below with a suitable American word. To help you, the English word is given in brackets after each sentence. Choose from the following. Not all the words will be used.

bill	grade	pants	streetlight
chips	hardware store	recess	subway
desk	janitor	restroom	thumb tack
downtown	license plate	semester	trashcan/garbage can
dresser/bureau	liquor store	shift	vest
drugstore	mailman	sports shoes	yard
flashlight	monkey wrench	streetcars	zeros
freshman	movie		

1 He handed the cab driver a $10 ________. (*note*)
2 He lived in an old house with quite a big ________. (*garden*)
3 Where can I throw these empty packets? The ________ is full. (*dustbin*)
4 She always went to work by ________. (*underground*)
5 We recently bought a new ________ for the bedroom. (*chest of drawers*)
6 Pass me a ________, please. (*drawing pin*)
7 We went to the ________ to get some nails. (*ironmonger's*)
8 He crashed his car into a ________. (*lamppost*)
9 A million is a one, followed by six ________. (*noughts*)
10 Has anyone seen my ________? (*spanner*)
11 There are still lots of ________ in San Francisco. (*trams*)
12 My uncle is a ________ at a High School. (*caretaker*)
13 He wore a red ________ with his suit. (*waistcoat*)
14 My son's in the 9th ________ at school. (*form, class*)
15 What do you think of my new ________? They're really cool, aren't they? (*trousers*)
16 It's dark in the woods, so take a ________ with you. (*torch*)
17 Excuse me, where's the nearest ________? (*chemist's*)
18 Shall we go and see the new James Bond ________ tonight? (*film*)
19 Can you buy some ________ for the party? (*crisps*)
20 Excuse me, where's the nearest ________, please? (*toilet*)
21 We could play bridge if someone has a ________ of cards. (*pack*)
22 I have a flat ________. (*in the city centre*)
23 We went to the ________ to buy some whisky. (*off-licence*)
24 My son's a ________ at Yale. (*undergraduate*)
25 The car had a California ________. (*number plate*)

2 PAIRS OF WORDS THAT ARE EASILY CONFUSED

A Choose the right word

Here are fifteen pairs of words that are often confused. Fill in the correct word in each sentence. Make any necessary verb changes.

shadow-shade

1 It's so hot! Let's sit in the __________.

2 Is it true that you can tell what time of day it is by the length of someone's __________?

conduct-direct

3 I've always wanted to __________ an orchestra.

4 The film, *Jurassic Park,* was __________ by Stephen Spielberg.

discover-invent

5 They say the Vikings __________ America.

6 Who __________ the first computer?

eventually-possibly

7 I'll see you one day next week – __________ on Friday.

8 After trying his driving test fourteen times, he __________ passed.

collect-gather

9 He went to the Far East to __________ material for his new book.

10 Not so many young people __________ stamps nowadays as they used to.

fit-suit

11 I don't think you should wear yellow. It doesn't __________ you.

12 These shoes don't __________ me. They're too big.

rob-steal

13 She told the police that two youths had attacked her in the park and __________ her mobile phone.

14 Three masked men __________ a bank early this morning.

fantasy-imagination

15 You need a pretty vivid __________ to write fiction.

16 Sherlock Holmes never existed. It's a work of __________.

admission-admittance

17 An enquiry is being held to find out how the man gained __________ to the White House.

18 There was a large sign on the door which said: '__________ £15'.

damp-humid

19 The climate in Singapore is always very hot and __________.

20 In many old houses, the cellar is __________.

avoid-prevent

21 He swerved his car to __________ hitting a dog.

22 Something must be done to '__________ such an accident ever happening again.

economic-economical

23 They say that small cars are far more __________ than big cars.

24 The Prime Minister agreed that the __________ situation had deteriorated in recent months. But he was confident that things would improve soon.

rise-raise

25 'All those in favour, please __________ your hands.'

26 Do you think house prices will go on __________?

check-control

27 She found it hard to __________ her feelings.

28 The immigration officer __________ her passport.

sensible-sensitive

29 If you've hurt someone's feelings, then the __________ thing is to apologize.

30 When it comes to detecting drugs, the customs and police rely on dogs and their very __________ noses.

B Choose one of two

Now fill in the missing words in the sentences below. Choose from the following. Only one word in each pair will be used and make any necessary verb changes.

affect-effect	effective-efficient	recipe-receipt
beside-besides	happy-lucky	remember-remind
blink-wink	match-suit	slander-libel
bring-take	nature-scenery	superstitious-supernatural
channels-canals	opportunity-possibility	
classic-classical	politics-policy	

1 Amsterdam is famous for its __________.

2 The __________ in the north of Sweden is very beautiful.

3 You should always keep the __________ when you buy something – just in case you need to take it back to the shop.

4 Could you __________ me to post this letter on my way home?

5 We've bought these curtains to __________ the carpet in the living-room.

6 Why don't you __________ your boyfriend next time? We'd love to meet him.

7 I never walk under a ladder – I'm very __________.

8 I used to love pop music, but now I prefer __________ music.

9 She is the most __________ secretary we have ever have. I really don't know how I managed without her. She's so good!

10 Parents who hit their children should realize that this could have a deep psychological __________ on them.
11 Having an English boyfriend is a wonderful __________ for you to learn English.
12 He always wins when he plays bingo. He's really __________.
13 I think that man over there fancies me. He just __________ at me.
14 Who else was at the party __________ John and the gang?
15 The government's __________ on immigration has changed a lot in recent years. They're far less generous towards asylum seekers than before.
16 If you print that story about me, then I'll sue you for __________.

Follow up

Work in pairs. Try and make up your own gapped sentences for 8 of the words that weren't used. Give them to another pair to try.

3 HOMONYMS AND HOMOPHONES

A Homonyms

A *homonym* is a word with more than one meaning.
Read through the following pairs of sentences and try to decide which words are missing. The same word is used for both gaps but with two completely different meanings.

Example
Our train __________ at 6.30
The lawn was covered with __________.
Answer = **leaves**

1 Buying shares in this company should be a very __________ investment.
I can't stand the __________ of the bagpipes!
2 Don't ask Paula to join the choir - she can't sing a __________!
He left a __________ for his mother saying he had popped down to the shops.
3 1066 is a __________ most British schoolchildren remember.
I'll always remember my first __________. It was with a girl called Janice and we went to the cinema.
4 Don't forget to __________ the cards before you deal them.
The old man walked with a slow __________.
5 The waiter was so friendly that I gave him a big __________.
It's only the __________ of an iceberg that is visible above the water.
6 Anyone over the age of 65 is __________ to a free bus pass.
His most famous book was __________ *The Assassin.*
7 This ticket will __________ one adult plus one child.
He refused to __________ that he was wrong.
8 We missed the last __________ home and had to walk.
She went to London to __________ to be a nurse.
9 We went to the cinema for a __________ last night.
He gave the taxi driver £5 and said, "Keep the __________!"
10 'This is my favourite __________ from the book. Shall I read it out to you?' she asked.
A narrow __________ ran between the two houses.
11 He was the __________ survivor when the boat sank in the middle of Loch Ness.
There was both cod and __________ on the menu.
12 Do you think the present prince will get the chance to __________ the country soon?
They should do away with the offside __________ in football. We'd see a lot more goals then!
13 He went on a French __________ before going to France for his holiday.
Is there a good golf __________ near here?
14 He was knocked out by a sharp __________ to the head.
I offered to __________ up balloons for the children's party.
15 A lot of British men find it hard to __________ their feelings.
We took the __________ train to London.

B Homophones

A *homophone* is a word that is pronounced the same way but is spelt differently and has a completely different meaning.

Read through the following pairs of sentences and try to work out which two words are missing. They'll sound the same but will be spelt differently.

Example
You are not __________ to walk about naked in public.
The teacher asked the pupil to read the poem __________.
Answer: **allowed-aloud**

1 The __________ of the holly tree is bright red.
Dogs love to __________ bones in the garden.
2 I need to __________ this dress – it's too long.
The priest was standing at the __________.
3 It's nice and sunny today. Let's go down to the __________.
He had a __________ tree at the bottom of his garden.
4 We're going on holiday next __________.
After the operation he felt really __________ and could hardly move.
5 The prison __________ was only 2 x 3 metres.
I need some money so I've decided to __________ my car.
6 The bride looked really lovely as she walked down the __________.
The __________ of Wight is just off the south coast of England.
7 The letter was __________ by airmail.
Flowers are chosen for their __________ as well as the way they look.
8 Her wedding ring was made of 22- __________ gold.
He gave a __________ to his pet rabbit.
9 A male __________ is called a stag and a female a hind.
The watch was too __________ so he decided not to buy it.
10 He ordered a plate of __________ at his favourite restaurant in Brussels.
You exercise lots of __________ when you go swimming.
11 Japanese people usually __________ when they greet one another.
He hit his head on the __________ of the tree.
12 The snooker player rubbed chalk onto the end of his __________ before potting the red.
There was a long __________ outside the cinema, waiting to buy tickets for the premier of the new *Star Wars* film.
13 A __________ of cattle came thundering past.
Have you ever __________ the sound of a nightingale?
14 Does Kathy __________ her hair?
Hundreds of people __________ on our roads every year.
15 Nowadays you don't usually feel any __________ when you have a tooth out.
The cricket ball broke a __________ in the window of a nearby house.

4 WORDS THAT GO TOGETHER (COLLOCATIONS)

A Adjective + noun combinations

Fill in the gaps in the sentences below by taking an adjective from A and a noun from B. Use each word once only.

A

active	golden	rough
ambiguous	haunted	thorough
confirmed	identical	torrential
deadly	infectious	unwritten
delicious	naked	vivid
fatal	narrow	worthy
flat	residential	

B

accident	guess	rain
area	house	search
bachelor	imagination	statement
cause	law	twins
disease	meal	tyre
escape	opportunity	volcano
eye	poison	

1 'That was a really ________ ________, Margaret' said Bob to his hostess.' You really must give me the recipe some time.'

2 'How many people were at the concert?'
'It's hard to say, but at a ________ ________ about 25,000.'

3 'I'm sorry I'm late. I got a ________ ________ on the motorway.'

4 They were ________ ________ and it was almost impossible to tell them apart.

5 To be a good writer, you need to have a ________ ________.

6 Mars and Venus are two planets that can easily be seen with the ________ ________. (You don't need a telescope.)

7 Don't eat those mushrooms - they contain a ________ ________ which will kill you in minutes.

8 The police made a ________ ________ of the area, but couldn't find any trace of the missing schoolgirls.

9 'Come on everyone - buy a raffle ticket for *Children in Need*. It's a very ________ ________ after all.

10 Two days of ________ ________ made the pitch so wet that the match had to be cancelled.

11 This is rather an ________ ________ You'd better rewrite it so that it's absolutely clear what we mean.

12 'This job offer in Canada is a ________ ________. for you James,' his father said. 'Certainly one you shouldn't turn down.'

13 'As measles is an ________ ________, you'd better keep your son at home until he's better,' the doctor said.

14 He had a ________ ________ when his car skidded on the icy surface and crashed into a hedge - just inches away from a steel lamppost.

15 I'm scared of ghosts, so you definitely wouldn't get me to stay at a ________ ________.

16 Mount Etna in Italy is still an ________ ________. So is Vesuvius.

17 He died in a ________ ________ while exploring the jungles of New Guinea.

18 There is an __________ __________ in this club that members do not borrow money from each other.
19 I don't think Andrew will ever get married. He's a __________ __________.
20 The nightclub was in the middle of a __________ __________, and was constantly receiving complaints about noise.

B Verb + noun combinations

Fill in the gaps in the sentences below by taking a verb from A and a noun from B. Use each word once only. Make any necessary verb changes.

A

bear	foretell	pay
catch	forge	play
change	have	quench
cook	hold	recite
commit	inherit	throw
cut	keep	undergo
foot	lose	

B

attention	future	operation
bill	fortune	party
books	fit	poem
change	grudge	signature
cold	line	thirst
crime	losses	truant
face	mind	

1 'Could you __________ the __________, please, caller? I'm just putting you through.'
2 'Atishoo!'
'Bless you! Have you __________ a __________ again?'
3 'Your mother will __________ a __________ when she sees that tattoo on your stomach!'
4 People who drive over the speed-limit don't always realize that they're __________ a __________ and certainly wouldn't think of themselves as criminals.
5 Forget beer! Water is the best thing to __________ your __________.
6 'I definitely didn't sign this cheque. Someone must have __________ my __________!'
7 'What do you mean you won't marry me? You said you would the other day. We've even picked the date of the wedding!'
'I know, but I've __________ my __________!'
8 'Cathy will __________ a __________ when her parents die. No wonder so many men want to go out with her!'
9 The student stood up and __________ a __________ by Robert Browning.
10 '__________ the __________!' he said as he paid and got out of the taxi.
11 He claimed he had psychic powers and could __________ the __________. (But he couldn't tell me next Saturday's winning Lottery numbers!)
12 'Could you all __________ __________, please! I have a very important announcement to make.'
13 My mother has to go into hospital next month to __________ a hip __________.
14 He __________ __________ a lot when he was a teenager. In fact, he was hardly ever at school.
15 The share prices were falling all the time so, in the end, he decided to __________ his __________ and sell most of them before they fell even more.

16 In Japan and many other cultures - especially in the Far East - it is very important not to __________ __________.

17 In Britain, it's customary for the father of the bride to __________ the __________ for his daughter's wedding. If he has more than one daughter, then this can be quite expensive.

18 Jack has never forgiven his brother for stealing and later marrying his girlfriend. In fact, he still __________ a __________ towards him.

19 On her 60th birthday, Norma decided to __________ a big __________ for all her friends and relatives.

20 The accountant was arrested and later sent to prison for __________ the __________.

5 WORDS OF SIMILAR MEANING (SYNONYMS)

A Find the synonyms

Look at the adjectives, verbs and nouns below. For each word, write two others that have a similar meaning. Choose from the following. Not all the words will be used. Use a dictionary, if necessary.

affluent	depressed	hideous	response
anecdote	detest	huge	rival
assassinate	enormous	irate	scare
bicker	exterminate	loathe	sunset
bold	feat	miserable	tale
cease	furious	peril	terminate
cheat	fury	quarrel	terrify
clutch	glare	rage	twilight
courageous	hazard	reply	weary
dawn	heartless	repulsive	well-off

ADJECTIVES

1 angry ____________ ____________
2 brave ____________ ____________
3 rich ____________ ____________
4 unhappy ____________ ____________
5 very big ____________ ____________

VERBS

6 argue ____________ ____________
7 frighten ____________ ____________
8 hate ____________ ____________
9 kill ____________ ____________
10 stop ____________ ____________

NOUNS

11 anger ____________ ____________
12 answer ____________ ____________
13 danger ____________ ____________
14 dusk ____________ ____________
15 story ____________ ____________

B Choose a synonym

Complete the sentences below with an adjective that is similar in meaning to the word in **bold type**. Choose from the following words. Not all of them will be used.

cloudy	keen	tasteless	unoccupied
complicated	mean	unavoidable	unpaid
conceited	priceless	unbelievable	unreadable
energetic	shy	unexpected	very bright
genuine	spacious	unfavourable	very drunk
helpful	stubborn	unfeeling	very strange

1 A **vivid** colour is ___________.
2 A **weird** person is ___________.
3 A **tight-fisted** person is ___________.
4 An **authentic** document is ___________.
5 A **bashful** person is ___________.
6 An **empty** flat is ___________.
7 A **big-headed** person is ___________.
8 An **adverse** report is ___________.
9 A **legless** person is ___________.
10 An **obstinate** person is ___________.
11 An **outstanding** debt is ___________.
12 An **unforeseen** event is ___________.
13 An **overcast** sky is ___________.
14 **Illegible** handwriting is ___________.
15 A **callous** person is ___________.
16 An **inevitable** result is ___________.
17 An **invaluable** object is ___________.
18 **Insipid** food is ___________.
19 An **incredible** story is ___________.
20 A **constructive** suggestion is ___________.

6 TWO WORDS MAKE ONE (COMPOUND WORDS)

A Compound nouns

Take a word from A and a word from B to form a new word. Write each word next to the correct definition below. Some words will be a single word, e.g. postman, while others will be two words, e.g. shop assistant.

A		**B**	
bar	hay	agent	moon
beauty	heart	alarm	neck
bottle	honey	attack	penalty
burglar	human	bow	rights
cat	life	chair	slaughter
contact	man	fever	spot
death	mother	gain	stroke
ear	rain	guard	tongue
estate	sun	house	walk
green	wheel	lenses	wig

1 ____________ What *Amnesty International* fights for all the time.
2 ____________ Something bought cheaply or for less than the usual price.
3 ____________ This might prevent people from breaking into your house.
4 ____________ Some people wear these instead of glasses.
5 ____________ A common cause of death.
6 ____________ An illness like a bad cold, caused by the pollen of flowers, etc. People usually suffer form this during the summer.
7 ____________ Something used by people who can't walk.
8 ____________ The 'ultimate' form of punishment.
9 ____________ What models walk along at fashion shows.
10 ____________ A kind of insect which, according to some people, likes to burrow into people's ears.
11 ____________ A person whose job is to buy and sell houses.
12 ____________ The coloured arch sometimes seen in the sky when rain is falling and the sun is shining at the same time.
13 ____________ Killing someone accidentally.
14 ____________ A place of great natural beauty.
15 ____________ A serious illness caused by being in very hot sunshine for too long.
16 ____________ A holiday taken by two people who have just got married.
17 ____________ A person whose job is to protect and rescue swimmers at the beach or at a swimming pool.
18 ____________ Your main language – usually the first one you learnt as a child.
19 ____________ A place in a road where the traffic can't pass easily, so that there are lots of delays.
20 ____________ A building, usually made of glass, in which plants are grown.

B Compound adjectives

Fill in the gaps in the sentences below using a suitable compound adjective. Choose from the following. Not all the words will be used.

absent-minded	cold-blooded	law-abiding	tight-fisted
air-conditioned	dead-end	light-fingered	time-consuming
badly-paid	drive-in	never-ending	two-faced
brand-new	duty-free	off-peak	whole-hearted
broken-hearted	far-fetched	part-time	
built-up	first-class	second-hand	
bullet-proof	house-trained	so-called	

1 Before he flew to Canada, he went into the __________ shop to buy a bottle of whisky and some chocolates.
2 For his protection, the Prime Minister wore a __________ vest.
3 The troubles in the Middle East seem __________.
4 Teresa was __________ when her boyfriend finished with her.
5 It was a really hot and humid day, so we were glad that the taxi was __________.
6 The __________ 'Irish' group playing at the pub was made up of an Englishman, a Welshman and two Italians.
7 It was a really __________ job. All I got was £3 an hour.
8 Telephone charges are lower during __________ periods, such as after 6 p.m. and at the weekend.
9 You're not allowed to drive more than 50 kilometres per hour in a __________ area.
10 Swedes, on the whole, are very __________.They don't usually break the law.
11 He was in a __________ job with no hope of getting promotion.
12 When you buy a puppy, make sure it is __________ first.
13 She never buys anyone a drink. She's so __________.
14 We couldn't afford a __________ cooker, so we bought a __________ one instead.
15 We didn't believe her story - it was too __________.
16 The professor was very __________ and was always forgetting things.
17 Keep your eye on Jack. He's __________ and often steals things.
18 My son has got a __________ job at weekends at a local supermarket.
19 At his summing up, the judge called the prisoner a __________ killer who deserved to be put away for life.

Follow up

Work in pairs. Make up sentences to show the meanings of the five words that have not been used.

7 PHRASAL VERBS 1

Choose a phrasal verb

Fill in the missing phrasal verbs in the sentences below. Choose from the following and make any verb changes that may be necessary. To help you, there's a Swedish translation in brackets after each sentence.

break down	count on	go down	keep off
break in	cut off	go in for	look out
bring up	do up	go off	look up
call off	dress up	go out	pass out
catch up	drop out of	go through with	pull through
close down	find out	go with	take after
come into	get on	hang up	
come round	get together	hold on	

1 'I won't let you down, Sandra. You can __________ me.' *(räkna med, lita på)*
2 'I'm sorry I'm late,' he said, 'but my car __________ on the motorway.' *(gå sönder)*
3 We didn't know when the next train left, so Jenny said she would go and __________. *(ta reda på)*
4 The *Titanic* __________ on her maiden voyage when the ship hit an iceberg. *(skjunka)*
5 There was a flash of lightning and seconds later all the lights __________. *(slockna)*
6 The two friends __________ like a house on fire. *(dra jämnt, komma bra överens)*
7 A last-minute injury forced her to __________ the race. *(hoppa av)*
8 Thieves __________ at the weekend and stole three valuable paintings. *(bryta sig in)*
9 They had to__________ the open-air pop concert because of bad weather. *(inställa)*
10 I was phoning my girlfriend when we were suddenly __________. *(/av/bryta)*
11 'If you could just __________ a minute, please, I'll see if Mr Carter is available.' *(dröja, vänta)*
12 If the factory __________ more than 1,500 people will be out of work. *(stänga)*
13 'Don't drink that milk - it's __________!' *(bli dålig)*
14 He planned to __________ the old house and then sell it for a huge profit. *(renovera, rusta upp)*
15 If you don't know what a word means, then __________ it __________ in a dictionary. *(slå upp)*
16 When her parents died, she was __________ by her grandparents. *(uppfostra)*
17 There was a sign in the park telling everyone to __________ the grass. *(hålla sig borta från)*
18 'Do we really have to __________ for the end-of-term party? Can't we just go in jeans?' *(klä upp sig)*
19 Bill is having second thoughts about emigrating to Saudi Arabia. I don't think he'll __________ it after all. *(genomföra, fullfölja)*
20 '__________! There's a car coming!' he shouted to the child who was about to cross the road. *(se upp)*
21 We try to __________ at least once a month - either for a drink or a meal. *(träffas, mötas)*

22 It took the boxer quite a while to ________ after he had been knocked out by his opponent in the fourth round. *(kvickna till, återfå medvetandet)*

23 When I phoned her, she didn't want to speak to me and ________ immediately. *(lägga på luren)*

24 The room was so hot and stuffy that she thought she was going to ________. *(svimma)*

25 His injuries were so serious that his doctors didn't think he'd ________. *(klara sig)*

26 'I'm thinking of ________ the London Marathon next year, so I'm starting to train for it already.' *(delta i)*

27 Sally will ________ quite a lot of money when her parents die. *(få, ärva)*

28 The race leader was too far ahead for the other runners to ________ her ________ . *(komma ikapp)*

29 'Your son has a very good voice, Mr Matthews.'
'Well, he certainly doesn't ________ me. I'm tone deaf and can't sing a note!' *(brås på, likna)*

30 'Do you think this blouse will ________ my black skirt?' *(passa till, gå till)*

8 PHRASAL VERBS 2

Choose a phrasal verb

Fill in the missing phrasal verbs in the sentences below. Choose from the following and make any verb changes that may be necessary. To help you, there's a Swedish translation in brackets after each sentence.

break down	grow up	look up to	send off
drop off	hand out	make up for	set out
fall for	hold down	pick up	settle down
fall through	hold up	play up	stand out
get through	keep up with	put in	take to
go down with	leave out	put off	turn in
go off	let off	put out	
go round	look down on	put up with	

1 She had bright green hair and really __________ in a crowd. *(framträda)*
2 When he heard the news of his wife's death he __________ and cried. *(bryta ihop, bryta samman)*
3 I tried phoning Channel 4 after the programme to protest, but I couldn't __________. All the lines were engaged. *(komma fram)*
4 The TV programme was so boring that she __________ half way through it. *(somna in)*
5 'You didn't __________ that old £5 note trick, did you? I didn't think you were so gullible!' *(gå på, låta sig luras)*
6 We __________ early to avoid the traffic. *(ge sig i väg)*
7 The player was __________ for punching the goalkeeper. *(utvisa)*
8 The teacher asked one of the students to __________ the exam papers. *(dela ut)*
9 'Sue can't come to the party. She's __________ measles.' *(få, drabbas av)*
10 'You're so childish sometimes, Gareth! Why don't you __________.!' *(bli vuxen)*
11 Thirty innocent people were killed and hundreds injured when the bomb __________ in the middle of the busy shopping centre. *(explodera, smälla)*
12 Gareth Bale was very disappointed when he was __________ of the team to play against Barcelona. *(utelämna, inte ta med)*
13 He __________ quite a lot of French when he lived in Paris for a year. *(lära sig)*
14 Our plans to hold a weekend rock festival __________ when local residents objected to it. *(misslyckas)*
15 There are some political leaders worth __________ these days. *(se upp till)*
16 The teacher was new and inexperienced, so the pupils __________ her __________. *(bräcka)*
17 The train was __________ for several hours because of an accident on the line. *(försena)*
18 'I'll probably __________ when I'm about 35. I'm too young to get married and start a family yet,' *(slå sig till ro, stadga sig)*
19 'By the way, Geoff, there's no meeting tonight. It's been __________ until next week.' *(skjuta upp)*

20 I tried playing golf once, but I never really __________ it. As far as I was concerned, it was just a good walk spoilt. *(bli förtjust i)*

21 'Share these sweets among you,' the mother said. 'There should be enough to __________.' *(räcka till för alla)*

22 It took the firefighters several hours to __________ the fire. *(släcka)*

23 My neighbour's a real snob and __________ anyone who is poor or working-class. *(se ned på)*

24 As you get older, you don't really worry about __________ the latest trends or fashion. *(hänga med, följa med)*

25 It was so cold last winter that we've decided to __________ a new central heating system. *(installera)*

26 'Honestly! The way he treats her! I don't know how she __________ it!' *(finna sig i, tåla, tolerera)*

27 There must be something wrong with Gerald. He just can't seem to __________ a job for long. *(lyckas behålla)*

28 As it was his first offence, the judge __________ him __________. *(låta slippa undan)*

29 'I'm feeling very tired. I think I'll __________ now.' *(gå och lägga sig)*

30 When Tom returned to school after a long illness, he had to work really hard to __________ the time he had missed. *(ta igen, hämta in)*

9 IDIOMS 1

Each of the sentences below contains an idiom. Unfortunately they're incomplete. Choose the missing word or words from the ones given (a, b or c).

1 'It can't possibly be true! No way! **You're** just **pulling my** __________!'
a) hair b) finger c) leg

2 We almost had an accident today. It was **a** __________ **shave**.
a) near b) thin c) close

3 'That's not what I meant at all! As usual, Paula, you've **got hold of the wrong end of the** __________!'
a) stick b) jug c) coin

4 'I'm too smart for you. You can't **pull the** __________ **over my eyes**.'
a) cap b) wool c) blanket

5 'Unless you **pull your** __________ up Harry, you're going to fail your exams next summer,' the teacher told him.
a) socks b) trousers c) sleeves

6 I said hello to Carol, but for some reason she **gave me the** __________.
a) back of her hand b) cold shoulder c) closed mouth

7 I've always **had** __________ for Asian women. It's probably because the first girl I ever fell in love with came from Thailand.
a) a sweet tooth b) weak lips c) a soft spot

8 'What's the matter with you, Pam? You're **like a cat** __________.'
'Yes, I know. I'm waiting for my test results.'
a) on hot bricks b) on thin ice c) in boiling water

9 Mr Brown's not looking too pleased. I think he's **got a** __________ **to pick with you**.
a) goose b) tooth c) bone

10 My father lost his job last week. There were fifteen people altogether who **got** __________.
a) the sack b) the cards c) the kick

11 Harry's really **gone** __________ since he lost his job and his wife left him.
a) to the cleaners b) down the drain c) to the dogs

12 'Joseph must be __________! Fancy turning down a free trip around the world!'
a) the worse for wear b) off his head c) up the pole

13 'I got paid £150 for helping out at the pub last weekend. All I had to do was collect the glasses. Honestly, Barry, It was **money for** __________.'
a) used cars b) broken glass c) old rope

14 My 15-year-old daughter wanted to go on holiday with her friends, but I soon __________ and made her come on holiday with us instead.
a) hit the nail on the head b) crossed my arms c) put my foot down

15 'It's supposed to be a secret, so make sure you **don't let the** __________ **out of the bag**.'
a) snake b) cat c) bear

16 'Hurry up or we'll miss the last bus home!'
'All right! All right! **Keep your** __________ on! I'm coming!'
a) hair b) knickers c) hat

17 Paul never wears a hat. He's **got** __________ **in his bonnet** about hats causing baldness.
a) a bug b) a bee c) a beetle

18 For some reason he **has** __________ **on his shoulder** about not having gone to university.
a) a chip b) an egg c) a weight

19 University students often find it hard to __________.
a) bake a whole loaf b) make ends meet c) stretch their legs

20 Honestly, darling, I don't know what all the fuss is about. If you ask me, they're **making** __________ **out of a molehill**!'
a) a pyramid b) a mountain c) a volcano

21 His new book is **selling like** __________. At this rate we'll have sold out of them by the end of the week.
a) melted butter b) fresh bread c) hot cakes

22 The owner was going abroad and wanted a quick sale, so I **got** his car **for** __________. I only paid £1,500 for it.
a) a song b) a smile c) a wink

23 My brother has always been careful with money and has never **lived beyond his** __________.
a) wallet b) means c) possessions

24 The headmaster __________ when he found three pupils hiding in the toilets when they should have been doing a French test.
a) hit the fan b) saw pink elephants c) blew his top

25 The English test was really easy. It was **a piece of** __________.
a) chocolate b) cake c) cheese

10 IDIOMS 2

Each of the sentences below contains an idiom. Unfortunately they're incomplete. Choose the missing word or words from the ones given.

1 It always seems to be very difficult to __________ **the waiter's eye** when you're in a hurry and want to pay the bill.
a) see b) catch c) hold

2 He deceived us. He **led us** __________.
a) down the aisle b) up the garden path c) over the mountain

3 'Don't tease her. She'll only **fly off the** __________.'
a) roof b) broom c) handle

4 'Trust you to **put your** __________ **in it**. How could you serve steak and chips when you knew she was a vegetarian!'
a) boot b) mouth c) foot

5 My uncle **had to** really pull __________ to get me a summer job at the local hospital.
a) belts b) strings c) his weight

6 'Of course the deal will go through. Don't worry. It's **in the** __________.'
a) dish b) bag c) frying pan

7 When I heard that Margaret had married Gary Day **you could have knocked me down with a** __________!
a) steamroller b) brick c) feather

8 I know the press are making a big fuss now, but it's probably just **a storm in a** __________.
a) teacup b) sherry glass c) bucket

9 She should take that job in publishing. It sounds just **up her** __________.
a) lane b) alley c) street

10 If you want a flat in the centre of Stockholm, then you have to **pay through the** __________ for it.
a) nose b) shirt c) table

11 'I hope you don't think I'm __________ when I say that I'm a very good voice and really ought to be in the school choir.'
a) beating my own drum b) blowing my own trumpet c) inflating my own balloon

12 She was **feeling** a bit **under the** __________, so her mother kept her home from school.
a) table b) colour c) weather

13 'I'm trying my driving test tomorrow, so **keep your** __________ **crossed** for me.'
a) legs b) fingers c) thumbs

14 He caught the last bus home **by the skin of his** __________. Another minute, and he'd have missed it.
a) neck b) nose c) teeth

15 Brenda was born and brought up in Liverpool and **knows it like the** __________.
a) tip of her tongue b) back of her hand c) nose on her face

16 He's going bald. He's **a bit** __________ **on top**.
a) thin b) scaly c) shiny

17 I don't think their success will last. They're just a __________.

a) needle in a haystack b) voice in the dark c) flash in the pan

18 My father **got** a bit **hot under the** __________ trying to explain the facts of life to me and my brother.

a) arms b) collar c) belt

19 I would never leave Britain – **not for all the** __________.

a) tea in China b) sand in the Sahara c) fish in the sea

20 He never buys his nephews or nieces birthday presents – he's really __________.

a) light-fingered b) stiff-necked c) tight-fisted

21 My father __________ when I told him that I'd lost the car keys. I don't think I've ever seen him so angry before.

a) hit the roof b) saw planets c) brought the house down

22 He's in a very bad mood today. He's **like** __________.

a) a dog in heat b) a bear with a sore head c) a tiger in a supermarket

23 I never prepare speeches. I prefer speaking **off** __________.

a) the cufflinks b) the top of my head c) the wrong foot

24 'I do wish you'd come to the point, James instead of __________ **about the bush** all the time!'

a) beating b) rushing c) leaping

25 'I'm going to be a famous film director one day.'

"Yes, and __________!'

a) penguins might dance b) pigs might fly c) cows might talk

USE OF ENGLISH

1 SENTENCE CHANGING 1

Complete the second sentence so that it has a similar meaning to the first sentence, using the words given. *Do not change the word given*. You must use between *two* and *five* words, including the word given.

1 We were surprised to see Pam at the concert.
EXPECT
We ________________________________ to see Pam at the concert.

2 I certainly won't go to that nightclub again!
LAST
That ________________________________ I go to that nightclub!

3 Everyone has heard about the hot springs in Iceland.
FAMOUS
Iceland ________________________________ hot springs.

4 I don't have much money so I can't go out this weekend.
COULD
If I ________________________________ go out this weekend.

5 Is it necessary for me to do the homework tonight?
HAVE
Do ________________________________ do the homework tonight?

6 Molly is very excited about going to the circus.
LOOKING
Molly is ________________________________ to the circus.

7 The hotel was full.
VACANCIES
There ________________________________ the hotel.

8 This is the best wine I've ever tasted.
BETTER
I've ________________________________ this.

9 The weather was so bad that we had to cancel the picnic.
SUCH
It ________________________________ that we had to cancel the picnic.

10 The food was so hot that we couldn't eat it.
TOO
The food was ________________________________ eat.

11 Are they Irish?
COME
Do ________________________________ Ireland?

12 He didn't kiss his wife goodbye when he left.

WITHOUT

He ________________________________ his wife goodbye.

13 It's a pity I didn't work harder at school.

WISH

I ________________________________ harder at school.

14 I completed that crossword puzzle in ten minutes.

TOOK

It ________________________________ complete that crossword puzzle.

15 Pam and Dave's wedding takes place next Saturday.

MARRIED

Pam and Dave ________________________________ next Saturday.

16 'I'm sorry I didn't phone to say I'd be late,' said Mark.

APOLOGIZED

Mark ________________________________ phoning to say he'd be late.

17 The only person who didn't come to the party was Clive.

EXCEPT

Everyone ________________________________ Clive.

18 Elvis Presley was forty-two when he died.

AGE

Elvis Presley ________________________________ forty-two.

19 The singer avoided the crowds of fans by leaving by a side door.

ORDER

The singer left by a side door ________________________________ the crowds of fans.

20 We watched TV the whole evening.

SPENT

We ________________________________ watching TV.

2 SENTENCE CHANGING 2

Complete the second sentence so that it has a similar meaning to the first sentence, using the words given. *Do not change the word given.* You must use between *two* and *five* words, including the word given.

1 It was the first time Sally had been abroad.
NEVER
Sally ______________________ abroad before.

2 'What's the time?' Danny asked.
KNOW
Danny ______________________ the time was.

3 Our way of living is not the same as theirs.
DIFFERENT
Our way of living ______________________ theirs.

4 It was really bad of you to drive after you had been drinking.
SHOULD
You ______________________ after you'd been drinking.

5 Harry was too short to join the police force.
ENOUGH
Harry ______________________ to join the police force.

6 After nearly half an hour the ambulance still hadn't arrived.
SIGN
After nearly half an hour ______________________ of the ambulance.

7 My brother hasn't contacted me for over two months.
HEARD
I ______________________ my brother for over two months.

8 Old people need less sleep than young people.
MORE
Young people ______________________ old people.

9 I don't really want to stay at home tonight.
PREFER
I ______________________ stay at home tonight.

10 You can stay with my sister if you're ever in Cardiff.
PUT
My sister will ______________________ if you're ever in Cardiff.

11 It's years since I saw Chris.
SEEN
I ______________________ for years.

12 They continued to play despite the bad weather.

THOUGH

They continued to play even ________________________ bad.

13 'Will you babysit for us tonight?'

ASKED

She ________________________ for her tonight.

14 'You really must have another drink,' he said to her.

INSISTED

He ________________________ another drink.

15 Don't work overtime if you don't feel like it.

POINT

There's ________________________ overtime if you don't feel like it.

16 Jamaica won the gold medal in the men's 4 x 400 metres relay.

AWARDED

Jamaica ________________________ gold medal in the men's 4 x 400 metres relay.

17 I didn't go shopping today so I couldn't buy any bread.

BOUGHT

If I'd gone shopping today ________________________ some bread.

18 Is this umbrella yours?

BELONG

Does ________________________ you?

19 Michael is the best player in the team.

BETTER

No one in the team ________________________ Michael.

20 I should very much like to be able to dance well.

WISH

I ________________________ dance well.

3 ONE WORD ONLY 1

Read the sentences below and think of the word which best fits each gap. Use **one word** only in each gap.

1 It's ________ easier to learn to play the guitar ________ a teacher ________ by trying to teach yourself.
2 She has ________ living in Brighton ________ 1991.
3 ________ he first lived in Italy it took him a long time to get ________ to driving ________ the right.
4 'How ________ do you go jogging?'
'Oh, about once ________ week.'
5 Peter doesn't sing ________ well as his brother, but he's a much ________ keyboard player.
6 Sally ________ come with us tonight ________ she's got a cold.
7 I ________ learning French five years ________, but I've ________ got a lot to learn.
8 I haven't smoked ________ ten years. In fact, I can't really remember what a cigarette tastes ________.
9 'Is that red Volvo ________?'
'No, it's ________ mine. I ________ drive.'
10 I'm ________ to get a job in television when I ________ university.
11 'How ________ does it take to ________ to London?'
'About twenty minutes ________ car.'
12 ________ was a Bank Holiday yesterday so, as usual, ________ were lots of cars on the roads.
13 He's been decorating the kitchen ________ last week and still hasn't finished it ________.
14 Which bus ________ you catch home ________ night?
15 In Britain, it is ________ cheaper to go by bus ________ to go by train.
16 ________ of my relatives live in Wales but ________ two of them speak Welsh.
17 How ________ people ________ there at the meeting last night?
18 '________'s the time, please?'
'It's ________ three o'clock.'
19 'Did you ________ anything interesting yesterday?'
'No, not ________ I just ________ some shopping in the afternoon, that's ________'
20 You will ________ to work much harder ________ you're going to pass your exam ________ the summer.
21 'Have you ever ________ to London before?'
'No, this ________ my first visit.'
22 She moved to Belgium two years ________ and has been living and working ________ ever since.
23 We didn't know that our flight ________ be delayed. We ________ to wait in the departure lounge for ________ than three hours.

24 You __________ have seen Mary in London yesterday. She's been in Canada __________ the past month.

25 I need __________ milk. I haven't got __________ left.

4 ONE WORD ONLY 2

In this text there are a number of gaps. Each gap is to be filled with **ONE** word that makes sense in the context and that is grammatically correct.

A Strange Prophesy

In 1975 three (1)__________the islands in the Comore group (2)__________ lies between Africa and Madagascar, declared (3)__________ independence (4)__________ France. Soon afterwards a man (5)__________ Ali Soilih declared himself dictator (6)__________ the tiny state with the military (7)__________ of a French mercenary, Bob Denard. Soilih proved to be a despot: he raised death squads, kidnapped and (8)__________ women and organized the destruction of (9)__________ machinery (10)__________ the islands.

Two years (11)__________ his reign Soilih consulted a witchdoctor in (12)__________ to know what the (13)__________ held for himself and his (14)__________. The witchdoctor was encouraging. Soilih could (15)__________ be killed by a man who (16)__________ a dog. Upon hearing this, Soilih acted (17)__________ any dictator (18)__________ and had his death squads kill all the (19)__________ on the island.

Nevertheless, a year (20)__________, he was dead – 'shot' while (21)__________ to escape by the forces (22)__________. his old comrade, Bob Denard. The French mercenary had (23)__________ a new contract, this time from one of Soilih's many (24)__________. And the witchdoctor had (25)__________ right. (26)__________ Denard's troops was his ever-present mascot – a large Alsatian dog.

5 ONE WORD ONLY 3

In this text there are a number of gaps. Each gap is to be filled with **ONE** word that makes sense in the context and that is grammatically correct.

How to Give Up Smoking

Here is a fifteen-step system that will allow you to (1)__________ control of your smoking habit.

Set a target quitting date. (2)__________ a day you think that stress will be minimal and you won't be around (3)__________ smokers. Then, once you've set a target date (4)__________ time in the future.

Keep a (5)__________ of your smoking habits, including the times and places you smoke. Keeping a 'smoking diary' (6)__________ help you to recognize how (7)__________ you smoke and why you smoke. Did a confrontation with a classmate or co-worker or an upsetting phone call make you (8)__________ for your cigarettes?

Designate a 'smoking place' and smoke (9)__________ in those places. Choose a place (10)__________ is inconvenient and uncomfortable. One person chose the corner of his basement, (11)__________ chose the front lawn. If it's raining or very cold, you might (12)__________ to stay indoors (13)__________ than smoke. And you will look silly standing there smoking on your front lawn.

(14)__________ ashtrays and lighters only in this designated smoking place.

Don't carry cigarettes with you. Ask non-smokers (spouse, friends) to hold your cigarettes. You will (15)__________ to ask for a cigarette (16)__________ you want one.

Smoke alone and do nothing (17)__________. No watching TV, drinking coffee or talking on the phone while smoking. Take the pleasure (18)__________ of the habit. Make smoking a chore.

Change smoking postures. If you (19)__________ hold your cigarette in your right hand, (20)__________ to your left. If you draw from your cigarette on the left side of your mouth, switch to the right. These changes (21)__________ make smoking more awkward and uncomfortable for you.

Buy one packet of cigarettes at a (22)__________ and change to a (23)__________ tar brand.

Delay your first smoke of the day and the first one (24)__________ a meal. Start with a half-hour delay and (25)__________ up to an hour.

When you want a cigarette, put (26)__________ lighting it for a while. Hold it in your hand and tell (27)__________, 'I don't need this just (28)__________.' Once you begin to take (29)__________ of your habit, the urge for a cigarette might pass.

Set up a support network. Choose sympathetic friends (perhaps ex-smokers) (30)__________ you can call when you (31)__________ the urge for a cigarette.

Start an exercise programme to help (32)__________ weight gain. But remember: quitting is the goal. You can (33)__________ about any extra kilos later.

Reward yourself often for (34)__________ your goals. If you (35)__________ down smoking before your target date arrives, quitting should be (36)__________ stressful.

6 WORD-BUILDING 1

Complete the following sentences by changing the words in **bold type** into a word (noun, adjective, adverb or verb) that fits suitably in each gap.

1 How much did they charge for ________ to the Van Gough exhibition? **ADMIT**
2 The reporter asked the Prime Minister for his ________ of the situation. **ANALYSE**
3 She wasn't feeling very well, so she made an ________ to see the doctor. **APPOINT**
4 Scotland is well-known for the ________ of its scenery. **BEAUTIFUL**
5 My wife and I are always having ________ about whose turn it is to do the hoovering. **ARGUE**
6 He'll never get the job; he lacks ________ in himself. **CONFIDENT**
7 Scandinavian Airways apologized for any ________ caused by the late arrival of flight SK 506. **CONVENIENT**
8 Cinema or theatre? It's your ________. I really don't mind where we go. **DECIDE**
9 To his great ________, he failed to get a place at university. **DISAPPOINT**
10 I seem to spend most of my time at work dealing with ________ from the public. **ENQUIRE**
11 He could give no satisfactory ________ for his behaviour. **EXPLAIN**
12 Burglaries seem to occur in this area with alarming ________. **FREQUENT**
13 'Life has not been easy for you,' began the fortune-teller. 'There seems to be a lot of ________ in your past.' **HAPPY**
14 The one thing you need above all else to be a successful writer is a vivid ________. **IMAGINE**
15 The job requires a working ________ of French and German. **KNOW**
16 My brother's ambition is to be a professional ________. **MUSIC**
17 Is there any ________ of us all getting together again on Friday? **POSSIBLE**
18 It was your own ________ and nothing else that led to the accident! **STUPID**
19 There can be little doubt that ________ in modern society is on the increase. **VIOLENT**
20 Switzerland and Austria are very ________ countries. **MOUNTAIN**
21 Which ________ do you prefer – Monet or Picasso? **ART**
22 Rugby is the ________ sport of both Wales and New Zealand. **NATION**
23 They say that money can't buy you ________, but it might help you to suffer in comfort. **HAPPY**
24 Ted's such a ________ driver, isn't he? I really can't understand how he hasn't had an accident yet. **CARE**
25 He seemed friendly, but in ________ he was only after her money. **REAL**

7 WORD-BUILDING 2

Complete the following sentences by changing the words in **bold type** into a word (noun, adjective, adverb or verb) that fits suitably in each gap.

1 I kept well away from the dog because it looked rather ______. **FRIEND**
2 If you have any ______ to make then go and see the manager. **COMPLAIN**
3 A loud cheer went up from the crowd at the sudden ______ of the President. **APPEAR**
4 Be careful how you drive. The roads are very ______ tonight. **ICE**
5 If you are in a position of authority, it must be a great ______ sometimes to misuse your power. **TEMPT**
6 Most of the people stared in ______ and horror as the two planes crashed into each other on the runway. **BELIEVE**
7 Their ______ was delayed because of bad weather. **DEPART**
8 It was a very important match and you could almost feel the ______ amongst the players. **TENSE**
9 It was very ______ of you to expect everyone to work overtime tonight at such short notice. **REASON**
10 To many people, pornography and prostitution are just two examples of men's ______ of women. **EXPLOIT**
11 We had to get special ______ to leave early. **PERMIT**
12 We've accepted their ______ so that's an end to the matter as far as we're concerned. **APOLOGIZE**
13 There was a ______ at the local post office at the weekend. **ROB**
14 Since her book became a best-seller, she has become quite a ______ and regularly appears on various chat shows. **CELEBRATE**
15 The sudden ______ of the chief cashier shortly after the bank robbery made the police very suspicious. **DISAPPEAR**
16 He spent his ______ in the Lake District. **CHILD**
17 Christopher Columbus is supposed to have ______ America in 1492. **DISCOVERY**
18 There was a history of ______ in her family. Both her grandmother and her uncle had gone mad. **INSANE**
19 When the fire broke out in the department store, there was a lot of ______ as people tried to leave the building. **CONFUSED**
20 ______ at the centre included hang-gliding, canoeing and rock-climbing. **ACTIVE**
21 Have you noticed that the new secretary bears a striking ______ to Lady Gaga? **RESEMBLE**
22 What do you think of this colour ______? **COMBINE**
23 I hate PVC windows and doors. I much prefer ______ ones. **WOOD**
24 You couldn't have seen John in London yesterday. It's an ______ He was here with me all day. **POSSIBLE**
25 Children who start smoking don't usually realize how ______ the habit is. **HARM**

8 WORD-BUILDING 3

Complete the following sentences by changing the words in **bold type** into a word (noun, adjective, adverb or verb) that fits suitably in each gap.

1 Many people find it difficult to tell the __________ between an Australian and a New Zealander. **DIFFERENT**
2 What did the man who attacked you look like? Can you give me a __________ of him? **DESCRIBE**
3 In __________ to England, the populations of Wales and Northern Ireland are very small. **COMPARE**
4 The crowd waited patiently for the __________ of the Queen and Prince Phillip. **ARRIVE**
5 The TV picture was too dark, so I tried to adjust the __________. **BRIGHT**
6 My sister's decided to take a course in __________ writing. **CREATE**
7 Do you think boys are more __________ than girls? **ENERGY**
8 'I hope you had an __________ evening at the theatre?'
'Yes, we had a wonderful time, thank you.' **ENJOY**
9 The canals in Amsterdam are often __________ during the winter. **FREEZE**
10 When the relief workers finally arrived at the site, a __________ sight greeted them of thousands of sick and dying refugees. **PITY**
11 Goodbye. It was a __________ meeting you. **PLEASE**
12 It was a very difficult problem - one that no one had a __________ to at the moment. **SOLVE**
13 There are still far too many hungry and __________ people in our large cities. **HOME**
14 Their arrival was totally __________ so we had nothing ready for them. **EXPECT**
15 Most people feel very __________ before making a speech. **NERVE**
16 The pop concert was so __________ that we left after half an hour. **NOISE**
17 In some countries, __________ without trial is quite common. **DETAIN**
18 The new drug was tested __________ before being put into mass production. **EXTEND**
19 It is perfectly normal for children to be __________ - when they are teenagers. **REBEL**
20 The police examined the __________ to try to find out the cause of the accident. **WRECK**
21 How could you say that to her? You ought to be __________ of yourself! **SHAME**
22 The talk he gave was very __________. **INFORM**
23 Punks used to shock older people with their __________ hairstyles and behaviour. **OUTRAGE**
24 If you're thinking of going to work abroad, there are some very __________ addresses at the back of this book. **USE**
25 The guest speaker's __________ was so bad that the audience couldn't understand a word she was saying. **PRONOUNCE**

9 FIND THE MISTAKES 1

Read the following text and look carefully at each line. Some of the lines are correct and some have a word that should **not** be there. If a line is correct put a tick (√) next to it. If a line has a word that should not be there, write down that word. The first two lines have been done for you.

Even pilots have a sense of humour

1	Passengers were very puzzled when the captain	✓
2	of the transatlantic airliner emerged out from the	*out*
3	flight deck holding two pieces of string. He was	______
4	backed slowly down the aisle unwinding the	______
5	lengths of the string, then stopped and handed the	______
6	ends to one of the passengers.	______
7	'Take over it will you?' he said. 'I've got to go to	______
8	the loo. If the plane veers to the right, give a tug	______
9	on the left-hand string. If it goes to the left, give	______
10	the right-hand piece a tug. You're in charge of	______
11	OK?' And with that he went out, leaving a dozens	______
12	of horror-struck passengers staring at the man	______
13	with the string, wondering if that he was going to	______
14	be able to 'control' the plane they were travelling up	______
15	in or not.	______
16	Ten minutes later the captain returned, took out	______
17	the string from the trembling passenger, thanked	______
18	him so profusely and disappeared back on to the	______
19	flight deck. The passengers were perfectly safe,	______
20	of course. The plane it had been on automatic pilot	______
21	all the time. The captain was just literally stringing	______
22	his passengers all along.	______
23	A more even frightening experience happened to a	______
24	party of business executives waiting for the pilot	______
25	of their chartered plane to turn it up. Finally, one of	______
26	them who jumped up and declared, 'Well, if the airline	______
27	can't find anyone to get this thing off the ground	______
28	then I'll have do it myself!' He said he needed a	______
29	navigator. Somebody who had not done car rallying	______
30	would do. Another person got up, said he had	______
31	done a bit of rallying and accompanied by the first	______
32	man to the flight deck.	______
33	The rest of the passengers sat petrified even as the	______
34	plane taxied, then took off! They were in the safe hands,	______

35 of course. The two 'executives' who were the plane's __________

36 proper pilot and navigator just having a bit of fun. __________

10 FIND THE MISTAKES 2

Read the following text and look carefully at each line. Some of the lines are correct and some have a word that should **not** be there. If a line is correct put a tick (√) next to it. If a line has a word that should not be there, write down that word. The first two lines have been done for you.

Dirty dog

1	A politician at the last General Election was	✔
2	canvassing for the votes and had come to a	*the*
3	terraced house with a ferocious pit bull outside. He	______
4	hated the dogs, and was a bit hesitant as he pressed the	______
5	doorbell. But he was being given a warm welcome by the	______
6	people of the house.	______
7	They told to him they always voted for him and,	______
8	were pleased to meet him, invited him in for a cup of tea.	______
9	He was feeling pretty thirsty after a tough	______
10	morning's door-to-door stepping and accepted their offer,	______
11	by edging past the growling pit bull.	______
12	The dog followed after him into the room and lay down	______
13	showing his teeth and staring at him from in the	______
14	middle of the floor.	______
15	He was so enjoying his cup of tea as much as he could	______
16	with the dog there, in chatting with his constituents	______
17	about local issues, when after the dog stood up, cocked	______
18	its leg and completely soaked over the carpet! His hosts	______
19	looked at the dog briefly, then carried on talking.	______
20	The politician was a bit shocked, but as no one didn't	______
21	else said anything, he just wondered a bit about if	______
22	what kind of supporter he was attracting to. Each to	______
23	be their own, he decided.	______
24	After a good chinwag, the candidate drained his cup,	______
25	thanked the family, and made out his way out of the	______
26	door. He'd just taken a few paces outside when he had	______
27	heard someone call out to behind him.	______
28	'Excuse me, aren't you not going to take	______
29	your dog home with you?'	______

11 FIND THE MISTAKES 3

Read the text below and look carefully at each line. Some of the lines are correct, and some have a word missing. If a line is correct put a tick (√) after it. If a line has a missing word, use a stroke (/) to show where a word has been left out and on the right suggest what the missing word might be. There are two examples at the beginning.

Fired for giving a present

1	Henry Ford, the founder of mass car production, was	✓
2	not the easiest / people to work for. He disliked	*of*
3	chewing gum, he banned it in his factories. Any	______
4	worker who disobeyed was sent to chew on the	______
5	street for an hour pay. Ford also demanded	______
6	complete silence and men were forbidden whistle,	______
7	sing or talk at their work. One man was sacked	______
8	asked what he done wrong. He was shown two	______
9	photographs of himself taken by a factory spy. One	______
10	showed him talking to a colleague. In other he	______
11	was looking into a doorway that workers not	______
12	allowed to pass through.	______
13	Ford ruled that when starting bell rung, men	______
14	should already standing by their machines,	______
15	wearing their overalls. They had to hang their street	______
16	clothes on hooks were promptly whisked high	______
17	out of reach. To anybody going home early,	______
18	the hooks weren't lowered the end of the day.	______
19	No chairs were provided. Furthermore, any worker	______
20	found sitting on the floor or leaning his	______
21	machine was sacked. Employees who failed to	______
22	their personal badges be sent home for up to	______
23	a fortnight.	______
24	But in spite of these rules, people clamoured for	______
25	work jobs in the 1930s were hard to come	______
26	by and Ford well. A teenager was so grateful at	______
27	being hired that he bought the foreman a present. He	______
28	was immediately dismissed because it was	______
29	the rules to make a gift a superior. That was his	______
30	lesson. When he learnt it, Ford gave him back	______
31	his job.	______

SOLID GOLD 2 WORD LISTS

GO-AHEAD

CRACKING THE CODE

crack knäcka
command of a language behärska ett språk
master bemästra, lära sig
assured tryggad, säkrad
native language modersmål
supplier leverantör
get a message across göra sig förstådd
primarily först och främst
decade årtionde
a fraction of a second en bråkdels sekund
tone tonfall; intonation
pitch tonhöjd
impact intryck, effekt
concept begrepp
congruence överensstämmelse; kongurens
increase öka
webinar webbkonferens
employee anställd
shareholder aktieägare
confident trygg, säker
investor investerare
negotiation förhandling
sufficiently tillräckligt
intention syfte, avsikt
adequate tillräcklig
persuasive övertygande
appropriate lämplig, passande
manager chef; manager
staff personal
adapt anpassa
self-awareness självkännedom
ability förmåga; skicklighet
at hand till hands; *ung.* som är aktuell
small talk småprat, kallprat
super-tool toppenverktyg

LETTER TO A FUNERAL PARLOR

award tilldela, belöna med
funeral parlor *AmE* begravningsbyrå
cremains askan efter kremering
deal with behandla; uppträda mot
startle göra bestört
sensitive känslig *h.* taktfull
in between dessemellan
whether om, huruvida
frankly uppriktigt sagt
substitute ersättning

chipped strimlad
beef oxkött
Porta Potti namn på barnpotta
pooper-scooper plastskyffel för att ta upp hundbajs
dish maträtt
cheerful glad
jovial gemytlig
alliteration alliteration (ord börjar på samma bokstav)
portmanteau word teleskopord (t. ex. motel av motorists' hotel)
be comforted låta trösta sig

WE BEAT THE STREET

obstacle hinder
apathy likgiltighet; slöhet
community samhälle
remarkable märklig, anmärkningsvärd
in retrospect när man ser tillbaka
daunting lätt skrämmande
undertake ta på sig
peer pressure kamrattryck, grupptryck
role model förebild
depend on lita på; vara beroende av
frequently titt som tätt, ofta
impulsive impulsiv *h.* okontrollerad
privacy privatliv
add lägga till
a beacon of hope en strimma hopp
in particular i synnerhet, särskilt
in general i allmänhet
flip through bläddra igenom
diverse mångfaldig
approach synsätt, inställning
bluntly rakt på sak
Hispanic latinamerikansk
seethe koka
occasionally då och då
reflect återspegla
cut the budget skära ned på utgifter
suburban förorts-
leftover överbliven
deserve förtjäna
walk out gå i strejk
seize upon kasta sig över
grab gripa
flyer flygblad
coordinator samordnare
troubleshooter medlare
participate delta, ta del
sidewalk trottoar
the Board of Education skolstyrelsen
lock arms kroka arm
chant sjunga
snarl trassla till
superintendent skolinspektör
timid-looking försiktigt, lättskrämt utseende
legitimate berättigad, rättmätig
concern angelägenhet
respectfully aktningsfullt
request begära; be
scurry kila
impatient otålig
surge våg
lobby entréhall
outspoken frispråkig
assemblyman medlem av lagstiftande församling
state senator statssenator
gradually undan för undan
detain hålla kvar
blanket filt
emphasize framhålla, trycka på
demand krav
victorious segerrik
curriculum kursplan
briefly i korthet
accomplish uträtta

LISTENING: WE BEAT THE STREET CONT.

push her buttons *sl.* provocera; hetsa upp (henne)
turn in lämna in
devilish djävulsk
get credit for tillgodoräkna sig
whine gnälla
grade rätta; betygsätta
according to enligt
insist hålla fast vid, insistera
shrug rycka på axlarna
ball up göra en boll av
assignment arbetsuppgift
toss kasta
tense bli spänd, bli nervös
ignore strunta i
roam ströva omkring
Silly String partysnöre på sprejburk
interrupt avbryta
aerosol can sprejflaska
sticky klibbig, kladdig
web nät
astonished förvånad
confusion förvirring
crack up bryta ihop, börja skratta
humiliate förödmjuka
principal rektor
insubordinate uppstudsig
suspended avstängd
indefinitely på obestämd tid
sacrifice offra
file lämna in
criminal charges polisanmälan om brott

uphold godkänna
expulsion relegering; avstängning
crumble falla sönder
statement yttrande
dropout studieavbrytare; utslagen
groan jämra sig, stöna
dignity värdighet
expel relegera, stänga av
thoughtful eftertänksam
deliberation övervägande
cooperative samarbetsvillig

CHALLENGES

I AM MALALA

public attention allmän uppmärksamhet
community samhälle
target göra till måltavla
miraculously mirakulöst
in recognition of som ett erkännande
courage mod
advocacy kamp
runner-up på andra plats *h.* finalist
award tilldela
champion kämpa för
access tillträde; tillgång
corncob majskolv
loudspeaker högtalare
emerge komma fram
collection samling; hop
pebble småsten
clamor skrika
in the front cab i förarhytten
persuade övertala
primary school lågstadieskola
tailboard bakläm, bakre kant
tantrum raserianfall
in a huff förnärmad, kränkt
dyna skolbuss (med hytt och täckt flak)
jumble virrvarr, röra
honk tuta
tricycle trehjuling
nuclear missile kärnvapenraket
shoo away schasa bort
Swatis folkgrupp i Pakistan
despite trots
cleanse rengöra
machine-gun nest kulsprutenäste
manning bemanna
checkpoint vägspärr; kontrollstation
valley dalgång
permission tillstånd
shortcut genväg
bounce studsa
van skåpbil
revision repetition
bullet kula
sever skiljas åt; *h.* nacka

LISTENING: INDIRA GANDHI ON EDUCATION

self-sufficiency självförsörjning
environmental policies miljöpolitik
contribute bidra
nickname ge öknamn
dumb doll dumdocka
swiftly snabbt
revise ändra
participation delaktighet
assassinate lönnmörda
ancient forntida
inadequate otillräcklig, bristfällig
neglect försumma, inte bry sig om
fairly ganska
recent nyligen
current aktuell
overhauling översyn, genomgång
demand efterfrågan
affluent rik, förmögen
salary lön
synthesize förena
valuable värdefull
neither... nor varken... eller
once and for all en gång för alla
enshrine bevara
superficial ytlig
rational förnuftig
soil mark; *h.* land
public allmän
content nöjd
enable sb to göra det möjligt för ngn
adjust anpassa sig

FRIDAY 4TH APRIL

numerous otaliga, många
DIY(Do-It-Yourself) shop affär med färg, verktyg etc
trolley kundvagn
distracted förvirrad
on special offer till extraerbjudande
part-time deltid
salary lön
tax skatt
tight knapp
fee avgift
contribution bidrag
mortgage betalning av huslån
single-sex enkönad
extravagant lyxig, påkostad
not good with figures inte bra på att räkna
emergency fiver fempundssedel i nödfall

delighted with förtjust över
half-smothered halvt kvävde
brillo (brilliant) *sl.* strålande
glow glöd; värme
poster affisch
festoon smycka med
raggy trasig
dog-eared med vikta hörn *h.* sliten
reverently vördnadsfullt
blu-tack häftmassa
glare skarpt solsken
spirit level vattenpass
mean snål; nedrig
pliers tång
nudge puffa till
lad pojke
pinnacle höjdpunkt
desirability åtråvärdhet
stray tillfällig
bless välsigna

FOR A LAUGH

hail hejda
pregnant gravid
understatement underskattning
slid gled
blurt slänga ur sig
up front rakt på sak
fresh fräck
disarming avväpnande
curb (kerb) trottoarkant
justification försvar; motivering
inquire fråga
display visa
wry smile tvunget leende
pillow kudde
bulge bula
nevertheless trots allt
be full of it *sl.* köra en grej
pretense (BrE. pretence) svepskäl; *h.* låtsasspel
offer erbjuda
exchange utbyte
novelty ovanlighet
nickel fem cent
challenge utmaning
back and forth fram och tillbaka *h.* dialog
bond band
self-esteem självkänsla
contribute bidra
drop out hoppa av studier
take off ge sig iväg
wind up (wound, wound) hamna
get something across få att förstå
quit sluta upp med
head off styra iväg
acknowledgment bekräftelse
be short on the exchange factor inte ge så mycket i utbyte

NO PLANS AT ALL

duvet duntäcke
yell skrika
pile hög
laundry tvätt
cupboard skåp
shove skjuta, fösa; *h.* köra
soiled smutsig
clothing kläder
weed rensa från ogräs
border kantrabatt
garden centre trädgårdscenter
bulb lök
annual ettårsväxt
key cutter nyckeltillverkare *h.* klackbar
mother-in-law svärmor
boot bagageutrymme
exceed överstiga
reach räckvidd
chop hacka; hugga
casserole gryta
fence staket
creosote kreosot; giftig trätjära
log fire stockvedsbrasa
foreseeable future överskådlig framtid
feed mata
innate medfödd
lure locka, lura
sagging nedsjunken
babble porla
brook bäck
pummel slå
sycamore mullbärsfikonträd
creak knarra
down-at-heel nedgången
rehabilitation återanpassning
unit enhet, avdelning
brogue rejäl sko med stickningar
manipulate hantera
simple enkla
dial knapp
fairy tale saga
stats (statistics) statistik
inflate blåsa upp
the string theory supersymmetry boys grabbarna som sysslar med en matematisk fysikalisk teori
Higgs boson teori inom partikelfysik
groom ansa
fiddle pyssla
twirl snurra
scraggy mager, *h.* tunn

remote fjärrkontroll
stab at måtta en stöt mot
stroke strykning (med handen)
off the menu *ung.* inte aktuellt

IN TRANSITION

FASTER THAN LIGHTNING

solid stark, säker
season säsong
track and field friidrott
thrive trivas, må bra
spark gnista
sensibly förnuftigt, klokt
attempt försöka att göra
off the scale otrolig
cat kille
trial försök
with serious game ordentligt motstånd
manager lagledare
winger ytterspelare
cuss förbanna; svära
accuracy precision
dedication engagemang, entusiasm
from afar fjärran ifrån
boundary gräns
achievement prestation, insats
landmark pace *h.* målhastighet
peak fitness toppform

NEXT STOP ALABAMA

promoter initiativtagare
charity välgörenhet
minor mindre viktig
boarding school internatskola
throw a party ordna ett party
underestimate underskatta
ragtag bunch *h.* brokig skara
geek tönt; nörd
cavernous mörk som en håla
persevere framhärda
awash på drift
delusion självbedrägeri, inbillning
artichoke kronärtskocka
festoon smycka
streamer vimpel
champagne popper smällare med konfetti
couch soffa
cavalry kavalleri
chunky bastant
charitably barmhärtigt
exhaust uttömma, göra slut på
excel utmärka sig, excellera
small talk kallprat
extend förlänga
awkwardness pinsamhet
rehearsal repetition
schedule schema
vastly väldigt
mull it over fundera över det
head vara på väg mot
simultaneously samtidigt
raise hell leva rövare
ace vara etta
flip bläddra
highlighted framträdande *h.* överstruket
quote citat
highlighter överstrykningspenna

LISTENING: NEXT STOP ALABAMA CONT.

humid fuktig
location plats
encounter stöta på
dorm (dormitory) room studenthemsrum
vicious våldsam, brutal
ferocity grymhet
modestly ringa
plush carpet tjock, lyxig matta
cinderblock slaggbetongblock
coat täcka
chequered rutig
bunk bed våningssäng
unfinished inte slutbehandlad
dresser byrå
Band-Aid plåster
minefield minfält
huddle hop, klunga
trial separation försöksseparation
overdue försenad
alumnus f.d. student
streak springa naken
whine jämra sig
badass *sl.* utåtagerande, vild

AT MUMBAI AIRPORT

extract utdrag
fluorescent light lysrörsljus
slump sjunka ihop
mould gjuta, forma
moulded *ung.* formpressad (i plast)
upholster klä, stoppa
maroon rödbrun
velour plysch
lackadaisical slapp, slängig
delay försena
proceed fortsätta
lounge stå och hänga
Diwali hinduisk högtid på hösten
rehoist lyfta upp igen
éclair petit-chou (ett slags bakverk)

tote släpa på
palm handflata
embrace kram, famntag
structure organisera
blurry-eyed med simmig blick
sheen glans, lyster
accessible tillgänglig
choke kväva
abandoned övergiven
irresistibly oemotståndligt
urge stark längtan; begär
inquisitive nyfiken
catlike kattlik
specious skenbar
shove knuffas, trängas
clutch hålla hårt i
nonsensically meningslöst
humidity fuktighet
laundry tvätt
intimacy förtrolighet; intimitet
runway start- och landningsbana
rickety skranglig
stow stuva
locker förvaringsfack
timbre klang(färg)
slender slank, smal
myriad otalig mängd
pointy spetsig landtunga

HEMI'S GIFT

tangi maori begravningsrit
unfold veckla ut
shuffle gå med släpande steg
solace tröst
batter illa medfaren
ancient gammal, ålderdomlig
sloppy slafsig
unmown oklippt
aisle mittgång
shrink sjunka ihop
pluck knäppa
pissed-off *sl.* utled
Pakeha icke-maori, vit
slump sjunka ner
permeate breda ut sig
tense spänd
register lägga märke till
rustle rassla
deliberate avsiktlig
humming and harring inte kunna besluta
seemingly till synes
entrance hänföra
fire it up *sl.* slå på
notification box meddelanderuta
FWD label märke med vidarebefordra
lame bristfällig
stroke hjärnblödning
cringe krypa ihop
snap...shut smälla igen
momentarily för ett ögonblick
shudder skaka
the last leg *ung.* sista biten
fridge kylskåp
wallet plånbok
stray enstaka
bugger *sl.* fan
amble gå i sakta mak
peer kisa
screwed ihopknipt
figure typiskt
chuck slänga
Once Were Warriors känd film om maoris
relief lättnad
hori nedsättande ord för maori
tar tjära
shoot a movie spela in en film
peeps *sl.* personer
spark up tända
snap *h.* skälla på
wither vissna; *h.* dö
chuck away kasta iväg
erupt bryta fram
swing gunga
lap knä
jandal flip-flop
index finger pekfinger
gentle mjuk, vänlig
buoyed *h.* styrkt
I am humbled jag blir ödmjuk
flawless fulländad
soothing lindrande, lugnande
grieve sörja
be comforted låta trösta sig
subside avta
moan gnöla

CLASSICS

GB

HAMLET, PRINCE OF DENMARK

extract utdrag
adaptation bearbetning
nephew brorson
foul gemen, motbjudande
twirl virvla omkring
battlement *ung.* bröstvärn
collar krage
cloak mantel, kappa

orchard fruktträdgård
seal up innesluta
tomb grav, gravvalv
courtyard gårdsplan
cunning slughet
turret torn
stroke slag
throb vibrera
beckon göra tecken, vinka
gasp flämta
armour rustning
circlet diadem
gleam glimma, glänsa
helm hjälm
despair förtvivlan
shudder rysning
backbone ryggrad
serpent orm
reel vackla
quiver darra
unwittingly omedvetet
brood ruva, grubbla
rumour rykte
wits förstånd
strain ansträngning
shatter förstöra, slå sönder
eternal evig
deceive bedra
bleak dyster
dagger kniv, dolk
sheathe sticka i slidan
concern omtanke
the Royal Chamberlain kunglig kammarherre
meddling rotande; *h.* en som lägger sig i
convent kloster
glimmer svagt sken
gleam stråle
casually i förbigående
purse pung
trap fälla
loathing avsky
resemble likna
pallor blekhet
torch fackla
underestimate underskatta
puzzled frågande
abandon överge
robe klädnad
wrist handled
skulk smyga omkring
plunge into kasta sig in i
fierce häftig, vild
glint glittra
mock håna
flicker skälva

LISTENING: HAMLET, PRINCE OF DENMARK CONT.

bundle into stuva ned
rattling skramlande
outwit someone överlista någon
lodging husrum
Elsinore Helsingör
ill tidings dåliga nyheter
blur göra suddig
plot sammansvärja sig
courtier hovman
idly sysslolöst
make wagers slå vad
slyly slugt
rapier värja
hover sväva
snick *ung.* skära
squeal skrika; *h.* klinga
menacing hotande
dodge hoppa undan
marshal vakt
drink to the dregs tömma till sista droppen
slash rispa
parry parera
snarl morrande
clutch at gripa efter
wrench rycka loss
lunge göra ett utfall
spurt stråle
reel vackla
crumple falla samman
topple falla
cringe krypa ihop

IRE

PYGMALION

playwright pjäsförfattare
note taker man som antecknar
pity oneself tycka synd om sig själv
in murmurs med mumlande röst
worrited (worried) orolig
chivied (chivy) plågad
brogue dialekt
ought to borde
coward ynkrygg
upstart uppkomling
cease sluta upp
detestable avskyvärd
boohoo böla, tjuta
instantly ögonblickligen
shelter skydd
feeble kraftlös
defiance trots

disgusting vedervärdig
divine gudomlig
articulate tydlig, artikulerad
native födelse-
croon gnola
bilious argsint, gallsprängd
pigeon duva
overwhelmed förkrossad
mingle blanda
wonder förundran
deprecation protest
in spite of trots
tickled *h.* road
garn skitsnack
kerbstone English rännstensengelska
in the gutter i rännstenen
duchess hertiginna
require kräva
profit förtjänst
scientific vetenskaplig
poet diktare
on Miltonic lines med rader i Miltons stil

NZ

SIXPENCE

sixpence äldre mynt
expatriate utvandrad
depict skildra
solitude ensamhet
impending annalkande, nära förestående
unaccountable egendomlig
creature varelse; människa
as a rule i regel
sensitive känslig
affectionate tillgiven, öm
obedient lydig
sensible förståndig
have moods ha humörsvängningar
hay hö
lawn gräsmatta
woodshed vedbod
dodge hoppa undan
peer kika
mossy mossig
apple trunk äppelträdstam
leap hoppa
sewing handarbete
drawing-room sällskapsrum
according to enligt
seize ta tag i
upside down upp och ner
clutch hålla fast
startled förskräckt
wobble vicka
sliver flisa
thimble fingerborg
chase jaga
damson krikon
undignified ovärdig
it's exasperating det är så man kan bli vansinnig
punish straffa
gather rynka (på tyg)
a whipping ett kok stryk
purse one's lips snörpa på mun
gentler measures mildare metoder
hiss väsa
take for granted ta för givet
impress gör intryck på
faintly svagt, matt
encouragingly uppmuntrande
make a remark fälla ett yttrande
cheery glad, munter
sigh sucka
on purpose med avsikt
reminder påminnelse
stagger vackla, stappla
pucker rynka
brim brätte
naughty stygg, elak
what-not allt möjligt
poke out one's tongue räcka ut tungan
scold skälla på
wail klaga högljutt
slip of a room *ung.* krypin
throb bultande slag
rage raseri, ursinne
flush rodna
properly ordentligt
huskily hest
bolt rusa iväg
hedge häck
barge into rusa in i
groan jämra sig
quiver darra
sprain vricka
fringe lugg
wrung *h.* plågat
lash ögonfrans
paw tass
buck up gaska upp sig
extraordinary särskild
snatch gripa tag i
twitch rycka
boundless gränslös
blot out utplåna

US

CAT IN THE RAIN

bench bänk
easel staffli
glisten glänsa
gravel path grusgång
crouch ligga hopkrupen
compact kompakt, sammanpressad
prop up stödja, palla upp
bow buga
complaint klagomål
dignity värdighet
eaves takfot
maid tjänsteflicka
tighten spänna
padrone ägare
momentary flyktig
supreme enorm
hand glass nackspegel
clip klippa
pretty darn nice rätt förbaskat snygg
smooth slät, jämn
knot knut
tortoise-shell cat sköldpaddsfärgad katt

SHOP TILL YOU DROP

A GOOD PRICE!

battle strida
vendor gatuförsäljare
stubborn omedgörlig, envis
submit to falla till föga för
entreaty enträgen bön
exert använda; utöva
slash sänka kraftigt
inimitable oefterhärmlig
wit kvickhet; intelligens
common sense bondförnuft
theatrics teaterkonst
homely-looking se alldaglig ut
throng massa, väldig mängd
booth stånd
frames glasögonbågar
neatly prydligt
flutter fladdra
gesture gest, rörelse
yelp tjuta; skrika
shrill gäll
sheepish fåraktig *h.* mjäkig
vacant frånvarande
discount rabatt
profit margin vinstmarginal
give sb a break ge ngn en chans
farang utlänning (i Thailand)
ridiculous löjlig
hint aning
mischief sattyg
bargain pruta, köpslå
in earnest på allvar
curtly kort
feign låtsas
courtesy artighet
browse gå runt och titta
aisle mittgång
fake förfalskad *h.* kopia
outrageous skandalös; *h.* hutlöst
substantiate bekräfta
snicker fnissa
tease retas
stunning jättesnygg
wallet plånbok
shrug rycka på axlarna
emphatically med eftertryck
bellow dåna
curt barsk, tvär
pallor blekhet
mute stum, tyst
standoff dödläge *h.* kraftmätning
flattery smicker
bettor vadhållare
ante insats
accessory accessoarer
optional valfri; *h.* onödig
raspy sträv

LISTENING: MEET NUNU NTSHINGILA-NJEKE FROM SOUTH AFRICA

Ogilvy företag inom reklam och marknadsföring
trainee program praktikantprogram
account manager kontoansvarig
work up the ladder jobba sig upp; göra karriär
chairman styrelseordförande
award pris
AdFocus Awards årliga sydafrikanska priser inom reklam, media etc.
my pleasure nöjet är mitt
determined fast besluten
advertising reklambranschen
honestly ärligt talat
stumble across råka på, ramla över
degree examen
be all set vara helt inriktad
land a job få tag i ett jobb
internship praktikperiod
executive chef
washing detergent tvättmedel
testimonial (skriftligt) bevis
stain fläck

resonate eka, genljuda, *h.* gå hem
gradually successivt, efter hand
equal jämlik
male-dominated mansdominerad
diverse mångfaldig, skiftande
agency agentur, *h.* reklambyrå
whereas då däremot, medan
management level ledningsnivå
work environment arbetsmiljö
be conductive to främja, befordra
cope klara det, stå pall
human behaviour mänskligt beteende
what makes people tick hur folk funkar
tenacity seghet; fasthet
bumpy ojämn, guppig
rebrand ändra eller uppdatera en image (av företag, organistaion)
gratifying tillfredsställande
fulfilling meningsfull
sit on a board sitta i en styrelse
logistics company logistikföretag (arbetar med transporter)
established etablerad, erkänd

CREATIVE DESTRUCTION

creative kreativ, skapande
destruction förstörelse
Polaroid kamera som framkallade bilder direkt
instant omedelbar
profit vinst
supply source anskaffningskälla
pioneer öppna vägen för
efficient effektiv
innovation nyskapande
driving force drivkraft
essential viktigast; nödvändig
ruined ruinerad
inevitable oundviklig
emerge uppstå; dyka upp
fundamental grundläggande
enterprise företagsamhet

SHOPPING, SEDUCTION & MR SELFRIDGE

seduction förförelse
gracefully elegant
encompass omfatta
emergent uppdykande
evolve utveckla sig
merge smälta samman
astutely skarpsinnigt
tap utnyttja
arguably *ung.* enligt mångas åsikt
grasp begripa
sensual vällustig
maverick ensamvarg; frifräsare
retailer återförsäljare
eponymous uppkallad efter en person
visionary visionär
modest blygsam
position placera
turnover omsättning
window-dressing skyltning
pioneer var först med
in-store i varuhuset
promotion marknadsföring
facilities resurser; inrättningar
infancy barndom
day out fridag
boast skryta
tantalize locka, förföra
display skyltning
consummate fulländad
celebrity kändis, celebritet
at close quarters på nära håll
invariably ständigt
cluster klunga
anticipation förväntan, hopp
approval gillande
curtain-raiser förpjäs
shortage brist
mastermind leda *h.* genomföra
imperial (brittiska) imperie-
capital huvudstad
acquire skaffa sig
scramble streta
cope with klara, orka med
insatiable omättlig
equip utrusta
prodigious ofantlig
conspicuous consumption skrytkonsumtion
crucial central; avgörande
catalyst katalysator, utlösande faktor
venture våga, tillåta sig
jeopardize äventyra, riskera
reputation gott rykte, anseende
further afield längre bort
enticing frestande
cater for tillgodose någons behov
carriage trade förmögna människor
egalitarian jämlikhets-
urban stads-
sale bargains rea till vrakpriser
infinitely oändligt
browse gå runt och titta
crèche dagis; barnpassning
justifiably rättmätigt
claim hävda
emanicipate frigöra

LISTENING: NEWS ITEMS

resort to ta till, tillgripa som utväg

boost öka, höja
illicit olaglig
prosecution åtal
wheelchair rullstol
disabled funktionshindrad
flotation device flytutrustning
accessible tillgänglig
clash drabba samman
riot police kravallpolis
erupt bryta ut
ahead före
anticipate se fram emot
rip up slita sönder
urinal pissoar
detained häktad person
ban förbjuda
access tillträde
radiation treatment strålbehandling
sapping tärande
topping garnering, topplager
be in charge vara ansvarig
weeds ogräs
disguise maskera, framställa i falsk dager
biopsy vävnadsprov
liquid nitrogen flytande kväve
wean avvänja
facility enhet
stray dog hemlös hund
gobble up glufsa i sig, sluka
predict förutsäga, förutspå
disaster katastrof
devour sluka
furry pälsklädd

THE ARTS

NIPPLE JESUS
nipple bröstvårta
screenwriter filmförfattare
exhibit utställningsföremål
controversial nature omstridd fråga
offend kränka
crown of thorns törnekrona
nail up spika upp
have a kip sova
screwed up förvridet
agony ångest
PG tillåtet för barn i föräldrars sällskap
R tillåten över 15 år
fuss ståhej, uppståndelse
pinch sno
dot punkt, prick
wanker idiot
bird *sl.* brud
give sb a hand hjälpa någon
offensive stötande
that's out of order inte ok, oacceptabelt
tosser *sl.* idiot
sentry duty vakttjänst
posh flott
floppy flaxande
braces hängslen
talk bollocks *sl.* snacka skit
royalty ekonomisk ersättning

PAINTING IS NOTHING NEW
span sträcka sig över
feature visa upp
retrospective *ung.* tillbakablickar
exhibition utställning
depict avbilda
image bild
scratch skrapa, rista in
available tillgänglig
man-made skapad av människohänder
adorn smycka
vessel farkost
attribute tillskriva
mankind mänskligheten
reaffirm bekräfta
genetic science genteknik
alter förändra
contemporary samtida
abandon överge
possess inneha
survival överlevnad

TWO LOVE POEMS
hook and eye hake och hyska (på kläder)
hook krok

LISTENING: THE CARRIE DIARIES
adapt omarbeta
bosomy *ung.* yppigt, stort
take a sip smutta
slyly slugt
excess överskott
interject utropa
beam stråla
potential möjlighet, potential
by rote av gammal vana
launch sätta igång
simulacrum imitation
middle-brow konventionell
meretricious prålig
dazed förvirrad
audible hörbar
fearful ängslig
ribbon band

impact intryck
in astonishment med förvåning
choke on proppa sig full med
poisonously giftigt
indicate markera
diaper byta blöja
guffaw flabba
in mirth uppsluppet
wink blinka
journal dagbok
stationery store affär för kontorsmaterial
randomly på måfå
on the other hand å andra sidan
perception uppfattning

FAREWELL, CAMDEN TOWN

in a daze omtumlad; förvirrad
according to enligt
tipsy lätt berusad
raise the alarm slå larm, varna
be in turmoil vara i ett kaos
lapse återfall
gradually gradvis
equate likställa
neatness ordningssamhet
recovery tillfrisknande
fiancé fästman
mortuary bårhus
paps paparazzi, sensationsjournalist
blotchiness fläckighet
seizure anfall
partition skiljevägg
foul play brott
shrine vallfartsort
police cordon polisavspärrning
comforting tröstande
bleak hours *h.* tidig morgontimma
post-mortem examination obduktion
inconclusive resultatlös
toxicology test giftprov
inquest förhör om dödsorsaken
adjourn skjuta upp
coroner ämbetsman som utreder dödsfall vid misstanke om mord
rally samla
eulogy minnestal

REHAB

rehab avgiftning
be on the mend vara på bättringsvägen

LISTENING: MEET JUDI DENCH

conscious medveten
on the dot prick, på klockslaget
dressing gown morgonrock
ironing strykning
nosy nyfiken
shed off lägga bort; *h.* glömma bort
repertoire repertoar, (spelas just nu)
word-run manusgenomgång
tedious tråkig, tröttsam
steam ånga
steamer ångkokare
spout pip
phial liten medicinflaska
royal jelly kunglig fruktgelé
vocal röst
chant skandera, mässa
tannoy högtalare
curtain-up ridåuppgång
decline förfall
remarkable anmärkningsvärd
appealing lockande
a tad en smula
treasure värdesätta

GLIMPSES OF ENGLAND

TORN ON THE PLATFORM

torn splittrad
the big smoke stadens avgaser
tramp luffare
slack spelrum
noose snara
beep pipa
momentarily för ett ögonblick
gap öppning, mellanrum

A LION WITH A PRICE TAG

price tag prislapp
lion cub lejonunge
assimilate införliva; *h.* ta till sig
drawcard dragplåster
prospect möjlighet, utsikt
extend sträcka sig
rehabilitate återanpassa
despite trots
incessantly oavbrutet
intrigued fängslad, intresserad
restrain hålla tillbaka, lägga band på
urge begär
demand kräva
snarl morra
irresistible oemotståndlig
enchanted förtrollad, hänförd
reminder påminnelse
expose utsätta
intuitively intuitivt, med omedelbar uppfattning
investigate undersöka
enquire höra sig för

available ledig
guinea mynt på 21 shilling
equivalent motsvarande
vast oerhörd
undaunted modig, oförskräckt
reasonable rimlig, skälig
pointedly tydligt
purchaser köpare
thoroughly grundligt
irresponsible oansvarig
skillfully skickligt
perceptively insiktsfullt
first option *h.* förtur

LISTENING: A LION WITH A PRICE TAG CONT.
assume anta
scramble klättra
frequently ofta
placate lugna
evade undvika
pad around tassa omkring
tentatively försiktigt
incredulously tvivlande
after hours efter stängningsdags
presumably troligen
resident bofast
hangers-on påhäng
serval cat mellanstort afrikanskt kattdjur
scatter beströ
ephemeral kortlivad
character egenskap
superficial ytlig
pretentious anspråksfull
self-conscious självmedveten
flamboyant praktfull
victim offer
amused road
embarrassment förlägenhet
surroundings omgivning, miljö
inhibition hämning
vanish försvinna
obviously helt klart
boisterous stojande
substitute ersättare
indifference likgiltighet
disdainful föraktfull
sociability sällskapande
superiority överlägsenhet
cuddle krama, kela med
tawny-coloured gulbrunfärgad
disproportionately oproportionerligt
placid fridfull
house-trained rumsren
fastidiousness kräsenhet
kitty litter tray kattlåda
indiscriminate planlös

puddle pöl
smack dask, slag

THE ROAD TO WIGAN PIER
dystopian mörk framtidsskildring
allegory bildlig
totalitarian diktatorisk
of long standing som har arbetat länge
obviously självklart
pit gruva
quantity mängd
detect upptäcka
wick veke
extent omfattning; *h.* längd
nevertheless trots det
crack spricka
crevice skreva
poke sticka in
spark gnista
blast spränga
pick hacka
gob fire pyrande eld
spontaneously spontant; av sig själv
smoulder pyra
disaster katastrof
hence därför, på grund av
tend to ha en tendens att
due to på grund av, *h.* bero på
pot hole potthål; tjälskott
promptitude snabbhet; *h.* hastighet
exception undantag
partly delvis
extract utvinna
remain förbli
unpropped utan stöttor
skill skicklighet
faint svag
creaking knakande
prop stöd
iron girder järnbalk
unexpectedly oväntat
devastating förödande
cranny skreva; vrå
extricate frigöra
drag släpa
gallery gång, ort
surface yta
cage hisskorg
delicate känslig
indicator visare
whizz slunga
blankness tomhet
snap slita av
clench pressa hårt samman
expectation väntan

NO BOUNDARIES

physicist fysiker
ALS nervsjukdom som gör att kroppen förlamas
estimate uppskatta
agreement överenskommelse
in return i gengäld
extend erbjuda
contract få
potential potential, möjlighet
accomplish åstadkomma
scientific vetenskaplig
prediction förutsägelse
quantum kvantum
emission utstrålning, utsläpp
verify bevisa
significance betydelse
despite trots
confirm bekräfta, bestyrka
asset tillgång
tedious tråkig, tröttsam
devote hänge
the wider public allmänheten
disabled handikappad
disguise oneself förklä sig
wig peruk
give someone away avslöja någon
besiege *h.*uppvakta
outweigh uppväga
anchor presentatör
detain hålla kvar
charge anklaga
continent världsdel
lecture föreläsa
singularity säregenhet

THE PEOPLE YOU NEVER HEAR FROM

broadcaster mediepersonlighet
dependent on beroende av
benefit bidrag
judge att döma av
fictional påhittade
presume förmoda
maverick frifräsare, oberoende
copper *sl.* polis
call-girl prostituerad
whimsical egendomlig
post-grad mastersstudent
kidult *ung.* halvvuxen
urban flat-share lägenhet i stan som man delar
sign on skriva in som arbetslös
cast member medverkande
Shameless brittisk komedi om arbetarklassen
bedrock grundval
prompt utlösa, trigga
response gensvar
cut skära ned på
support system skyddsnät
at random på måfå
intriguing intressant
by and large på det hela taget
tend ha en benägenhet
paramount dominerande
encapsulate in inkapsla i
whine about gnälla om
presumption antagande
broadsheet columnist morgontidningsskribent
bail someone out utverka frihet *h.* understödja
dismantle avveckla
grain spannmål
powdered milk mjölkpulver
well connected (med) bra kontakter
grumpy butter
unfailingly ständigt
optional valfri
ad hoc från fall till fall
pauper fattig
parish handouts allmosor
admin kortform administration, pappersarbete
winsome trevlig
source ge medel
needful behövande
free up frigöra
PA personlig assistent
DSS ett beslutsstödjande system
sibling syskon
alter förändra
sorely i högsta grad
squint skela
subsequently senare
Electric Boogaloo en typ av dans
body-pop dansa (en slags gatudans)

YES OR NO!

THE MOTHER´S PRAYER FOR ITS DAUGHTER

FSU Florida State University
logo logga
stain befläcka
haunch ländrygg
damaged förstörd
creepy läskig
meth kortform för amfetamin
restroom toalett
escalator rulltrappa
Ferris wheels *ung.* Pariserhjul
roller-coaster berg- och dalbana
log flume vattenrutschkana
Hell Drop ett slags dataspel
Tower of Torture tortyrkammare
The Death Spiral en hårdrockskonsert

feature presentera
Aerosmith ett amerikanskt rockband
high heels högklackat
midwifery barnmorskearbete
fiery eldig
sinewy kärnfull
grant även om så vore
a rough patch *ung.* en tuff period
dry-humping petting
invective glåpord
peer jämnårig
stabbed knivskuren
yank rycka
poop bajs
feces bajs
gratitude tacksamhet
peep kika

CHICKY

fence stängsel
drill såbädd
soothe lugna
provide tillhandahålla
cave grotta
ancient lastgammal
dress up klä ut sig
insurance office försäkringsbolag
knitting factory stickfabrik
garment plagg
Aran sweater mönsterstickad ulltröja
retail outlet detaljhandel
flashing blixtrande
in stock på lager
intend to ha för avsikt att
endearing älskvärd
wilds vildmark
take a vow svära på
immense ofantlig
row gräl
upset bråk
tramp luffare; *h.*fnask
sainted helgonlik
scourge plåga
maid hembiträde
reckless hänsynslös
drop out of hoppa av
in spite of trots
bring shame on so dra vanära över
infatuation dårskap
adamant orubblig
blessing välsignelse

LISTENING: ONLINE ALL THE TIME

case report fallbeskrivning
previously tidigare
nosedive störtdykning
properly ordentligt
fate öde
zap into susa iväg
robotic robotliknande
servile slavisk
compulsion tvång
instant ögonblicklig
transformative föränderlig
preserve privilegium
mainstream huvudfåra
device apparat
tablet handdator
ambivalence vacklande
application användande
spam-spewing skräppostspyende
reveal uppdaga, visa
widespread concern allmänspridd angelägenhet
AOL America online (företag som erbjuder internet-tjänster)
survey enkät
respondent svarande
lavatory toalett
habitual vanemässig
disruptive splittrande
recover återhämta sig
incredibly otroligt
habit-forming vanebildande
variable-interval växlande intervall
reinforcement förstärkning
capture fånga
office supply company kontorsföretag
obsessive tvångsmässig
rubbish skräp
sorely i högsta grad
juicy läcker
tittle-tattle skvaller
CEO Chief Executive Officer, VD
appointed avtalad

EVERYTHING YOU NEED TO KNOW ABOUT GENERATION Z

in a nutshell i ett nötskal
stubborn envis
pragmatic praktisk
be in a rush ha bråttom
unaware omedveten
a million miles removed *ung.* en miljon mil från
previous tidigare
hooked into hakad i; fast i
nickname ge ett öknamn
mutant en person med förändrad DNA
simultaneously samtidigt
pay through the nose bli uppskörtad d.v.s. betala för mycket
turn up their nose rynka på näsan åt
blockbuster dundersuccé

twerk typ av dans
pepper with peppra med
acronym initialord som uttalas som vanligt ord, t.ex. FN
incomprehensible obegripligt
in the know vara invigd
pal *sl.* kompis
obsolete omodern, föråldrad
ultimate definitiv
consultancy konsultbyrå
be in the loop vara i framkant
poison gift
flagging dalande
omnipresent allestädes närvarande
grand storslagen
attention span koncentrationsspann
start-up eget företag
hierarchy rangordning
achieve prestera
aim to med målsättning
outlook inställning
bleak dyster
innovative nyskapande
ethical moralisk

LISTENING: NEWS ITEMS

reward belöning
tale historia
pickup körning
bundle bunt
verify kontrollera, bestyrka
enlist ta i sin tjänst
get to grips gå i närkamp med
endemic inhemsk
cultural shift kulturell förändring
congestion trafikstockning
cobbled street kullerstensgata
wind slingra sig
ensue bli följden
pedestrian crossing övergångsställe
barbarity omänsklighet, barbari
intervene ingripa
fine böter
bid vadslagning
yacht segelbåt
voyage sjöresa
hard shoulder väggren
roar past dåna förbi
mow down meja ned
4x4 truck truck med stora hjul
in a bid i ett försök
carriageway tvåfilig väg
roundabout rondell
slip road på/avfartsväg till motorväg
deliberately avsiktligt
be alerted by larmad av, uppmärksammad på
forestry skogs-
relocate förflytta
reinforce förstärka
stray ströva
path stig
patch fläck, område
cheeky fräck
crouch krypa ihop
hearse likbil
alleged utpekad
foyer foajé
trolley rullbår
pursue följa efter
aghast förskräckt
hilarious lustig, dråplig

OUTLOOK ON US

QUIET STRENGTH

sensible förnuftig
erectly rakryggat
dingy sjabbig, mörk
ignite tända
conviction fällande dom
disorderly conduct störande beteende
The Montgomery Improvement Association en förening startad 1955 med syftet att motverka rassegregation
hold a rally hålla ett massmöte
pew kyrkbänk
trample trampa
oppression förtryck
amidst mitt bland
piercing stickande
mere blott, bara
presence närvaro
galvanize sporra
trudge traska
carpool samåka
stately ståtlig
bold djärv
glowering blängande
obituary minnesruna
small in stature liten till växten
humility ödmjukhet
fortitude mod, styrka
implicit underförstådd
courageous modig
paradox motsägelse
assumption antagande
give credit to sätta tro till

THE NEGRO MOTHER

playwright pjäsförfattare

seed frö
yield lämna ifrån sig
labor arbeta
blessing lycka, glädje
trudge släpa sig fram
nourish ge näring åt
smother tysta ned
despair förtvivlan
torch fackla
ignorance okunnighet
banner fana
whip piska
slaver slavhandlare
track spår
strife kamp
bar stänga av, spärra av; hinder, spärr
impel driva

WE ARE THE FUTURE

brainteaser nöt att knäcka
honoree *ung.* stjärnelev
vast oerhört stor
Intel stort elektronikföretag
hail from vara från
virtue fördel
blue collar arbetskläder (industriarbete)
formula recept
high-aspiring uppåtsträvande
retain hålla kvar
orderly metodisk
first-round draft choice förstahandsval
aspirational ambitiös
the choices de bästa
enable möjliggöra
solar system solsystem
efficient ändamålsenlig

LISTENING: KAVES – THE GRAFFITI AND TATTOO MASTER

pioneer föregångsman
elaborate raffinerad
deem anse
make one's bones där man kommer ifrån
vivid levande
nostalgia längtan tillbaka
round the way närbelägna
clientele kundkrets
turbulent orolig, stormig
blank slate tom tavla
cut it for sb passa någon
marker märkpenna
tag tagga, märka
dude *sl.* kille
Rocky Baloa boxare i filmen Rocky
Flatbush ett område I Brooklyn, New York
induct uppta, introducera

rare unik
crude obearbetad
in my opinion enligt mig
canvas duk

THE AGE OF EXCITEMENT

account berättelse, redogörelse
soothe lugna
jangly *h.* orolig
jaded minds trötta hjärnor
benign välgörande
penetrate genomtränga
ray stråle
tissue vävnad
bathe in bada i
the Heimlich manoeuvre manöver för att få loss ngt som fastnat i luftstrupen
child safety cap barnsäkert lock
bleach blekmedel
combust självantända
purr spinna
convenient bekväm
preposterous absurd, omöjlig
assure försäkra
thud dunsa
nosecone-first med nosdelen först
prevailing rådande
proposition förslag
stand to attention stå i givakt
shear off klippa av
flat-top platt topp
endearing älskvärd, rar
innocence oskuldsfullhet, naivitet
vanish försvinna
dishevelled ovårdad
lucid normal
roam ströva omkring
the Executive Mansion det beslutsfattande huset
instantaneous ögonblicklig
sustained ihållande
lavish frikostig
posthumous efter någons död
into the custody under uppsikt; i förvar

THE BIRTH OF HELA

biopsy report vävnadsanalys
malignant elakartad
right up direkt
admissions desk inskrivningsdisk
consent medgivande
operative procedure operativt ingrepp
anaesthetic bedövning
illegible oläslig
tube slang
bladder urinblåsa
invasive angripande

cervical livmoderhals
carcinoma cancer
eerie spöklik
hail välkomna, hylla
dial visare
mutation förändring
conducted by utförd av
tuck into stoppa in i
slot öppning
canvas pouch tygpåse
plaque platta
oversee övervaka
wheel into rulla in
glaring skarp
in stirrups *ung.* i gynekologstol
dilate *h.* öppna, utvidga
cervix livmoderhals
rolls of gauze rullar med gasbinda
catheter kateter (rörformat instrument)
chart diagram; *h.* patientjournal
tedious tråkig, *h.* alldaglig
vein blodåder
distress smärta, nöd
in culture i en odling
drill rutin
mythological mytisk
intensity intensitet
spread like crabgrass spridas som ogräs

LISTENING: WHAT'S THE TOPIC?

cue ge en vink
inability oförmåga
visualization åskådliggörande
replacement ersättning
rejuvenate vitalisera
dim svag, matt
emit ge ifrån sig
survey enkät, undersökning
in principle i princip
striking slående
in public life i det offentliga livet
polled intervjuad
study undersökning, studie
conducted by utförd av
lecture föreläsning
a ripe time lämplig tidpunkt
attempt försök
plain-old gamla hederliga
quiz frågesport
write in longhand skriva för hand
outperform överträffa
verbatim ordagrant
be inclined to vara benägen att
capture fånga, uppfatta
admission tillträde
grandstand enclosure inhägnad huvudläktare
fascinator huvudsjal
strapless utan axelband
strap dress fodral
adhere hålla sig till
comply with rätta sig efter
midriff midja, mage
venture äventyr
boobs bröst
awkward obekväm, pinsam
judgement kritik
endeavor försök
compatibility förenlighet
intercept fånga upp
encrypt kryptera
spoof falsk
hotspot allmän plats där man kan ansluta till internet
corporate företags-
vishing lurendrejeri via telefon
courier kurir, ombud
fraud bedrägeri
compromise utsätta för fara
fraudster bedragare
abbreviation förkortning
dispel skingra, ta bort
capital versal, stor bokstav
omission utelämning
literacy läs- och skrivkunnighet
gait gång
strides kliv
alluring lockande
exert utöva
regardless utan hänsyn till, oavsett
nocturnal nattlig, sen
subdued dämpad
premature förhastad
multi-layered i flera lager
varnish fernissa
humdrum alldaglig
equipped utrustad

ACKNOWLEDGEMENTS

Every effort has been made to make this list of copyright holders complete and correct. Any necessary amendments are welcome. We are grateful for the permissions granted by the following publishers and agents.

From Cracking the Code by Allie Edwardsson, © Liber. Reproduced by permission. (p. 10)

From The Collected Stories of Lydia Davis by Lydia Davis (Hamish Hamilton 2010) © Lydia Davis 2010. Reproduced by permission of Penguin Books Ltd (p. 13)

From We beat the Street by The Three Doctors, © Puffin Books. (p. 15)

From *I Am Malala: The Girl Who Stood Up for Education and Was Shot by the Taliban* by Malala Yousafzai with Christina Lamb. Copyright © 2013 by Salarzai Limited. Used by permission of Little, Brown and Company. (p. 20)

Indira Gandhi on Education, © Quercus Editions Ltd 2005, 2010: Quoted from Indira Gandhi's Speech 'What Educated Women Can Do' given on 23 November 1974 in New Delhi. Reproduced by permission of Quercus Editions Limited.

Extract from the novel *Sister ... No Way!* by Siobhan Parkinson, The O'Brien Press Ltd, Dublin, © Copyright Siobhan Parkinson. (p. 23)

Extract from Confessions of a New York Taxi Driver by Eugene Salomon, © Harper Collins. (p. 26)

Excerpt from THE WOMAN WHO WENT TO BED FOR A YEAR by Sue Townsend (Michael Joseph, 2012). Copyright © Lily Broadway Productions Ltd, 2012. Reproduced by permission of Penguin Books Ltd. (p. 29)

Excerpt from THE WOMAN WHO WENT TO BED FOR A YEAR by Sue Townsend. Audio rights. © Curtis Brown.

Excerpt from Faster than Lightning by Usain Bolt. © Harper Sport (p. 34)

Excerpt from Looking for Alaska by John Green. © Dutton Books. (p. 36)

Excerpt from Saraswati Park by Anjali Joseph. © Harpers Collins. (p. 39)

Excerpt from Hemi's Gift from Huai Short Stories 10 by Tj Corrigan. © Huai Publishers. Reproduced with kind permission. (p. 43)

Excerpt from Hamlet, Prince of Denmark from *The Orchard Book of Shakespeare Stories by Shakespeare.* (p. 50)

Excerpt from PYGMALION by George Bernard Shaw used by permission of The Society of Authors, on behalf of the Bernard Shaw Estate. (p. 56)

Excerpt from Six Pence from Katherine Mansfield's Short Stories by Katherine Mansfield. © Random House. (p. 59)

Excerpt from Cat in the Rain from The Complete Short Stories by E Hemingway. © Simon and Schuster. (p. 66)

Excerpts from *Sightseeing*, copyright © 2005 by Rattawut Lapcharoensap. Used by permission of Grove/Atlantic, Inc. Any third party use of this material, outside of this publication, is prohibited. (p. 80)

CREATIVE DESTRUCTION taken from 30-SECOND ECONOMICS by Donald Marron, copyright © Ivy Press 2011. Used by kind permission of Ivy Press. (p. 84)

Excerpt from Shopping, Seduction & Mr Selfridge by Lindy Woodhead. © Profile Books. (p. 85)

Excerpt from 'Nipple Jesus' in SPEAKING WITH THE ANGEL edited and with an introduction by Nick Hornby (Penguin Books, 2000). Copyright © for this collection, Penguin Books, 2000. Copyright © Introduction, Nick Hornby 2000. (p. 90)

Excerpt from 'Nipple Jesus' Audio rights: Copyright © Nick Hornby 2000. Published by Penguin 2000. Reproduced by permission of the author c/o Rogers, Coleridge & White Ltd., 20 Powis Mews, London W11 1JN.

Excerpt from Painting Is Nothing from Ketih Haring Journals by Keith Haring. © Wylie Agency (p. 94)

You Fit into Me from Power Politics by Margaret Atwood © House of Anasi Press. (p. 96)

Farewell, Camden Town taken from "'Dad. I've had enough of drinking': Mitch Winehouse tells congregation that Amy hadn't touched alcohol for three weeks" by Georgina Littlejohn (freelance writer). Originally published in MailOnline 27/07/2011. (p. 97)

REHAB. Text & musik: Amy Winehouse. © EMI Music Publishing Ltd. Publicerad med tillstånd av EMI Music Publishing Scandinavia AB/Notfabriken Music Publishing AB. (p. 100)

Excerpt from Carrie Diaries by Candace Bushnell © Harper Collins

Excerpt from AND FURTHERMORE by Judi Dench. Copyright © Orion Books, 2010. Used by permission of The Orion Publishing Group Ltd.

TORN ON THE PLATFORM. Musik och text: Jack Peñate. © Universal Music Publishing Ltd. För Norden & Baltikum: Universal Music Publishing AB. Tryckt med tillstånd av Gehrmans Musikförlag AB. (p. 104)

From A LION CALLED CHRISTIAN by Anthony Bourke and John Rendall. Published by © Bantam Press. Reprinted by permission of The Random House Group Limited. (p. 106)

From A LION CALLED CHRISTIAN by Anthony Bourke and John Rendall. Audiorights. By kind permission of Peter Fraser & Dunlop.

Excerpt from THE ROAD TO WIGAN PIER by George Orwell (Victor Gollancz 1937, Martin Secker & Warburg 1959, Penguin Books 1962, 1989, Penguin Classics 2001) Copyright 1937 by Eric Blair. This Edition copyright © the Estate of the late Sonia Brownwell Orwell, 1986. Reproduced by permission of Penguin Books Ltd. (p. 108)

Excerpt from THE ROAD TO WIGAN PIER audio rights: *The Road to Wigan Pier* by George Orwell (Copyright © George Orwell, 1937) reprinted by permission of Bill Hamilton as the Literary Executor of the Estate of the Late Sonia Brownell Orwell.

Excerpts(s) from MY BRIEF HISTORY by Stephen Hawking, copyright © 2013 by Stephen W. Hawking. Used by permission of Bantam Books, an imprint of Random House, a division of Penguin Random House LLC. All rights reserved. (p. 111)

Excerpts(s) from MY BRIEF HISTORY by Stephen Hawking, copyright © 2013 by Stephen W. Hawking. Audiorights. Used by permission from Writers House, US.

Excerpts from The People you Never Hear from Moranthology by Caitlin Moran © Harper Collins (p. 114)

Excerpt from BOSSYPANTS by Tina Fey, copyright © Little, Brown Book Group Ltd. Used by permission of Little, Brown Book Group Ltd. (p. 120)

Excerpt from A WEEK IN WINTER by Maeve Binchy. Copyright © Orion Books, 2013. Used by permission of The Orion Publishing Group Ltd. (p. 123)

Listening Exercise ONLINE ALL THE TIME taken from MAKING HABITS, BREAKING HABITS, copyright Oneworld Publications, 2013. Used by permission of Oneworld Publications.

Excerpt(s) from QUIET: THE POWER OF INTROVERTS IN A WORLD THAT CAN'T STOP TALKING by Susan Cain, copyright © 2012, 2013 by Susan Cain. Used by permission of Crown Books, an imprint of the Crown Publishing Group, a division of Random House LLC. All rights reserved. (p. 130)

Excerpt from The Negro Mother from Selected Poems of Langston Hughes, By Langston Hughes. © Random House. (p. 135)

Excerpt from "The Terrible Twos" from "Part IV: Political Failure" from THAT USED TO BE US by Thomas L. Friedman and Michael Mandelbaum. Copyright © 2011 by Thomas L. Friedman and Michael Mandelbaum. reprinted by permission of Farrar, Strauss and Giroux, LLC. (p. 137)

Excerpt from SKIN GRAF. MASTERS OF GRAFFITI TATTOO. Michael Mcleer/Billy Burke, Skin Graf. © 2013 Prestel Verlag, München, in der Verlagsgruppe Random House GmbH.

Excerpt(s) from THE LIFE AND TIMES OF THE THUNDERBOLT KID: A MEMOIR by Bill Bryson, copyright © 2006 by Bill Bryson. Used by permission of Broadway Books, an imprint of the Crown Publishing Group, a division of Random House LLC. All rights reserved. (p. 139)

Excerpt from The Immortal Life of Henrietta Lacks by Rebecca Skloot. © Crown Publishers (p. 142)

Excerpt from Brand Strategy for a New Generation by Amanda Slavin. © The Huffington Post, Feb 6, 2015.

The Parrot Sketch from Monthy Python's Flying Circus.

Excerpts from W.H. Auden edited by Edward Mendelson. © Curtis Brown.

A Parents and Teenagers Alphabet Book by David Crystal from All in the Family, poems by John Foster. Reproduced with kind permission of John Foster.

Excerpts from Americanah by Chimamanda Ngozi Adichi by David Annand. Telegraph UK. Reproduced with kind permission.

ILLUSTRATIONER

Ingrid Frölich

BILDFÖRTECKNING

s. 8-9 View Apart/Shutterstock
s. 10-11 Richard Whitcombe/Shutterstock
s. 16-17 The all Nite Images The three doctors foundation Costcutters
s. 19 Costas Anton Dumitrescu/Shutterstock
s. 20 JStone/Shutterstock
s. 26-27 Stockelements/Shutterstock
s. 33 Shutterstock
s. 35 KCS Presse/IBL
s. 41 Aina Jameela/Shutterstock
s. 49:1 Rue des Archives/IBL Bildbyrå
s. 49:2 Rue des Archives/IBL Bildbyrå
s. 49:3 Bridgeman/IBL Bildbyrå
s. 49:4 Georgios Kollidas
s. 79 pcruciatti/Shutterstock
s. 84 KPG_Payless/Shutterstock
s. 86-87 Jewish Chronicle/Heritage Images/IBL Bildbyrå
s. 89 Ferrari Press Agency/TT
s. 94-95 catwalker/Shutterstock
s. 96 Hintau Aliaksei/Shutterstock
s. 99 Nando Machado/Shutterstock
s. 102-103 S.Borisov/Shutterstock
s. 105 pisaphotography/Shutterstock
s. 106 Derek Cattani
s. 109 Library of Congress, Lewis Wickes Hine
s. 114-115 Suzanne Tucker/Shutterstock
s. 118-119 Igor Stevanovic/Sshutterstock
s. 121 Auremar/Shutterstock
s. 128 Aleutie/Shutterstock
s. 130-131 Patrick Rolands/Shutterstock
s. 137:1 Faiz Zaki/Shutterstock
s. 137:2 KPG_Payless/Shutterstock
s. 137:3 leungchopan/Shutterstock
s. 138:1 SnowWhiteimages/shutterstock
s. 138:2 KPG_Payless/Shutterstock
s. 138:3 Apollofoto/Shutterstock
s. 138:4 KPG_Payless/Shutterstock
s. 140 Angela Boatwright National Archives and Records Administration Wikimedia
s. 143 National Institutes of Health
s. 186 Richard Whitcombe/Shutterstock
s. 191 Costcutters
s. 198 JStone/Shutterstock
s. 200 Bridgeman/IBL Bildbyrå
s. 206 Stockelements/Shutterstock
s. 218 Aina Jameela/Shutterstock
s. 246 Brian Gibbs/Ogilvy & Mather
s. 249 KPG_Payless/Shutterstock
s. 250 Jewish Chronicle/Heritage Images/IBL Bildbyrå
s. 259 Catwalker/Shutterstock.com
s. 261 Hintau Aliaksei/Shutterstock
s. 264 Nando Machado/Shutterstock
s. 268 Andrea Raffin/Shutterstock
s. 276 Derek Cattani
s. 281 Library of Congress, Lewis Wickes Hine
s. 285 Suzanne Tucker/Shutterstock
s. 290 auremar/Shutterstock
s. 293 Aleutie/Shutterstock
s. 296 Auremar/Shutterstock
s. 311:1 Faiz Zaki/Shutterstock
s. 311:2 KPG_Payless/Shutterstock
s. 311:3 leungchopan/Shutterstock
s. 313 BrooklynMade Tattoo
s. 318 National Institutes of Health

Övriga bilder Shutterstock